# A HERO *for the* ATOMIC AGE

# The Past in the Present

# A HERO *for the* ATOMIC AGE

Thor
Heyerdahl
and the
*Kon-Tiki*
Expedition

AXEL
ANDERSSON

Peter Lang Oxford

First published in 2010 by

Peter Lang Ltd
International Academic Publishers
Evenlode Court, Main Road, Long Hanborough, Witney
Oxfordshire OX29 8SZ
United Kingdom

www.peterlang.com

Axel Andersson has asserted his moral right under the Copyright, Designs
and Patents Act of 1988 to be identified as the Author of this Work.

A catalogue record for this book is available from the British Library

ISBN 978-1-906165-31-4

COVER ILLUSTRATIONS:
Front: A bearded Heyerdahl on the mast of the raft. © Kon-Tiki Museum, Oslo
Back: The 'real Kon-Tiki'. © Teresa Gisbert

Every effort has been made to trace copyright holders and to obtain their permission
for the use of copyright material. The publisher apologizes for any errors or omissions
in the above list and would be grateful for notification of any corrections that
should be incorporated in future reprints or editions of this book.

Printed in the United Kingdom by the MPG Books Group

# Contents

vi

# Plates

The plates are located between pages 116 and 117.

1. Heyerdahl and his wife-to-be Liv Torp in the Norwegian mountains. © Kon-Tiki Museum, Oslo

2. Heyerdahl and Liv Torp bathing in a river on Fatuiva. © Kon-Tiki Museum, Oslo

3. King Heyerdahl of Fatuiva. © Kon-Tiki Museum, Oslo

4. The *Kon-Tiki* under construction in the dockyard of the Peruvian Navy in Callao. © Kon-Tiki Museum, Oslo

5. The crew of the *Kon-Tiki*. © Kon-Tiki Museum, Oslo

6. The *Kon-Tiki* on the open seas. © Kon-Tiki Museum, Oslo

7. Haugland and Raaby doing maintenance work on one of the four radio sets. © Kon-Tiki Museum, Oslo

8. Heyerdahl with one of the countless sharks that he and his crew caught during their Pacific crossing. © Kon-Tiki Museum, Oslo

9. Map showing Heyerdahl's three journeys of experimental archaeology in the footsteps of a vanished itinerant race. © Kon-Tiki Museum, Oslo

10. Hesselberg plays guitar for Raaby on the raft. © Kon-Tiki Museum, Oslo

11. A group of Swedish booksellers and Adam Helms on an excursion, 3 September 1950. © Adam Helms Collection, Stockholm University Library

# Preface and Acknowledgements

We all need heroes and heroines, whether we treasure them secretly or propagandize publically on their behalf. Certain figures become larger than life because we crave for guides to lead us through complex realities. Culture creates heroes, not the other way round, but at some point it becomes impossible for those accorded heroic status to live up to our unreasonable expectations. The failed hero is as common as the redeeming one. Reality is always too multifaceted, too mercurial, for any guide to show the way. The figure that used to be larger than life now becomes associated with the meanest and pettiest of life's attributes. This ancient mythological pattern has been speeded up to a dizzying tempo in the modern media environment with its cult of celebrity. The heroes and heroines of the twenty-first century experience the cruel destinies of mayflies. Years in mud, and then a day-long Icarus flight to soaring heights before being burnt by the sun.

I had a hero. His name was Thor Heyerdahl. The Norwegian experimental archaeologist who stunned the world with his 1947 *Kon-Tiki* raft journey across the Pacific inspired me to dream of far-away adventures. It was Heyerdahl that made me dare to travel the world when I was old enough to leave the safe confines of home. Many years later I decided to study his life and writings in order to understand what kind of hero I, and so many like me, had made him become. I focused on his first major expedition, the *Kon-Tiki*, and tried to reconstruct how this eccentric voyage on a balsa-wood raft two years after the Second World War became a worldwide media sensation.

The first thing I learnt when studying Heyerdahl was that heroic legends are total systems. A hero cannot be believed 'a little bit', but most be admired as a whole. There were things about Heyerdahl and the

*Kon-Tiki* that were fantastic and worth celebrating like the creation of a new benign conception of the sea that he pioneered. There were also less appetizing aspects. That Heyerdahl the storyteller conscientiously created a narrative of his life was easy to forgive; most of us do the same. What was much more problematic was a jarring presence of a 'white race' in the *Kon-Tiki* story. Heyerdahl and his fellow Scandinavian expeditionaries came as young white men to South America and Polynesia and they sometimes behaved, as the saying goes, as children of their time. There was also another white race, Heyerdahl argued, a culture-bearing race of white teachers that had travelled the world in ancient times. It was their fabled voyage that Heyerdahl wanted to reconstruct. The idea of race, and of hierarchies of races, was contentious in the postwar period and remains so now. There is nothing innocent in the idea of a white race that had brought into being all the world's great civilizations. It is a dangerous racist myth.

But this book is about more than Heyerdahl's problematic white race; it tries to explain how heroes are made and how certain periods crave different adventures. I hope that it can be seen as both a celebration and a questioning of this process. It has however been with some remorse and sadness that I have tried to expose the different nuts and bolts of the legend. I know that it is easier to pick something apart than to put it together, and humbly take my bow in front of the storyteller Heyerdahl even though his theories were at times appalling. The time has now come to study the Heyerdahl legend. We need to understand how reality is, and was, far too intricate for a one-dimensional image of him to persist. This work has already begun in earnest in Norway where Roar Skolmen published a book criticizing Heyerdahl as a scholar in 2000 and in 2005 and 2008 Ragnar Kvam Jr published a probing two-volume biography that shed new and not always flattering light on Heyerdahl the private man. To these books can be added a loving parody on the *Kon-Tiki* from 1999 by Erlend Loe entitled *L*. In contrast to these books my interest is in Heyerdahl as a modern hero and the *Kon-Tiki* as a media phenomenon. It is my hope that this focus will add another strand to the rendering of a more complex idea of Heyerdahl and his greatest adventure.

For those who wish to read the full Heyerdahl legend I would like to recommend Arnold Jacoby's biography *Señor Kon-Tiki*, or Heyerdahl's autobiographical text *In the Footsteps of Adam*, both available in English. For a description of the *Kon-Tiki* voyage nothing could ever rival Heyerdahl's own narration that is continuously being published in new editions. The Kon-Tiki museum in Oslo, which Heyerdahl helped create, also offers an exhibition about his theories and travels. It is here that the *Kon-Tiki* raft has its home, appropriately close to other remnants of Norwegian maritime history with their own museums such as the Gokstad Viking ship and Nansen and Amundsen's *Fram*.

Writing this book has entailed a number of journeys for me, both real and intellectual. Many have accompanied me and given me support along the way. I owe gratitude first and foremost to Victoria de Grazia, who supervised the dissertation out of which this work grew. Without her encouragement I would never have got up and walked so boldly. Thank you also to Bo Stråth, Aleksandra Djajic Horváth, Simon Toubeau, Clemens Maier-Wolthausen, Lucy Turner Voakes, Maria Graciela Lombardo and Siddhartha Della Santina who helped me so much with the dissertation, to Karine Grinde for the great times in Oslo and to my parents and sister for all their encouragement. That the Kon-Tiki Museum in Oslo granted me access to its archive proved invaluable for me, and special thanks go to Paul Wallin, who helped me get started with the sources. In Stockholm I was greatly assisted by Bodil Edvardsson at the Adam Helms Collection of Stockholm University Library. I also thank the Reading University Library, the Explorers Club in New York, Brooklyn Museum of Natural History and the Newberry Library in Chicago, as well as the Albert Bonniers Förlag Archive and the Swedish Film Institute Library in Stockholm for letting me study their archives. Even though I have been helped by many, any errors in this work are mine and mine alone. For those who desire a more comprehensive discussion on sources and literature please consult my dissertation 'Kon-Tiki and the Postwar Journey of Discovery' at the European University Institute in Florence.

This book and the dissertation on which it is based were written in Pian di Mugnone in Fiesole, Campo di Marte in Florence, Bercy, Le Marais and Île Saint Louis in Paris, Giudecca in Venice, Reitano on Sicily, King's Parade in Cambridge, Gràcia in Barcelona, Wilmersdorf in Berlin, Pueyrredon in the Argentinean Córdoba and the small village of Bo in the Swedish forest. If only one could thank places; I owe so much to all of them. But I can at least end by thanking the one who walks by my side through a wondrous world; Tania Espinoza, precious companion.

# Introduction

On Monday afternoon 28 April 1947 a strange vessel was towed out of the naval dockyard in Callao, the harbour town of the Peruvian capital Lima. Fifteen large balsa logs, almost fourteen metres long, tied together and covered with bamboo matting, made a small raft. There was a nine-metre-tall mast of mangrove wood that would later hold a sail decorated with a drawing of a bearded human head. Six men formed the crew, five Norwegians and a Swede. They were to live on board for 101 days in a small hut plaited from bamboo strands and banana leaves as their raft drifted more than 4000 nautical miles in the Humboldt Current, from the shores of South America to the islands of French Polynesia.

A little more than half a year before the raft's departure from Callao, a young Norwegian, Thor Heyerdahl, had arrived in New York. In his suitcase he carried copies of a manuscript in which he had collected evidence that the Polynesian islands had first been settled through prehistoric migrations from the Americas by a white race, and not from Asia as the prevailing scientific opinion decreed. The young Heyerdahl was not a scientist. He had decided to discontinue his university studies and instead carry out research of his own. Nine and a half years before he had travelled to Polynesia in a failed attempt to abandon civilization. Now he wanted to return on a raft from South America, just like the people who had settled the Pacific. It was a crazy idea. The year was 1946, and the bloodiest war in the history of mankind had just come to an end. Heyerdahl had left behind his wife and two children and a good chance to establish himself in his native Norway. Instead of putting his pre-war years of anxious wayfaring behind him, he had decided to take the final step towards making his life into an adventure, whatever the cost.

In 2002, many years and adventures later, we find Heyerdahl in the small Italian village of Colla Micheri in the green hills of Liguria. He is 87 years old and has been diagnosed with terminal cancer. There will be no more daring exploits, no more crazy ideas to realize. Maybe his thoughts return to how it had all begun, and how it was that he had become an international celebrity through that first raft journey. The book about the adventure had sold tens of millions of copies worldwide and had been translated into more than 60 languages. This success had enabled him to devote his life to adventures in the name of popular science. He had carried out excavations all over the world and sailed experimental reconstructions of primitive vessels across the Atlantic Ocean and the Arabian Gulf. Heyerdahl had brought his gift for making stories to the international stage and the popular audience that he had sought since his youth. It might only be a poetic conjecture, but one can imagine that Heyerdahl's thoughts of the past mingled with chagrin. Now it was time to go, time to give up control of his story. As all storytellers know, the key to success is to be the one who casts the spell.

I was one of the many people who read Heyerdahl. It all began during one of those childhood Christmases that for the most part appear indistinguishable from each other. The taste of the ginger wafers and the smell of the freshly cut spruce tree were the same and even though there was not always snow, I invariably colour the fields and forests outside my childhood home fluffy white with hibernal nostalgia. Everything, in short, flows together in some common measure of time. One winter a new edition of Heyerdahl's book about that raft journey that had begun in Callao, *The Kon-Tiki Expedition*, lay under the Christmas tree with all its mesmerizing decorations. Both my father and my grandfather were at hand to tell me of their own experiences of reading this classic that I had not known existed. I do not remember whether I reflected that being introduced to the book was a masculine rite of passage. What I do remember is that I spent the following days on the blue, warm Pacific, on a creaking balsa raft.

Many years later I was on the west coast of Norway, together with a group of other people in front of the expedition leader of that adventurous journey from Peru to Polynesia. By that time I had in my imagination crewed on every subsequent vessel of this adventurer and explorer, and believed that I had a comprehensive grasp of his theories of prehistoric ocean migrations and his philosophy of the interconnectedness of humanity that necessitated a commitment to the issues of peace and the environment. The Christmas gift had even prompted me to collect books about travel and adventure, and had strengthened my own wish to go beyond the confines of my rural home. When Heyerdahl finished speaking I could not, however, bring myself to walk up to him. I had the curious sensation that the frail white-haired man with a stoop was someone, or something, quite different from my childhood hero.

Later in life I decided to get to the bottom of my interest in adventurous journeys and the figure of Heyerdahl. The fascination had, after all, not been mine alone. It was not only my grandfather and father who had shared it, but generations around the world. Heyerdahl was one of a long line of atavistic figures who seemed to have braved the most extreme elements on behalf of the less daring. Soon it became clear for me that this fascination could best be understood by studying the phenomenon of exploration and travel in general, rather than the details of the individual tortuous journeys of specific hardy adventurers. The *Kon-Tiki* voyage and Heyerdahl the person were less interesting than *Kon-Tiki* the event and Heyerdahl the concept. My only starting premise when I returned to Norway to begin my researches was that adventure and adventurers are created; they do not simply come into existence.

I did not know what to expect to find at the Kon-Tiki Museum on Bygdøy (see plate 15). The short boat ride across the beautiful Oslo fjord had almost been enough to make me content. The small balsa raft displayed there, on which Heyerdahl and his crew of five had drifted across half of the Pacific Ocean, appeared to have sunk into a Sleeping Beauty-like slumber from which I could not rouse her. It was only when I was let into a windowless back room, full of green filing cabinets, that I sensed something alive among the relics. There I found the paperwork, meticulously preserved, that began to explain how a young de-mobbed university drop-out who looked quite a bit like Kirk Douglas created a media sensation in the late 1940s and early 1950s around an adventure undertaken to prove a rather fantastic theory that Polynesian culture was the result of migrations from the Americas. This was what would end up as dreams of adventure like the one I had been gripped by for so many years.

The onion-leaf, thin carbon copies of correspondence with backers, publishers and the various others who helped to make the *Kon-Tiki* expedition possible became the real stuff of my story. Here were the traces of how one of many adventurous journeys had been made; if only the material at the museum could be unravelled it might say something about the fascination with extreme travelling that has been such an important feature in so many of the world's cultures, not at least in the West ever since Odysseus left Ithaca. But the thin, brittle paper and massive scrapbooks of articles, in many cases neglected for almost 60 years, required a context. To be understood they had to be inserted anew into the universe from which they had been taken when they were put into their stout green time capsules. This is how my story of the *Kon-Tiki* came to be as much about the immediate postwar period in the USA and Europe as about primitive rafts, timeless oceans and itinerant gods. Hence this book's only somewhat ironic title: *A Hero for the Atomic Age*.

The journey of the *Kon-Tiki* was a highly orchestrated event whose beginnings are interwoven with the historical and cultural fabric of the time in which it was created. It was not the same as the story that caught the world's imagination and ended up as a timeless adventure under my family's Christmas tree. Heyerdahl had worked hard to secure the greatest possible impact for his first major expedition. He had left a war-torn Europe and travelled to the USA, where the Pentagon and other institutions like the new United Nations had given him the support he needed. As he drifted across the Pacific he wrote articles, filmed and began his book about the journey even before it was over. When he returned to 'civilization' he lectured tirelessly in the USA and Europe, as well as securing publishers for his book and help with making his documentary film. It took Heyerdahl only a few years to reach an audience of millions in the West. By the mid-1960s the *Kon-Tiki* book had sold an estimated 50 million copies around the world.

In the early 1950s 'Kon-Tiki' became a by-word for the exotic, for adventure, for bravery, and for a spirited, commonsensical and democratic challenge to dusty scientific dogmatism. The name of the young Norwegian adventurer's creation was on everybody's lips. Heyerdahl had transformed the journey of a small, flimsy raft across the Pacific into the leading adventure of the era, and himself into the updated embodiment of the explorer of yesteryear. He had come from nowhere and created one of the most important events in postwar popular culture. It is true that his 'nowhere' was an upper-class background replete with crucial contacts, and that he was also helped by favourable circumstances, but Heyerdahl's achievement should not be understated. He had set his mind to creating a legendary story, and he succeeded.

One of the most fortuitous factors beyond Heyerdahl's control was that he did not receive the immediate recognition in the USA that he had hoped for. His inability to secure a US publisher for his book and a distributor for his film forced him to return to Europe in order to launch his *Kon-Tiki* story there. But Heyerdahl never gave up trying to break into the huge North American media market, and one day it happened. As Heyerdahl crossed and recrossed the Atlantic the *Kon-Tiki* became an event that belonged as much to the USA as it did to Europe. It was in the USA that the expedition had been planned and funded, and it was in Europe that Heyerdahl assembled both his campaign to sell the book and his documentary film before they were brought back to the USA. His Pacific journey had a marked Atlantic character, and illustrates above all the interconnectedness of the popular culture of the postwar West.

This book tells the story of how the *Kon-Tiki* grew from a dream into a spectacular reality in the late 1940s and early 1950s. It seeks to explain why the *Kon-Tiki* book still appears under Christmas trees and why it continues to inspire fantasies of exotic adventures. There is however a price to pay, as anyone who interrogates fantasies knows. The *Kon-Tiki* story is not as simple and innocent as the legend it has become, but its most problematic aspects are not in any hidden unpleasant details that have been buried in some filing cabinet or in some family secret. When it comes to Heyerdahl's *Kon-Tiki* there is an elephant in the room in the form of a highly articulated racist theory that has for a long time remained almost perfectly invisible.

It is possible to castigate Heyerdahl for being a bad scientist, and for experts in his chosen fields of study – I am not one – it is easy to find fault with his theories of prehistoric ocean migrations. The focus of this book is not upon Heyerdahl's science but upon his story; for the present purpose it does not matter whether the first Polynesians arrived from the east or the west, north or south. The disturbing kernel of Heyerdahl's theory went well beyond questions of geography. He argued that it had been an itinerant race of white and blue-eyed culture-bearers that had journeyed from some centre in the Old World to jump-start the world's great civilizations. The god and king Kon-Tiki had been a leader of this people. This was more than cranky pseudoscience; it was an articulation of a belief in the cultural superiority of a white race that drew its inspirations from the murky depths of nineteenth-century race 'science'. It was also a story that made disturbing allegorical sense on a number of levels. The advance across the Pacific of Heyerdahl's all-white crew mirrored the postwar US frontier movement in the same ocean, and the argument that development required white skin was a reactionary comment upon the struggles against Western colonial domination around the world that continue to this day.

Race was an important part of the *Kon-Tiki*. Heyerdahl the mythmaker constructed his stories through reconciling apparent opposites, be they reason and sentiment, adventure and science, the exotic and the primitive, or the beautiful and the sublime, but when it came to race there was little to reconcile: culture and history belonged to the white. To discuss Heyerdahl's racist message does not amount to a gratuitous and politically correct admonition. Heyerdahl was not simply a child of his time. It is true that ideas of white supremacy were legion in the 1940s and 1950s. At the same time a world war had recently been fought against racist ideologies, and many publicly recognized scientists of the time dismissed the concept of human races in general and the supremacy of the white one in particular. Heyerdahl had at his disposal the intellectual tools to see how ideologically tainted his theories were, but he failed to grasp this. That he was not the only one who failed can help us to understand Heyerdahl the person, but it cannot excuse his theories. Unfortunately Heyerdahl was almost never challenged when it came to the racism of his theories, neither at the time of the *Kon-Tiki* nor, surprisingly, at any time later. Though the idea of white supremacy was not unquestioned, it retained a strong position in the Western political unconscious. The racism in the *Kon-Tiki* theory that was so clearly articulated by Heyerdahl became invisible with a disturbing ease. That it also remained equally uncommented on throughout the second half of the twentieth century shows the stubborn persistency of racial theories. Now the time has come not to dismiss Heyerdahl as a racist but to uncover the sooty kernel at the heart of Heyerdahl's fantasy, and our fantasy of Heyerdahl.

# 1

## The Man and the Myth

### The Evening Prayer

The low white house at Steingata 7 was made of wood, as were many of the houses in the small Norwegian coastal town of Larvik in the first years of the twentieth century, and like all wooden houses it resonated like some great instrument. The wind that swept up the street from the nearby fjord made it groan and sigh. The members of the Heyerdahl family also gave rise to their own distinct squeaking noises when walking across a room or using the staircase leading to the upper floor where the son of the house was sleeping. Young Thor knew without a moment's hesitation who it was that was approaching his room as he lay in bed waiting to fall asleep.

First the boy would hear the footsteps of his father, Thor senior, moving up the flight of steps and then stealing into his son's room. They were both well aware of the ritual that would unfold. The father would signal his son to be silent and then they would kneel together and begin the Lord's Prayer: 'Our Father, who art in heaven …'. Sometimes they would also read from the Bible or talk about God. This was a God referred to as *Fader Vår*, 'Our Father', and nothing else. Throughout the proceedings their voices remained hushed. This was their shared secret.

In the end it would hardly matter how silent father and son tried to be. The staircase would soon announce the arrival of someone else. Now the footsteps were unmistakably those of Alison, the young boy's mother. This signalled the end of the fragile communion. The father hurried out, and the boy jumped back into bed. Outside his room he could hear his mother sharply admonishing his father. What kind of nonsense was it that he had been teaching the boy?[1]

Heyerdahl's resolute mother had strong reasons to object to the invocation of 'Our Father'. She was convinced that He did not exist. Religion, she held, was nothing short of childish superstition. Her allegiance was to science, rationalism and Charles Darwin. Alison Lyng was born in Trondheim in 1873 and had in her youth been sent to England to study. She returned to Norway influenced by popular understanding of the evolutionary theory first articulated in Darwin's 1859 work, *On the Origin of Species*. Taking her cue from a radical interpretation of Darwin she was now an atheist with a firm belief in progress. Moreover she had become a committed anglophile who detested everything German. The Norway she returned to was in the midst of its own heated debate over Darwin's thesis after a Norwegian translation of his work in 1890 by Ingebret Suleng had made it accessible to the nation as a whole.[2]

Thor senior's trajectory was in many ways the reverse of his wife's. He was born in the Norwegian capital Christiania, present-day Oslo, in 1870 and had gone to Germany to receive an education in chemistry that would launch him into a career as a brewer. From Germany he had returned not with Darwin but with Martin Luther, and though not doctrinaire in issues of theology he preserved a strong faith. He did not object to progress, but remained ambivalent as to whether humanity was developing for the better. The Great War that had begun just before his son Thor was born led him to pessimistic conclusions about the future.[3]

A central theme of Thor Heyerdahl's construction of his own legend, the 'Heyerdahl story', is the conflict he inherited from his parents. On one side stood Darwin and sharp empiricism, and on the other an earnest pietistic belief in 'Our Father'. Towards the end of his life Heyerdahl addressed this split, writing that 'the warmth of my father's simple belief penetrated my heart, and my mother's scientific reasoning penetrated my brain'.[4] This dichotomy could also be understood as an allegory of the relationship between England and Germany. This made poetic sense for a person born in the shadow of one major war involving those two nations, and who would experience another in his early adulthood. Symbolically, the position also echoed that of Norway, a nation as tightly knit culturally, politically and economically with Germany as it was with Britain.

The split between reason and sentiment was to have a clear function when Heyerdahl crafted a legend of his life. It was to become a master metaphor, and all that he did could be interpreted as different attempts to negotiate this fundamental divide. His writings are full of mediations between opposing terms that could be put under the same categories: wilderness versus civilization, private versus public, honesty versus corruption, individuality versus the mass, adventure versus passive science, the primitive versus the exotic and the sublime versus the beautiful.

Simply put, the French anthropologist Claude Lévi-Strauss argued that myths in 'primitive' societies help to mediate between binary opposites like earth and sky, life and death. Through myths people identify the antagonisms in their societies and then resolve the apparent contradictions between extremes.[5] Lévi-Strauss made little distinction between folktale, myth and legend, yet binary oppositions are not peculiar to myth and are found in most stories.[6] The important thing here is not what to call it, but to understand what it does. Lévi-Strauss's greatest insight is to be found in his discussion of the function of myths in narratives: they can help us reconcile ourselves to dramatic opposites in our lives. Lévi-Strauss believed politics had taken the place of religion in modern society; even so it can be argued that myths are still needed in the same way they always have been. Heyerdahl's construction of his own story is a clear illustration of the power of myths and legends to help navigate through multifaceted realities.[7]

Heyerdahl later used his parents' conflict as a crucial metaphor in his autobiographical writings, as did his friend Arnold Jacoby in his biography of Heyerdahl written in 1965; this does not mean that Heyerdahl invented it, however. The evening prayer was most probably broken up in the way he so vividly described. His parents' marriage was however problematic for many other reasons. Heyerdahl made a complex reality into two simple and carefully delineated dramatic opposites between which he mediated through his life and works, thus making his own persona embody the functions of a myth that symbolically reunited his parents.

Heyerdahl's parents had from the outset also a lot in common. Not only were they from wealthy upper-class Norwegian families, they were also new to the town of Larvik, situated on Norway's southern coast. Thor senior moved there in 1894, buying the brewery Vestfolds Bryggeri- og Mineralvandfabrik with his inheritance. Alison came in 1912, when the two married. Both had previous marriages behind them, as well as children from these earlier unions. Alison's situation of having been through two failed marriages was especially unorthodox in a culturally conservative provincial town. She had given birth to seven children of whom five survived. Her daughter Ingrid came with her when she left her second husband in 1911 after having fallen in love with Thor senior. The second divorce did however come at great cost. One of her children, Jacob, was so traumatized by her departure that he tried to commit suicide.[8] Alison and Thor were united also by their advanced age. They were well into their forties when their last child, Thor junior, was born on 6 October 1914.

The Heyerdahl family constellation might have caused raised eyebrows in Larvik, but the affluence and urbane affability of Thor senior laid fears to rest. The marriage was soon all but undone, however. When Thor junior was four his fifteen-year-old half-sister saw her stepfather fondling the maid. Ingrid decided to tell her mother.[9] Alison would never forgive her third husband for whom she had sacrificed so much, but yet another divorce was unthinkable. She left the marital bed and promptly moved in with her son, sharing a bedroom with him all through his childhood. Her attention was now completely directed towards Thor junior, and she continued to live close to her son until he left for his first major journey at the age of 22.[10] Thor senior and Alison eventually separated, but the father kept a strong and affectionate bond with his son.

In Heyerdahl's own story, his mother's dominance would translate into a childhood attraction to science and collecting. His father tried in vain to interest him in hunting and outdoor activities. He wanted to make 'a man' out of the boy.[11] In an emblematic and symbolic story of the child's scientific awakening, and of his mother's success, Heyerdahl constructed his own zoological 'museum' in one of the buildings on the family property.[12] Influenced by his mother's constant talk of the evolution of species he developed a great interest in animals. He collected whatever small creatures he could find in the neighbourhood and drowned them in jars filled with formalin. His father, eventually reconciled to this less manly interest, brought him gifts of stuffed animals from his many trips abroad, and took him down to the harbour to let him buy curious sea creatures from the fishermen returning with the catch of the day. The 'museum' collection grew, and the ultimate recognition came one day when a biology teacher took a school class to admire Heyerdahl's creation.

Heyerdahl's alignment with the reason and empiricism of his mother, a great collector herself, serves in his story to add another pair of opposites to sentiment and Christianity versus reason and science: the private versus the public. It is important to note that Heyerdahl's creation was not a simple, private, juvenile cabinet of wonders. Even though the museum was a childish affair, it was presented and arranged as a public display. Much later, during the *Kon-Tiki* expedition, Heyerdahl used the scientific and public dimension of the enterprise to lend legitimacy to a partly sentimental story and also to present it to a larger public. Heyerdahl's religious beliefs would always, in his writings, be shrouded in images of the private, the exclusive and the frail; much like the story of the evening prayer with his father. Sentiment needed one type of address, science another.

## The Call of the Wild

The child collecting animals for his museum was, as Heyerdahl paints him, pampered, weak and insecure. His manhood lay before him to be conquered, and that masculinity would not come to him through reason and science. Nature, irrational and wild, would beckon to him. Heyerdahl equated nature with hardiness and culture with the feminine and soft, an understanding that found its clearest articulations in nostalgic late nineteenth-century ideas of a frontier that industrialization had for the most part already erased. It is not improbable that Heyerdahl in his youth read books like Jack London's *The Call of the Wild,* translated into Norwegian in 1907, in which the anthropomorphized spoilt dog Buck from the 'soft' civilized California was abducted and brought into the wild and 'primitive' Yukon and Alaska. In the wilderness he overcame the weakness that was the result of an urban life.

Another story that lay even closer to Heyerdahl's was that of Theodore Roosevelt, the twenty-sixth president of the USA. Whereas London's Buck had been kidnapped and brought to the frontier, Roosevelt's own story, tailored to appeal to a rapidly industrializing and changing nation, hailed the idea of free will.[13] In Roosevelt's masculine legend the future 'rough rider' grew up as an urban, sick and weakly child, suffering from severe asthma. He was fascinated by zoology in his childhood and opened his own museum, as Heyerdahl was to do, grandly naming it the 'Roosevelt

Museum of Natural History'.[14] Later, with the help of his father, Roosevelt managed to overcome his physical feebleness and fulfil his desire to become a 'real man' in the wild.

Heyerdahl might have not been familiar with London's and Roosevelt's stories, but as a young boy growing up in the 1920s countless similar ones surrounded him. His desire to 'return' to a wild and masculine nature was not instinctive, even though this is how he later liked to present it. In his biography Jacoby put forward evidence for Heyerdahl's innate attraction to the wild, informing us that as a child Heyerdahl would wish for a coconut every Christmas, not as a novelty to admire or to eat, but as a symbol of the primitive. Later, in a drawing by the seven-year-old Thor showing his future house, we can see a hut on stilts on what appears to be a South Sea island.[15] Heyerdahl was to become one with the wild; the house was for him to live in. In Heyerdahl's story his instinct to abandon civilization was suppressed in childhood, but would return in adolescence.

Around the time when Heyerdahl started secondary school in 1928 his interests are supposed to have begun to shift from rational science to romantic wilderness. He became disenchanted with biology as the teaching became more and more technical; the marvels of the plants and animals waned when they were displayed in a dissected and schematized form. He turned his attention, like Roosevelt, to overcoming his own physical weakness and delicateness. One of Heyerdahl's inspirations was Edgar Rice Burroughs's creation Tarzan; he dreamt of being strong enough to swing from tree to tree in the jungle. Heyerdahl's father seized the opportunity and constructed a makeshift gym in the back yard, just as Roosevelt's had done for his son.[16]

With the help of some neighbours Heyerdahl's attention soon turned to sport. Jacoby stresses, however, that it was the exercise and not the results that interested him. If Heyerdahl saw animal tracks when he was out running he would leave the path to follow these instead.[17] Heyerdahl was becoming a primitive. It was a substitute father figure, Ola Bjørneby, who would complete this 'return' to nature. Bjørneby lived in the mountains close to Heyerdahl's mother's favourite chalet in Hornsjø, north of Lillehammer, where mother and son usually spent the summer. One day they stumbled over this upper-class non-conformist who spent his life as a roaming vagabond in the mountains. At the age of fourteen, Heyerdahl was allowed to stay with Bjørneby for the summer. Without his mother at last, he was now initiated to the mysteries, and also the hardships, of living with, and in, nature.[18]

For the young Heyerdahl Bjørneby was a Tarzan come to life. Ever since meeting him Heyerdahl became a dedicated hiker in the mountains, a place that in his legend became 'the very symbol of freedom'.[19] Civilization, represented by Larvik, school and bourgeois expectations, was the inverted mirror of the mountains: an over-rationalized world, enfeebled, superfluous, stagnant and doomed. In Heyerdahl's story Bjørneby and the wild north replaced his father, who had by this time left the household. Up in the mountains he could leave behind, in the words of London's dog Buck, 'the soft Southland'.[20]

It was not surprising that Heyerdahl encountered an inspiring wilderness in the craggy peaks of Norway's interior. The wind-swept plateaux of Rondane and Jotunheimen were well established as the romantic frontier in the Norwegian national story. It was here that the two polar pioneers Fridtjof Nansen and Roald Amundsen had prepared themselves for their expeditions after abandoning their safe upper-class homes in the south. A generation later Heyerdahl was to do the same. He hiked, skied and slept in snow bivouacs. The mountains became for Heyerdahl the essence of Norway, and the home of the nation's spirit of adventure and freedom, just as it had been for the heroes of the previous generation.[21]

Heyerdahl had already decided to become famous, to become another of his young nation's great explorers. He used the mountains as his explorer-school, as he was supposed to do. When he returned to Larvik and civilization he told his friend Jacoby that he would soon head out on journeys and expeditions to far-away and mysterious corners of the world. It did not matter that there were no more uncharted spots on the map left to explore. Heyerdahl claimed that it was not only in geography that one could make discoveries. The world held many mysteries other than unmapped territories, like the strange statues on Rapa Nui (Easter Island).[22] In other words, the Norwegian history of masculine adventure could continue despite what Amundsen had finally discovered in the Arctic: that there was no more land left to claim and map. In Heyerdahl's story his desire to become an explorer merged with the rejection of the effeminate bourgeois urban world represented by the south of Norway. While his friends were thinking about how they would enter the professional world he decided to travel so far that there was no turning back. Convinced that civilization was doomed, he was now, according to Jacoby, contemplating a complete return to nature.[23] Even exploration would only be in the service of a world he detested. He wanted to make the ultimate discovery by finding his own paradise in nature and beginning anew.

After having modelled himself on Amundsen and Nansen, Heyerdahl decided to become a new Adam. For this to succeed he needed an Eve. Heyerdahl met Liv Coucheron Torp at a matriculation ball. Friends had brought them together and he had nervously suggested a walk, as he dreaded dancing. They strolled down to the waterfront, the noise of the party cutting through the night behind them, and headed towards the moored ships in front of them. Convinced that he had found the right person, he asked her what she thought about returning to nature. She accepted with a condition: it would have to be all the way. From that moment their agreement was sealed through their commitment to the possibility of a primitive paradise.[24]

Even the most uncritical and hagiographic of Heyerdahl's biographers has said that the story of the ball sounds like sentimental romantic fiction, while nevertheless claiming that this was how it happened.[25] The story's romantic nature is however less important than the fact that Liv, who became Heyerdahl's wife, is reduced to a function of Heyerdahl's own legend. The rib of which Liv was made was Heyerdahl's myth. This central character in his life would be forced to stay forever in the shadow of Heyerdahl's intrepidity and greatness.[26]

Heyerdahl encountered a problem in using the Genesis story to provide a framework for his own escape to the wilderness. If the wilderness was where a man became a man, then there was not much room for the woman. First of all, she had to declare that she also wanted to quit the effeminate civilization, and this Liv had done. This, however, was not enough. In his writings Heyerdahl treated her as a creature whose subjectivity was unimportant and who could be controlled and cancelled out. In contrast to his mother, whom he discussed repeatedly, Liv was only an accomplice, a symbolic Eve, in an escape that was his alone.

By the autumn of 1933 Heyerdahl had toughened himself in the mountains and found a woman willing to follow him in his endeavour. He was not yet even nineteen, however, and Liv was two years younger. They would have to wait – wait and prepare. Two years passed before Heyerdahl could resume planning his escape. He did not see his future wife during this time. Reason, science and urban life claimed him once again. He had started studying at the University of Oslo, focusing on zoology like both Roosevelt and Nansen. His parents bought him a flat in the leafy and affluent residential area behind the Royal Palace, and his mother moved in with him. But all of this was a smokescreen. He had chosen to study zoology as his major in order to have a reason to go on a field trip that could be turned into an abandonment of civilization, and geography as a minor in order to discover which place on earth was most like paradise.[27] He had, in his mind, already left.

Predictably, Heyerdahl found out that dissections, microscopes, test tubes, scientific method and lectures bored him in just the same way as they had bored Roosevelt, who in his 1913 autobiography lashed out against his professors at Harvard for constructing an over-specialized 'science of the laboratory'.[28] The university would not teach Heyerdahl about the romantic nature that he was interested in. Whenever he could, he left for the mountains.

Life in the 'big' city of Oslo could only reinforce Heyerdahl's hatred of a modernity he believed was doomed, as did the reports of a world ablaze from China to Spain. His own legend prompts us to believe that he was convinced that the apocalypse was coming in the shape of a new war that would be worse than any hitherto seen.[29] The prophetic nature of this knowledge underlines the legendary nature of the story. This is not to say that Heyerdahl did not, even as a small child, dream of the South Seas that he was to visit, or that as a young man he was not genuinely afraid of a new world war; but the story could have contained so much more than this – other dreams, other fears. His time in Oslo was probably marked by loneliness and worries about not being able to fit into society – commonplace adolescent experiences – but Heyerdahl wanted to invest these events with more significance than their being simply part of the passage to adulthood. He did this through an allegiance to the good simple story rather than the messy reality of existence, but also through a rare literal interpretation of this story. If he tapped into an image of the superiority of nature over civilization then he would act on it. The importance of this impulse is vital when understanding Heyerdahl's narration of his life and work. All of his stories were built around simplicity and action – themes that he would later perfect in his first major success: the *Kon-Tiki* expedition of 1947.

## An Apprentice Explorer in the South Seas

In December 1936 Heyerdahl married Liv and began a voyage that would eventually take the young couple to the middle of the Pacific Ocean. In Heyerdahl's story he left a wintry Norway never to come back. He quit civilization after seven uninspiring semesters at the university. At the age of 22 he felt ready to sever all ties with his native land. He was finally going to become a Tarzan (or 'white skin' as the name meant in the language of the apes) in the jungle (see plate 3).[30]

There were many reasons why Heyerdahl decided that his wilderness would be on a Polynesian island. Polynesia had had an iconic status as a paradise ever since Denis Diderot wrote a fanciful supplement to Bougainville's account of his 1767 visit to Tahiti. But there were several inspirations closer to home, as the author Roar Skolmen has pointed out in his book *I skyggen av Kon-Tiki* (In Kon-Tiki's Shadow).[31] In 1926, when Heyerdahl was twelve, the first Norwegian scientific expedition to Polynesia left under the leadership of Ørjan Olsen. The expedition resulted in two popular books in 1930 and 1931; the second presented the French geologist Jules Garnier's thesis that South Americans, traversing a now-sunken land link, had settled Polynesia. The idea that travellers from South America had reached Polynesia in prehistoric times was going to be part of the theory that Heyerdahl would try to prove with the *Kon-Tiki* expedition.

Two years later, to the excitement of Heyerdahl and the local boys, the bohemian sailor Erling Tambs fitted out his ship *Teddy* in the harbour of Larvik for a trip to the Pacific. This journey also gave rise to articles and books. A more crucial meeting would come after Heyerdahl's move to Oslo, however, when he became acquainted with Bjarne Kroepelien, a wealthy wine merchant. Kroepelien had travelled to Tahiti in 1918–19, and had become fascinated with the island and profoundly moved by the carnage of the influenza pandemic of the period that killed one tenth of the island's population. His Tahitian lover had been among the victims. Kroepelien never had the heart to go back and instead built up a substitute in the form of an extensive collection of books on Polynesia that he let Heyerdahl study. In this library Heyerdahl could not only read romantic accounts of life in the South Seas, but also discover a mystery in anthropology that he would eventually make his own: the origins of the Polynesians.

Heyerdahl had selected the island of Fatuiva in the remote Fenua Enata, or Marquesas, group of islands in French Polynesia.[32] But he needed the excuse of a field trip that would help him prepare for a doctorate. His professors suggested that he should follow in Darwin's footsteps and study the evolution of species on Fatuiva just as Darwin had on Galapagos.[33] This was fortunate for Heyerdahl, as the invocation of Darwin could help to convince his protective mother to lend her support. It worked. If any doubts remained Heyerdahl also had the recommendation of his professor Kristine Bonnevie, an emancipated woman who had become the first female professor at the University of Oslo and who was one of his mother's idols.[34] After she became convinced, Alison managed to get her estranged husband to agree to the trip and to pay for it, mostly through assenting to see him again. The couple had not met since Thor senior had left the family home in Heyerdahl's childhood. It was then Heyerdahl's father who in turn charmed Liv Torp's parents to allow their twenty-year-old daughter to accompany his son.[35]

Heyerdahl had met Liv again two years after their romantic vows. Liv was studying, and Heyerdahl believed she was being corrupted by life in the capital. As she was still enthusiastic about the planned return to nature he proceeded to help her adapt to the wilderness. In 1935 Heyerdahl took her up into the mountains where they fried fish on rocks, roasted potatoes on embers and learnt how to live without modern conveniences (see plate 1). Heyerdahl might have followed in the footsteps of both Adam and Darwin, but Liv had to follow in his. In order to harden herself she walked after him barefoot through the rough terrain until blood gushed from the soles of her feet.[36] The scientific aim of the voyage was both an excuse and a fallback plan. If they had to return to Europe Heyerdahl could at least justify his trip. He took the preparations seriously; in the autumn after that summer with Liv in the wilderness he left with his father for a study trip to Berlin. In Kroepelien's library he might have had all the texts he wanted, but at the Dahlem ethnological museum in south Berlin he could see the artefacts of a real Polynesia. In the German capital he also met one of the most prominent race scientists of the Third Reich, Dr Hans F. K. Günther, who was married to a friend of Liv's mother and had lived in Norway for some time in the 1920s.

A Nazi Party member and Nordicist ideologue, Günther was the author of several influential pseudoscientific tracts that divined mental characteristics from physical attributes. He was a personal favourite of Adolf Hitler who had attended his inaugural lecture when Günther had been made head of race 'science' at the prestigious University of Jena in 1930 by the Nazis who had joined the Thuringian legislature after the state elections in December 1929.[37] A month before Heyerdahl visited Berlin in October 1935 the anti-Semitic Nuremberg Laws had been passed in Germany; Günther's venomous rhetoric had helped provide the arguments for them.[38] After Heyerdahl returned to Oslo Günther in a letter asked him to bring him some craniums from Fatuiva as he wanted to test the nineteenth-century hypothesis that the Polynesians had been part of the Aryan race.[39]

There is no reason to believe that Heyerdahl was at this stage particularly interested in the racial politics of the Third Reich. He seemed too consumed with his preparations for the Polynesian adventure and abandonment of civilization to care for politics. There is however scope to suspect that the meeting with Hans Günther introduced Heyerdahl to the theory that the world's great civilizations had emanated from one white culture-bearing race that had migrated to the most distant corners of the world, a staple of the Aryanism or Nordicism so linked with the Nazi project – if he was not already familiar with it. Heyerdahl would have reasons to return not only to the Third Reich and Professor Günther, but also to that murky racist theory of the white race.

On Christmas Eve 1936 a priest married Heyerdahl and his young bride in the Torp family home in Brevik. Heyerdahl had already bid farewell to his few friends in Larvik. The following day the couple stepped onto a train that took them first to Oslo and then to Marseille. There they boarded the ocean liner *Comissaire Ramel*, bound for Tahiti. Now their voyage to 'the time before the dawn of history' had commenced.[40] It began in style; Heyerdahl's father had bought them first-class tickets.[41] Thor and Liv experienced all the decadent glory of civilization during black-tie dinners before they commenced their own re-enactment of the biblical Genesis. It has been argued that the trip was a honeymoon that was written up as a mythic attempt to return to nature, and that it was not Heyerdahl's intention to abandon civilization forever.[42] In his 1974 book about this journey Heyerdahl did stress the one-way nature of the escape much more than in his first account from 1938, something that supports this argument. Ultimately it is the myth rather the truth that is interesting. The voyage to Polynesia would come to symbolize Heyerdahl's most overt choice of the primitive wilderness over the rational. It is an instructive story, for it shows the dangers of going too far. Heyerdahl's aim was to mediate between the poles of culture and nature, to become the symbolic incarnation of their synthesis. This is why his voyage to Polynesia in the late 1930s needed to be a failed escape. The couple's first spell on Tahiti was pleasant enough. Kroepelien had given Heyerdahl a letter of introduction to the native chief Teriieroo a Teriierooiterai, who took care of them and tried to prepare them for life on isolated Fatuiva. However, soon after arriving in Fenua Enata the problems set in. There was to be no simple Robinson Crusoe existence in store for the Norwegian youngsters; 'the snake had entered Eden' as Heyerdahl later said.[43] Like anyone living out the fantasy of returning to the innocent time of Genesis (see plate 2), Heyerdahl and Liv were inevitably too late. The apple had already been eaten, and the island of Fatuiva was a decadent tropical nightmare riddled with disease, social feuds and insects.

Heyerdahl thus found out, like so many others before him, that Polynesia was not an easy place to set up camp for a bourgeois European with hazy romantic dreams. For a start the 'real savages' had 'decided', as he puts it in a letter home with great irritation, to give up their traditional life.[44] He seemed unable to make friends with any of the natives, except for the 'lonely cannibal' Tei Tetua. For this failed integration he blamed not himself but the island's inhabitants.[45] During his stay he collected not only animals and plant specimens but also archaeological treasures from the island. It is a testament to his youthful ignorance and low opinion of the Polynesians that he did not link the indigenous people's resentment with the fact that he was, at times even through deceit, pilfering their cultural heritage.[46] On the contrary, according to Jacoby, his fear that the islanders would 'steal' what he had 'collected' seems to have been a great source of anxiety during the stay.[47] Heyerdahl saw not only a scientific but also a monetary value in this collection, a source of income that would help him establish himself if, or when, he had to return to Norway.[48] That he and Liv had to do just this became painfully clear when both fell ill and needed modern medicine. Soon two ostracized and sick Norwegian youngsters covered with tropical ulcers were hiding in a damp cave waiting for the first boat out.

The biographer Ragnar Kvam Jr has argued that Heyerdahl's treatment of the natives of Fatuiva was simply a sign that Heyerdahl was a child of his time, when racism and colonialism were uncontroversial subjects.[49]

This is a considerable simplification of events. Heyerdahl was behaving, if anything, as a child of nineteenth-century European imperialist aggression. But how he used this derogatory view of the Polynesians is more interesting than the racism potentially implied in it. In his Polynesian adventure Heyerdahl constructed an image of the 'primitive' as already being lost, corrupted by the same civilization that he had just tried to leave behind. Importantly for his account, this meant that Heyerdahl's failure to return to paradise was not his own fault, because such a regression was impossible. Civilization could not be challenged and exited by trying to become primitive with the real contemporary primitives, by being a Tarzan in the jungle. Other measures were necessary. It is not difficult to conjecture that Heyerdahl was thinking of the mysterious white race of Professor Günther and his fellow Nordicists during the long voyage home. What if the true Polynesians had at one time been white? When he and Liv arrived back in Marseille they boarded a train bound for Berlin.

## Tackling Primitives

It was early 1938 when Heyerdahl returned to Europe. He was a thin and haggard 23-year-old who had realized the impossibility of turning his back on modernity.[50] One year had passed, a year spent on Fatuiva and in the more urban setting of Tahiti. Now Heyerdahl, according to the logic of his story, had to return to science after his failed escape to the romantic wild. It was therefore fitting that he brought with him what he called a novel solution to the old question of the origins of the inhabitants of the Polynesian islands. In the beginning of the *Kon-Tiki* book, written a decade later, Heyerdahl describes the moment when the idea that the Polynesians had come from South America, and not from Asia, came to him as an epiphany on Fatuiva. It is night and Heyerdahl cannot sleep; the sound of the ocean is trying to tell him something. He is thinking about what his native friend Tei Tetua has told him of the Polynesian god Tiki who travelled over the sea. Suddenly he realizes the similarities between the stone figures of Fatuiva and those he has seen in photographs of South America. He turns to his wife and asks whether she has ever thought the same, but the reader is not told what Liv's response was; in the place of her voice the breakers of the ocean roar out their agreement to the connection that Heyerdahl has made, and he falls asleep.[51]

In the story of Heyerdahl's return to science he was careful to establish himself as the deductive mind at the centre of the narrative. Tei Tetua, Heyerdahl's 'cannibal' friend, is brought in as a dramatic sidekick whose primitive belief in Tiki can be contrasted with Heyerdahl's rationality that is capable of producing a solution to the mystery of the god. Heyerdahl cannot allow any other conclusion than his own at this momentous time. He even seems unwilling to incorporate Liv, whose voice is replaced by a description of majestic nature. The white man, Heyerdahl, creates a world in which natives and women are rendered equally speechless in his presence.

Heyerdahl's new 'scientific' theory was in fact anything but original. The possibility of the Polynesians' American origins had been discussed throughout the nineteenth century, as Heyerdahl would have known from his studies in the Kroepelien library in Oslo. Most scholarship had rejected the idea, however, and the consensus view was that the links to Asia were much stronger. Even so, would Professor Hans Günther in Berlin be receptive to Heyerdahl's recycled theory if the Polynesians had been white? Heyerdahl put great hope in Günther, 'one of the leading men of the new regime' as he describes him in a letter to his mother. Heyerdahl was also thrilled to come back to Germany after having dealt with the French in Polynesia and en route to Germany. In another letter he described the French as 'filthy, uneducated, egotistic, immoral, and rude' as opposed to the 'cleanly, amiable, helpful, educated, and polite' Germans, a people belonging to a 'race with integrity'.[52]

Hans Günther, or the *Rassenpapst* (Race Pope) as he was nicknamed in the Third Reich, was very pleased with Heyerdahl's gift of a Polynesian cranium that bore signs of the primitive brain surgery known as trepanation, common in ancient Mesoamerica and Egypt.[53] Heyerdahl's eagerness to discuss his theories with this man was not the result of simple political naiveté. Günther, as Heyerdahl would have known, was well connected with both the Nazi movement and Norwegian race theorists such as Jon Alfred Mjøen and Halfdan Bryn, as well as Karl E. Schreiner and Alette Schreiner (who had however already dissociated themselves from Günther in the early 1930s because of his involvement with the Nazis).[54] Much more problematic than this is that the theory of a white culture-bearing race would become integral to Heyerdahl's universe, a theory with which he would score his greatest successes when the Third Reich had been reduced to rubble and Günther interned in an Allied camp for his involvement with the Nazi Party. Heyerdahl was lucky that time in Berlin. Günther might have been thrilled with his gift, but he could not give Heyerdahl, who had hoped at least to sell him his collection of Polynesian artefacts, anything more than encouragement. Maybe he pointed Heyerdahl to the work of the Norwegian eugenicist Mjøen, who argued that the blond race had ruled not only the ancient Egyptian, Assyrian, Persian and Indian civilizations, but also the Peruvian one.[55] Heyerdahl and Liv were almost penniless and had no choice but to buy a third-class train ticket for Oslo. Heyerdahl thus escaped a more profound stain from his contact with the German scientific racism that, while often no different from the one encountered in many other places, would inspire and legitimize the horrible crimes of the Nazis.

Though Heyerdahl's return to Norway signalled a return to science, he decided to abandon academia and resume his studies alone. At this point he appears to have been careful not to be taken over by any narratives that lay outside his control. Even though he had collected a considerable amount of scientific material on Fatuiva for his doctoral studies, he disposed of this to the Zoological Museum of the University of Oslo. He was through with zoology. Heyerdahl kept the anthropological artefacts, but even though he was now more interested in the Polynesians than in their animals and plants he did not enter the university's department of anthropology. He was to be free and independent, a self-made man.

In the *Kon-Tiki* book Heyerdahl outlined his new programme in the following way: 'I wanted to give up my animal studies and tackle primitive people.'[56] Considering Heyerdahl's inability to deal with the 'natives' in Polynesia it is possible to detect a certain vindictiveness in his wish to 'tackle' them now. No longer interested in reaching some spiritual unity with their world, he wanted to strip away their mythologies and dispassionately dissect them. His new objective was to find rational solutions to the mysteries of the Pacific Ocean, and he was to devote all his energy to identifying 'Tiki', the god of the Polynesian legend that he had encountered on Fatuiva. Heyerdahl assumed the role of the rational West bent on unravelling the enigma of the natives' myth. It was as though he was getting back at the islanders of Fatuiva for crushing his own myth of paradise.

Heyerdahl's rejection of the university as an environment in which to explore the anthropological issues that interested him was in part because he had set his eyes on a much more public arena. His stories would not be only for crusty academics. Already during the time on Fatuiva he had written articles for the Norwegian press about the adventure, something that had brought him substantial remuneration.[57] Now he toured the country giving lectures, and he also sat down to write a book. Heyerdahl prepared a writer's den in a mountain chalet bought with the publisher's advance, sharpened his pencils and wrote *På jakt efter paradiset* (In Pursuit of Paradise) during the late spring and summer of 1938.[58] It was a short book contrived in a classical travel-narrative form, nothing more or less spectacular than the great number of books written by Western mock-primitives in Polynesia. In it he did not acknowledge help or inspiration from any source, not even Kroepelien.[59] The Norwegian publisher Harald Grieg at Gyldendal released the book on 20 October 1938, but it was not particularly successful. Heyerdahl's Norwegian lecture tour during the spring of 1938 did go well, however.[60]

The 'return' to civilization was not complete; Heyerdahl continued to live and study in the mountains where he had written his book. To be closer to her son and her daughter-in-law, now expecting a child, Heyerdahl's mother sold her flat in Oslo and moved into a house 300 metres from their chalet.[61] This pastoral scholarly period of Heyerdahl's life did not, however, last long. He had arrived back in Norway in the spring of 1938 and in September the following year he and his small family, now enlarged by a son, boarded a liner bound for Vancouver, Canada. The war that Heyerdahl allegedly predicted was about to begin. Heyerdahl had returned to Norway from Polynesia in March 1938 when the Third Reich annexed Austria. The rounds of the Munich conference and faint hopes of peace had dominated that summer. In the autumn the Nazis stunned the world with barbaric pogroms against Jews. The hopes from Munich were then finally crushed as Hitler bullied Czechoslovakia into submission and took over the country in March 1939. In September German tanks crossed the Polish border and started the Second World War. Heyerdahl was leaving a sinking ship. Who in Europe would now be interested in where the Polynesians came from?

Canada was a good option, as Heyerdahl could continue his studies there. The Pacific Indian tribes of British Columbia had previously been linked to the Pacific islands. In 1778, on his third voyage, James Cook had observed that the Nootkan (Nuu-chah-nulth) people living on Victoria Island shared many characteristics with the Polynesians. In 1901 John Claus Voss had sailed with his friend Norman Luxton in a 38-foot modified Nootkan canoe, the *Tilikum*, from British Columbia to Fenua Enata and then on to Fiji. The possibility of a cultural contact between North America and Polynesia had thus already been explored.[62] Heyerdahl also had a cousin, Jens Heyerdahl, who had lived in British Columbia since the 1920s working as an outdoor guide and a lighthouse operator.[63] Heyerdahl was therefore familiar with British Columbia for a number of reasons when he contacted the shipping magnate Thomas Olsen of the Fred Olsen line, a friend of the family, who granted him financial support to do fieldwork on the Canadian Pacific coast.

When Heyerdahl later described his voyage to Canada in 1939 he did not mention Captain Cook, John Voss, or his cousin, nor did he discuss his own voyage as an escape from the war.[64] In his own legend it was another epiphany that had precipitated his leaving, just like the one on Fatuiva when the theory of the South American link came to him. The day after a radio interview with Heyerdahl was broadcast in October 1938 he went to buy milk from a neighbouring farm. The farmer, who had heard his story of Fatuiva on the radio, congratulated him. Over a cup of coffee, the man showed him some photos that his visiting brother, Ivan Fougner, had brought from Canada. The photographs were of carvings, totems and tools from the Nuxálk nation in Bella Coola, British Columbia, where Fougner had been an Indian agent. Now Heyerdahl suddenly 'realized' that Polynesia had been settled by two migrations from the Americas, not one: one that originated in South America, and the other in present-day British Columbia.[65]

This story is little more than a legend. There is nothing to suggest that the meeting did not take place, but it could probably not have taught Heyerdahl anything that he did not already know. He needed a good excuse to escape a war in which he did not want to get caught up. Heyerdahl wished to write his own story now that he had decided to break through to a large audience outside the academic world, and if he was going to remain in control of that story, his only option was to leave.

## Suburbia or Barracks? Dilemmas of War

The Norwegian consul in Vancouver would not hear anything of Heyerdahl signing up to fight for Norway. His name was von Stahlschmidt, and he spoke with a German accent. It would be best for Heyerdahl to return to 'his Indians', he advised him.[66] It was April 1940, and Norway had just been invaded by that 'race of integrity', as Heyerdahl had called the Germans two years earlier. He had arrived in Vancouver in November 1939 and at Christmas travelled north to the Bella Coola valley, where he had waited for the snow to thaw in order to start his fieldwork. When he heard of the German invasion of Norway at the beginning of April he quickly made his way down to Vancouver again with Liv and their son Thor. He was going to enlist. Even though the war was only the product of a corrupt modern civilization Heyerdahl could not abandon his country in its hour of need. When he was rejected at the Norwegian consulate he was reduced to having to do manual work for his subsistence until he could arrange to go to the USA to sign up.

Heyerdahl's version of events at this time, recounted above, is problematic. To begin with, the consul for Norway and Sweden in Vancouver at the time was Charles B. Stahlschmidt, who in all likelihood had been born in British Columbia in 1865.[67] The German accent and the 'von' appear to have been Heyerdahl's inventions. But even if the consul had been a Canadian Nazi this did not explain why Heyerdahl did not try to enlist elsewhere in Canada instead of trying to go to the USA. Canada had been in war with Germany since September 1939; the USA would not join the war until after Pearl Harbor in December 1941. It is more likely that as Heyerdahl had just escaped the war by going to North America he was not about to return to it now.

Heyerdahl was cut off from his father's money, and Liv was about to give birth to their second child. He was lucky to have contacts with Thomas Olsen, the wealthy industrialist who had helped him come to Canada. In the summer of 1940 Olsen offered a monthly allowance to the Heyerdahl family, by now living in a rented room in Vancouver. Soon afterwards another Norwegian contact, the engineer Robert Lepsøe, arranged a job for him at the Consolidated Mining and Smelting Company up in the Rocky Mountains.[68] In the spring of 1941 the Lepsøe family offered the Heyerdahls, now four after the birth of their son Bjørn, their cabin in Arrow Lake in the Selkirk Mountains.[69] After working for ten months, first as a labourer and then as a foreman, Heyerdahl had had enough. In late spring 1941 he was offered both a better job at the factory and another as a curator at the Museum of Anthropology at the University of British Columbia.[70] Heyerdahl turned down both offers, however; according to his own story he was to report for duty at the Norwegian consulate in New York.[71]

Heyerdahl left his family in Canada and travelled to the USA in the summer of 1941. He did report to the Norwegian authorities, but it did not seem as though he was asking to become a soldier. The Norwegian Embassy in Washington helped him with permits and arranged a job for him in Baltimore that he turned down because it did not pay enough.[72] He managed to get other jobs in the same city, first at the Reid-Avery metal factory and then at the Bethlehem-Fairfield shipyards that built Liberty ships for the war effort. Soon Liv and the children followed, and the Heyerdahl family entered US suburbia. They got a dog, made friends and went for car trips in the weekends.[73] Heyerdahl made some much-needed money by selling his collection of Polynesian artefacts from Fatuiva to Dr Herbert Spinden, the curator of American Indian Art and Primitive Cultures at the Brooklyn Museum. In a letter home to his parents in October 1941 Heyerdahl stated that he and Liv would of course remain in the USA until the end of the war.[74]

In the summer of 1942 Heyerdahl changed his mind; he was after all going to enlist in the Norwegian Army in exile. What prompted him to do this? One motivation could have been that the war was going badly for the Allies; the Allied victory in North Africa and the German defeat at Stalingrad were half a year away. In Norway the situation was dire. 1942, or the 'Big Year' as it was to be called later in Norwegian occupation history was characterized by the brutal clumsiness with which Vidkun Quisling's small indigenous fascist party tried forcefully to co-ordinate the whole society as well as by German mass arrests and arbitrary punishments. On 26 April 1942 a gun battle between two British-trained Norwegian commandos and the Gestapo in the small village of Telavåg southwest of Bergen gave the German occupation force an excuse to embark on an infamous collective punishment. The village was destroyed and all men between sixteen and 60, 72 individuals, were sent to the Sachsenhausen concentration camp north of Berlin where many would die. The women were interred in Norway. Sixteen Norwegian prisoners unrelated to Televåg were also executed as retribution.

Two days before the tragedy at Televåg the Commander of the Norwegian Air Force Hjalmar Riiser-Larsen, who had explored the Arctic with Amundsen in the 1920s, spoke to his countrymen on the BBC. He argued that the mobilization order from 9 April 1940 was still in force, and that it was the duty of all Norwegians wherever in the world they might be to report to the army in exile. If they failed to do this they were skivers and truants.[75] To mobilize Norwegians abroad had not been an easy task for a government in exile; a draft order for Norwegian men on US and Canadian soil had been passed in November 1941, but the Norwegian authorities had to rely on emotional arguments rather than coercion.[76] Heyerdahl could not have helped realizing that it was becoming untenable to remain in the USA and hope that the war would pass him by. This storm was more than he could hope to weather; even if it were possible to stay out of the fighting that decision entailed the risk of being seen as someone who valued his personal well-being higher than that of his nation. The war was a story larger than him, and he momentarily had to surrender control of his life.

Heyerdahl's decision proved a wise one. Immediately after the war he was careful not to exaggerate his wartime effort, especially as he surrounded himself with real Norwegian resistance heroes on the *Kon-Tiki* raft. This did not, of course, stop sensationalist newspapers at the time of the raft expedition from making him into a war hero with years behind enemy lines, a development that Heyerdahl did not seem to mind. His martial exploits were left in the hands of the public-relation firms employed by his publishers, and Heyerdahl's service to his country often became embellished. For example, in 1956 Harshe-Rotman Inc., acting for Heyerdahl's US publisher Rand McNally, would claim that he had fought the Germans from 1940 to 1945.[77] At certain points later in his career Heyerdahl too slipped into this more comfortable story. In a new epilogue written for a 1996 British republication of the *Kon-Tiki* book, Heyerdahl claimed that he abandoned his Pacific research for four years of fighting the Nazi menace, extending his service with a bonus year.[78]

In the *Kon-Tiki* book Heyerdahl simply and briefly stated that the war had interrupted his fieldwork in Canada, and that he had then been trained and sent to Norway.[79] The story would certainly be more heroic if the readers filled in the details for themselves. Later in life, though, he did describe the inglorious muddle in which he had actually ended up. It took two and a half years from the moment when he stepped into the New York recruitment office of the Norwegian armed forces before he was even close to the theatre of war. First he was sent back to Canada to be enrolled as a private and start his training; the US adventure was over. At the Norwegian Army base Lunenberg in Nova Scotia and the Air Force Camp Little Norway in Toronto, as well as at St Andrews and Dumfries in Scotland, he was trained to become a radio operator in a small group working behind enemy lines. In late 1944 Heyerdahl was finally shipped out to Finnmark in the north of Norway via Russia to help establish radio communications. When he arrived back in his homeland in December 1944 the Nazis were already retreating. However, he did not stay long. There had been a bureaucratic mistake: the Norwegian Army had promoted Heyerdahl Second Lieutenant just before departure but the Russian authorities had only given a permit for a 'Sergeant Heyerdahl' to enter, meaning that he was almost immediately sent back on the same perilous Murmansk convoy route that had brought him there.[80] The next time he made it back to Norwegian soil was less than a month before the German surrender in May 1945. He had been sent from London on 6 February to set up a parachuting school on the air base of Kallax in northern Sweden for the Norwegian Army which, disguised as 'police-troops', was training in the neutral country.[81] On 10 April he was flown with 26 men to the airport of the liberated city of Kirkenes.[82]

Heyerdahl had to spend most of his three years in the Norwegian armed forces marching up and down squares, scrubbing stairs, washing dishes and digging holes in the ground that he then had to fill up again. He was even court-martialled and sentenced to a 60-day probationary jail sentence for refusing to serve as a busboy in the officers' mess.[83] The story of his days in uniform is a catalogue of mistakes, absurdities and pettiness that could have been written by Joseph Heller, author of *Catch-22*. Heyerdahl himself said in 1998 that the only thing he could boast about after the war was that he had not killed anyone.[84] Already in 1945 he had privately confided to Herbert Spinden that his old mother, who had aided the secret Norwegian resistance movement, had contributed far more to the war effort than he had.[85]

Heyerdahl constructed a neat allegorical story of how he gained control over his life when peace came in 1945. The Norwegian Army had refused to discharge him, but did grant him leave to travel to see Liv and the children who came back to Norway after having spent the war in North America. In the story he walks into army headquarters in Oslo and orders two clerks of lower rank than him, second lieutenants, to fill in and stamp discharge papers for a certain Lieutenant Thor Heyerdahl.[86] He had now used the Kafkaesque army bureaucracy against itself, and left behind a twisted life in uniform. Finally he was free to decide the course of his own life's story. It has been suggested that the truth was more prosaic than this: that it had been Heyerdahl's friend, and later *Kon-Tiki* crew member, Knut Haugland, who received and granted this request for discharge.[87]

Whichever way Heyerdahl came by his discharge, the event still meant that his long and tedious time in uniform was over. Now he was not going to lose another minute, and he quickly resumed his studies on prehistoric migrations from the Americas to Polynesia. One thing the war had given him was time to think. When Heyerdahl had met Haugland in Britain he had told him of a fantastic new idea. His theory that the Polynesians had come from the Americas was so revolutionary that he might need to carry out a practical experiment to prove it.[88] In 1945 he informed his old backer Thomas Olsen of this project.[89] Olsen's financial support would come in handy if he was to carry out his plans.

In Heyerdahl's story he was forced to adopt this fanciful idea of sailing a balsa-raft replica from South America to Polynesia because he could not get academic support for his thesis. He had however proved on several occasions that he was not interested in academia. Whatever happened, Heyerdahl was set on stunning the world with a sensational story. The inactivity forced upon him by the war had instilled in him a great desire to break out at last. Academia was useful as an anonymous enemy that he could blame for having to brave the Pacific on a raft. The end goal for Heyerdahl was in any case much grander than simply becoming a scholar. He wanted to create a great adventure for the mass audience he craved as a storyteller. The sojourn in Polynesia before the war had given him a first taste of what it was to be an impresario of dreams. Now the work could continue.

In the summer of 1946, a little more than a year after the end of the war, Heyerdahl packed his bags and stood ready to leave Norway a third time. He was returning to the USA. The *Wehrmacht* had retreated and surrendered, but Norway was industrially and financially crippled.[90] It was a move that many would have envied, away from the drudgery of economic and social misery. Across the nation, people dreamt of better lives elsewhere. As late as 1949, 35 percent of the Norwegian population stated in an opinion poll that they would emigrate if they could.[91] Heyerdahl did not have in mind a modest new abode elsewhere as he set off over the Atlantic. He simply had three copies of his manuscript, *Polynesia and America: A Study of Prehistoric Relations*, in his suitcase. His dream was to make an epic story his home. The USA was where dreams were made, especially now that most of Europe was in even worse condition than Norway was. Germany was crushed and Hans Günther had already spent one year in Allied custody for putting his scientific clout and the theory of the superiority of the white race in the service of the Nazi Party.

# 2

## Making the *Kon-Tiki*

### Scientists, Soldiers and a Crazy Idea

Idle time in the barracks gave Heyerdahl opportunity to dream about a raft expedition across the Pacific. It was a fanciful dream that he hoped would launch him into stardom when the interruption of the war was over. The idea of experimental archaeology was, however, not as original as it is easy to believe. Heyerdahl knew of the 1901 journey of Captain John C. Voss from Vancouver to Polynesia in a converted Native American dugout canoe. Voss had already showed the possibility that there had been contact between North America and Polynesia. In Heyerdahl's theory this was the second migration to Polynesia that had taken place around 1000 or 1100 AD. What remained for him to do was to prove the possibility of what he argued had been the first stage, namely the one from South America around 500 AD, and it was for this reason Heyerdahl wanted to reconstruct a raft of balsa wood, native to the Pacific coast of the Andean nations.

The first famous reconstruction of a historical vessel had taken place shortly before the journey of Voss, and it had been Norwegian. In 1893 a replica Viking ship sailed from Bergen in Norway to the World Fair in Chicago. The World's Columbian Exposition, as it was also called, was an attempt to appropriate and incorporate Columbus into the narration of the US national trajectory. This did not prevent the voyage of a Viking ship, 'proving' the possibility of a pre-Columbian contact between Europe and America, becoming a massive sensation.[1] In the 1920s the Norwegian adventurer Gerhard Folgerø carried out more journeys on reconstructions of Viking ships, and he gave popular lectures around Norway in the 1930s. Folgerø even planned to use his Viking ship *Roald Amundsen* to smuggle people from Nazi-occupied Norway to England during the war but he was intercepted and interned by the Germans in August 1940.[2] Heyerdahl never mentioned Folgerø in his writings but he would most certainly have been familiar both with his story and with the 1893 journey to Chicago.

Voyages in historical vessels are travels in time, and the exploration of the past became a way for Heyerdahl to continue the classic journey of discovery at a point when no blank spots remained on the map. It was in any case not the practical results of geographic expeditions that attracted the great masses. Journeys of discovery were pretexts for presenting dramatic stories. The failed polar expedition of Roald Amundsen in 1925 had been his most popular. It was adventure that audiences craved, together with the promise that heroes still existed.[3] The same was true for Charles Lindbergh's solo flight over the Atlantic in 1927. But heroic adventures still needed a claim that they were more than simple attempts to propel the protagonist into stardom. The hero had to be martyred for a worthy cause. John Alcock and Arthur Whitten Brown had already flown non-stop over the Atlantic in 1919. That Lindbergh proved that one could do it alone was not a very elaborate excuse for adventure, but it sufficed. Daredevils who did not care about the why and went over the Niagara Falls in barrels for the thrill of it received notoriety rather than stardom. Heyerdahl, for his part, had already decided to make a fight against scientific dogmatism the thing that would give meaning to his exploit. The dismissed scholar would take to the oceans.

In Heyerdahl's own story he arrived in New York in the summer of 1946 and tried to present 'his' theory to academics throughout the autumn. The rejection was unanimous, and based on a blind reverence of scientific dogma. Heyerdahl distilled his encounters with the scholars in the field to a single one that he described in more detail. In this episode an old and unnamed scientist refuses to read Heyerdahl's manuscript as he had already decided that his belief that the Polynesians migrated from Asia could not be wrong, regardless of whatever evidence Heyerdahl could present to the contrary. The old academic rejecting Heyerdahl is stereotypically described as white-haired and surrounded by obscure books in his study.[4] After this meeting it soon becomes clear for Heyerdahl that if he is to be listened to he has to prove his thesis practically.

In 1965 Heyerdahl's biographer Jacoby named the unidentified scientist as Dr Herbert Spinden of the Brooklyn Museum of Natural History.[5] This was the same Spinden who had bought Heyerdahl's Fatuiva collection during the war and helped Heyerdahl to become a member of the exclusive Explorers Club in New York in 1942. Spinden had even let Heyerdahl borrow his own flat for a period in the same year.[6] In 1998 Heyerdahl admitted that he had been living in Spinden's flat during part of the autumn of 1946, the same time when the meeting described in the *Kon-Tiki* book supposedly took place.[7] If anyone had been kindly disposed to listen to Heyerdahl it would have been Spinden, who helped him so much despite disagreeing with the Norwegian's theory.[8]

Heyerdahl used Spinden to epitomize an ossified academic world because he needed that opposition in order to appear as a scientific rebel. In the *Kon-Tiki* book and in letters home he upheld the image of being an impoverished, misunderstood genius without any support, but he never defined what the 'support' could entail. He had not previously appeared interested in any academic positions. Heyerdahl did no doubt meet with scientists during that autumn in New York but they could not have told him anything other than that his theory was neither original nor convincing. And in any case they would have been suspicious of someone who held institutional learning in such low esteem that he had not even graduated. Heyerdahl himself seemed relieved when he could finally give up the staged fight against academia. He wrote to his sponsor Thomas Olsen and said that now he needed to make a name for himself through a bit of a sensation so that his voice could be heard.[9] He had received the rejection he needed to get on with his task.

One of the most important figures in the build-up to the raft expedition, Bjørn Rørholt, a captain in the Norwegian Army, had arrived in Washington not long after Heyerdahl had come to New York. Rørholt had for a time during the war been Heyerdahl's commanding officer and he had encouraged him to start planning for the raft expedition.[10] Heyerdahl was, however, not the reason why Rørholt came to Washington. He was there to study, and it was a coincidence that they were in the USA at the same time. The Attaché Colonel Otto Munthe-Kaas himself had appointed Rørholt, his nephew, as the assistant Military Attaché at the Norwegian Embassy, which meant that Rørholt had an official position with institutional backing.[11] Heyerdahl already had contacts in the USA since his year-long sojourn there during the war, but now the situation dramatically improved. Rørholt became the entry point into the resources of the Norwegian Embassy in Washington.

Heyerdahl started in earnest with the preparations for a raft expedition in November 1946. His main problem was how to raise enough funds for an enterprise that would be far beyond even the substantial means that could be supplied by his father and Thomas Olsen. In late November Heyerdahl tried to convince the National Geographic Society that they should support his expedition. In return he would write an article about it in the society's magazine.[12] Here he had already published an article about the Fatuiva adventure in 1941 with the romantic title 'Turning Back Time in the South Seas'. Now his plea received a discouraging answer. J. R. Hildebrand, a third-ranking editor, declined the offer as he thought, ironically enough, that the resulting article would be too scientific.[13] Later Heyerdahl made this into a better story when he claimed to have been rejected because the society thought his journey was too dangerous, even suicidal.[14]

Heyerdahl's fortune would turn only days later when he entered the sumptuous New York premises of the Explorers Club in the Majestic building by Central Park. A Colonel Haskin of the US Air Force Material Command was offering the explorers the survival gear developed in his laboratories in exchange for detailed reports.[15] For Heyerdahl it was a major break-through. The US armed forces remained, a little more than a year after the Second World War, an enormous organization. The National Geographic Society was no longer crucial.

Bjørn Rørholt was just the kind of person that Heyerdahl needed to gain access to the new and exciting potential institutional support of the US armed forces, a war hero decorated with the British Distinguished Service Order (DSO), the highest military award granted to foreign soldiers. He had been in and out of Nazi-occupied Norway during the war, even taking part in the important operation of sinking the German battleship *Tirpitz* off the coast of Tromsø in the north of Norway in 1944. He had served with both the British Special Operations Executive and the Special Intelligence Service, and had contacts in the US armed forces. Some time in early December Rørholt called his friend Major Gordon W. Ross, a foreign liaison officer, and asked if the Pentagon had an interest in the expedition. The response was enthusiastic. With the help of Captain John Oppenheimer in the Public Relations Section, Ross set up a meeting with various bodies of the US Army and Navy such as the US Army Research and Development

Division, US Army Quartermaster, US Army Signal Corps, US Air Force Material Command and US Navy Hydrographic Department.[16]

The meeting took place on 12 December in the Pentagon.[17] Heyerdahl, flanked by Rørholt and Munthe-Kaas, came armed with a wish-list for equipment, and he came away having been promised practically every single item free of charge: field rations, technical equipment (including radios and cameras), emergency life rafts, sleeping bags, ropes and cooking utensils.[18] He had struck gold. It was through this meeting that Heyerdahl's expedition was transformed from a wild idea to a distinct possibility. He left the Pentagon with not only promises, but also a list of new contacts, both individuals and institutions, that could be of help. The US military machine had now given its firm approval to the Norwegian raft expedition across the Pacific.

## A Curious Military Exercise

Heyerdahl's use of the US armed forces was in some ways paradoxical. The reluctant soldier came to the Pentagon presenting a pseudoscientific idea of an itinerant culture-bearing white race that would have fitted without problems into the conception of the world held by the vanquished Nazis. Yet Heyerdahl's journey of discovery soon acquired a military garb, as reflected in his choice of crew. Besides a Norwegian refrigeration engineer, Herman Watzinger, whom he had met in New York, and a childhood friend, the painter Erik Hesselberg, Heyerdahl wrote to two Norwegian resistance heroes he knew from the war. One was Knut Haugland, who had participated in the sabotaging of German heavy-water production in Rjuken, later immortalized by the 1965 Anthony Mann film *The Heroes of Telemark*. The other one was Torstein Raaby, who had been in on the sinking of the *Tirpitz* together with Rørholt. Both had worked with the British and US military intelligence, and were decorated with DSOs. Heyerdahl was about to change snow for sea, guns for harpoons – transforming, tapping into and continuing the story of the heroic Norwegian fighting spirit of so much wartime fame in Britain and the USA. It would help him in his contact with the top brass at the Pentagon if the crew were 'good guys', brothers in arms.

It would have been impossible to carry out an expedition on the scale Heyerdahl wanted without a large backer. He was going to carry five tonnes of equipment on his raft, most of which he tried to obtain from the Pentagon, but also from the British armed forces whom he contacted in December 1946.[19] He also needed to move people and material over large distances. In January 1947 he estimated the cost of the venture to be $15,000 after the military contribution, which was probably a conservative estimate as he was in November 1948 still $14,500 in debt.[20] *Kon-Tiki* was remarkably cheap as the dollar was roughly ten times today's value. The main reason for the low costs was the US and British armed forces funding.

The US armed forces as well as the British provided Heyerdahl with the only kind of institutional stability he was used to as he came straight from the war. For the Fatuiva journey he had only needed to organize himself and Liv; this was an expedition on a much larger scale. The military connection gave him a framework within which to work and helped to align the expedition with the Norwegian war effort by using the aura of heroism and epic adventure that surrounded it. The manly, brave and fast-thinking figure of the soldier-adventurer could be further used to cast institutional science as effeminate, cowardly (not even daring to read Heyerdahl's 'thesis') and dogmatic. None of these stereotypes bore much similarity to Heyerdahl's experience in either the army or the academic world, but they helped him to construct a good story for public consumption.

In his subsequent book about the expedition Heyerdahl did not deny the involvement of the US and British armed forces, but he downplayed its importance. He devoted fewer than five pages to humorous descriptions of meetings with the US and British officers, compressing rounds of negotiations into single dramatic events in a style that can best be described as the mythic singular. He put forward two explanations for the interest that the military institutions showed in his expedition. The voyage supposedly provided an opportunity for the military laboratories to test their equipment in a realistic setting. Furthermore, Heyerdahl claimed that it, more significantly, also meant a welcome break from the drudgery of peacetime office work for the officers that became engaged in the expedition.[21] More than anything Heyerdahl didactically described these officers as his first audience, an audience that became enthralled with his theory and his adventure. But this was a simplification of reality.

Heyerdahl received substantial support backed by generals and admirals, and it is hard to imagine that he caught their interest simply by proposing to test military equipment, however adventurous and thrilling his *Kon-Tiki* idea was.

It is easy to understand what Heyerdahl got out of the military connection, but it is much more difficult to understand what he could possibly have given back in exchange. Sometimes there was a real material use of Heyerdahl's expedition that was not as innocent as he made it out to be. The contacts with the British armed forces went through Colonel 'Bertie' Lumsden. Lumsden was the Washington representative of Major-General R. E. Laycock, Chief of Combined Operations and responsible for amphibious operations in the British armed forces. Lumsden wrote to his superiors in Britain that Heyerdahl's crew of well-known Norwegians could after completion report back as to the military dimension that their voyage might have had.[22] The response he got from Laycock was that the expedition could provide ideas as to how to carry out raids with small vessels.[23] The Combined Operations had quite a history of eccentric projects. At the height of the war they tried to develop warships of reified ice, and now they were interested in a prehistoric raft that no one knew would float or could be steered.[24]

At the US Navy Hydrographic Office the distinguished Rear Admiral Cato D. Glover gave the crew charts of currents in return for having them corrected. The meeting with this 'good-natured old sea-dog' is narrated in the *Kon-Tiki* book.[25] There is good reason to suspect that the navy's oceanographers were indeed interested in the data that Heyerdahl could collect, as it would help them to understand the great ocean that was now virtually all under their control. Maybe they even thought it could be useful in helping to construct models with which to calculate the fallout of the atomic bombs that were being tested in Micronesia. Or it could have been the case that Rear Admiral Glover was just genuinely excited by the primitive raft that was to explore a Pacific so different from his of carnage and modern technology. Glover had commanded the aircraft carrier *USS Enterprise* during the war and travelled back to the Pacific in July 1946 to observe the atomic bomb tests, Operation Crossroads, on the small Micronesian atoll of Bikini, or Pikinni, from his flagship, the amphibious force vessel *USS Blue Ridge*. Through a curious coincidence Colonel Lumsden had been the British War Office observer at the Bikini atoll that same summer.[26]

The investment of the US armed forces in the *Kon-Tiki* stemmed in part from an expected exchange of information, but there probably existed a much more important explanation for this backing. One way to understand the military support is to see it as a transaction between Heyerdahl and various military bodies in which the latter offered him goods in return for publicity, or 'popular credit'. This credit had become increasingly difficult to earn after the end of the war when huge armies had gone from fighting to occupying. Policing was much less easy than battles to make into heroic stories – heroic stories that the military-industrial-media complex needed to fight for recognition and budget allocations. Heyerdahl's reason for mentioning the army contacts in his own narration could, apart from lending weight and legitimacy to his argument, have been part of an implicit agreement between the two parties over much-coveted publicity. One indication pointing to this is the early involvement of the US War Department Public Relations Divison in the project, and its eagerness to put Heyerdahl in contact with the various parts of the US Army and Navy that would help him with equipment.[27] That the US Navy was so active might in itself point towards this conclusion since there was ambiguity over the atom bomb (in particular over the virtue of the Bikini tests) and the Navy's postwar role in the USA at the time.[28] According to a National Opinion Research Centre Poll in 1946 70 percent of the US population wished to see a prohibition on the production of atomic weapons, and a majority of that group wished to see the USA destroying its existing arsenal.[29]

The Second World War had seen the public relations side of fighting grow into a fully fledged industry. For all the official rhetoric, and amidst an ideological vacuum, troops and officers could at least all agree that they were fighting for recognition and the credit of the folks back home.[30] Public relations officers, like Eisenhower's media expert US Navy captain Harry Butcher, and journalists, like Ernie Pyle, became key figures in a war in which the achievement was real only if it became a heroic story.[31] It was on the point of heroism that the interests of the military machine and Heyerdahl overlapped. Since the psychological and proxy wars of the immediate postwar period that were developing into the Cold War failed to provide heroic battles, Heyerdahl was welcomed by public relations officers.

The media savvy of the US War Department Public Relations Division took even Heyerdahl by surprise.[32] After one of his meetings with the War Department in the Pentagon (26 December 1946) Heyerdahl was paraded before a well-attended press conference in full holiday season. The following day the news of the expedition was cabled out over the USA and the world. The press release had the War Department Public Relations Division's letterhead and stated that the 'noted Norwegian explorer' had entered into an agreement with the War Department concerning an expedition across the Pacific and then proceeded to outline what army and air force equipment the raft would be carrying.[33]

That Heyerdahl's expedition was about publicity was something that was clear for Rørholt and his uncle at the military mission of the Norwegian Embassy in Washington. The only difference between them and the Pentagon was that they conceived of the event in terms of publicity for Norway. Both men tried to secure leave of absence for Haugland and Raaby so that they could join the expedition. Rørholt wrote home to his commanding officer saying that Heyerdahl's expedition could remedy the problem that Norway had received so little credit in the USA for its wartime contributions to the Allied cause.[34] When Haugland and Raaby had been granted their leaves Rørholt wrote to them and told them to travel in military uniforms so that they could greet the press upon arrival as representatives of Norway. They should not let modesty affect them but instead freely market themselves as they were on a mission for the good name of Norway and its armed forces.[35] When it came to publicity there were gains to be made by everyone, especially Heyerdahl who was riding on the crest of the momentum that he and Rørholt had created.

The story that the young Norwegian adventurer brought to the Pentagon was deeply allegorical. The US Navy had after the Second World War made itself the suzerain of virtually the entire Pacific Ocean, and it controlled outright the Micronesian territories that had formerly been in the hands of the Japanese. It was only in 1951 that the US Navy relinquished this control to the US Department of the Interior. The Micronesian acquisition led to the opening of a new frontier in the history of US geographical expansion, which also fulfilled old desires that the Pacific might one day be opened to the USA as the mainland was firmly settled.[36] Even though the islands in question were only small ones in Micronesia, their possession by the Navy transformed the Pacific into an 'American lake'.[37] The USA had acquired these territories with a strategic reasoning uncannily like the one Heyerdahl employed for his thesis on Polynesian migration. The argument was that, after Pearl Harbor, the world's oceans could not be seen as 'defensive barriers'; they were 'open highways' to both positive and negative cross-cultural interaction.[38]

After the end of hostilities in the Pacific the US Navy was effectively, and later officially through the UN, to rule an area the size of the continental USA. The three groups of islands with a population of 50,000 people, and a vast sea between them, constituted an area considered as the beginning of an imagined oceanographic freeway leading back to the US mainland. A host of military and academic bodies were enlisted in trying to understand these territories and the sea surrounding them. In June 1946 the Pacific Science Conference was held in which US academia aimed to co-ordinate with the armed forces in exploring the new territories. At the same time the Pacific Science Board (PSB) was formed to organize this exploration in the field. Although the PSB mainly dealt with 'exploration', a large part of the US effort in the new territory was centred on the area as an atom bomb test ground. Heyerdahl's expedition became a way for the Navy to supplement other efforts to understand the Pacific.

Heyerdahl had tried to impress a representative of Nazi race science with his concept of an itinerant white culture-bearing race, but it was only when he brought the same idea to the USA that he achieved a breakthrough. Heyerdahl's thesis that it was a folk with white skin and blue eyes that had been the first settlers of Polynesia, as the first War Department press release claimed, rang poetically in an era of new US expansion into the vast Pacific formally under Asian control.[39] In the wartime propaganda book *America,* distributed to the liberated areas of Europe, Stephen Vincent Benét claimed that the USA did not want to 'rule the world or set up an American empire in which Americans will be the master race and other people subject race. If you ask any real American whether he believes in a master race, you will get a long stare or a long laugh. Americans do not believe in master races.'[40] Heyerdahl did not get any 'long stares' or 'long laughs'; he got several tonnes of equipment as well as logistical support from the Pentagon in order to prove his thesis about a culture-bearing white race that dovetailed into the US project in the Pacific with allegorical perfection.

## To the White House via the United Nations

At six o'clock in the evening of 5 December 1946, Heyerdahl entered an exclusive Manhattan flat together with the young engineering student Herman Watzinger whom he had enticed into becoming part of his crew. A trio consisting of Robert C. Durham, a US airman that Heyerdahl and

Rørholt had met in Russia during the war, and the two journalists John D. Withmore and Egil Tresselt, was waiting for them.[41] These three men had proposed to manage and finance Heyerdahl's expedition. It was a support that in the end did not materialize, but the minutes from this meeting are fascinating reading. The conversation mostly revolved around the necessity of spending a lot of money on promotion, on the future book and on how to get radio messages with news for press distribution from the Pacific. But maybe more interesting is the persistence with which the need for diplomatic support was underlined. It was agreed that the key to gaining this support was to get in contact with the Norwegian Secretary-General of the new United Nations, Trygve Lie. Tresselt, also Norwegian and the UN correspondent of Norsk Telegrambyrå (NTB), promised to try to visit Lie as soon as he possibly could.[42]

If Heyerdahl had sailed from the shores of the USA the assistance from the US armed forces would have been enough, but he wanted to set sail from Peru on a raft of balsa logs he would need to acquire in the Ecuadorean jungle. He would have to transport a great quantity of equipment, much of it military, through customs in two South American countries. For this task it was necessary to try to gain diplomatic support. And there was no lack of diplomats in New York at the time. The new United Nations' modest temporary headquarters had recently been set up in a disused ice ring in Queens. This was not the only fortuitous circumstance: the organization was also led by Heyerdahl's countryman Lie, who had previously been the foreign minister in the wartime Norwegian government in exile.

Heyerdahl visited the UN together with Tresselt sometime between 5 and 11 December. In the *Kon-Tiki* book Heyerdahl described how they managed to speak to not only the Peruvian and Ecuadorean representatives, but also the assistant secretary Dr Benjamin Cohen from Chile and the Norwegian ambassador Wilhelm von Munthe af Morgonstierne. Upon hearing that countrymen were in the building Lie stopped for a chat.[43] This was probably a simplification of events, as the meeting with Lie would almost certainly have been arranged before. Tresselt had access to Lie, and Rørholt knew his daughter. Lie gave his blessing to the enterprise, and his assistant Tom Gjesdal put Heyerdahl in contact with Cohen.[44]

Benjamin Cohen, a Chilean diplomat and amateur archaeologist, was the assistant secretary of the Department of Public Information, the 'propaganda' branch of the UN. Cohen received a tenth of the UN's budget for spreading a message of international dialogue and understanding.[45] The *Kon-Tiki* was a versatile story; prehistoric contacts between people who had hitherto been seen as cut off from each other could be viewed as an international exchange of sorts. Cohen did not hesitate to give his whole-hearted support to Heyerdahl and his expedition and sat down to write him letters of introduction to the presidents of Peru, Ecuador and also, for good measure, Chile.[46]

After Heyerdahl had gained the support of Cohen he could proceed to establish the remaining contacts that he needed. He travelled to Washington for meetings with the Peruvian and Ecuadorean ambassadors. By 20 December the Ecuadorean ambassador to the USA, Dr Francisco Yllescas, had issued courtesy visas to Heyerdahl and Watzinger, and the vice-consul at the Ecuadorean Embassy, Cristobal Montero, had written to the customs administration of Guayaquil to let the expedition and its material into the country without any problems.[47] By early January 1947 the Ecuadorean delegate to the UN, Manuel A. Navarro, had written to the balsa manufacturer Gustavo von Buchwald introducing Heyerdahl. In early January Heyerdahl also received the green light from the Peruvian authorities, and the Peruvian Navy put its resources at Heyerdahl's disposal.[48]

The imprimatur of the new UN opened the doors to South America for Heyerdahl, but he ensured a good reception by selling his story to yet more parties. The white or mestizo managerial elites in South America had for a long time nurtured theories of a prehistoric white master race as a way to disenfranchise the indigenous populations.[49] Heyerdahl could play the racial and nationalist card. This strategy is evident in a letter to Rear Admiral Frederico Diaz Dulanto of the Peruvian Navy. Heyerdahl claimed that the admiral's country had been the most important seat of an advanced civilization of culture-bearing white men who had from its shores colonized Rapa Nui and then the rest of Polynesia. The history of Peru, Heyerdahl guaranteed, would become known to the world as being every bit as extraordinary and captivating as that Egypt or any Old World country. Heyerdahl promised that he was the man who could give Peru its long-overdue recognition through the publicity his expedition would generate.[50] On this occasion Heyerdahl clearly spelt out how popular credit was used in transactions over material support.

In his letter to Dulanto Heyerdahl also promised that the expedition would make all its scientific findings available to the Peruvian authorities.

This was a not unimportant point. On 28 September 1945 the United States had proclaimed the right to control both the territory under the sea as far as the continental shelf, as well as a lot of the sea above it.[51] Soon Mexico, Argentina and Panama took the same measures to protect mineral as well as fishing resources, mostly from encroachment of US vessels. One thing that Heyerdahl incidentally was to discover on his expedition, a discovery he presumably shared with the Peruvians, was that the Humboldt Current off Peru's coast, contrary to popular belief, was full of fish. The Peruvian president, José Luis Bustamente y Rivero, whom Heyerdahl met before setting out on the expedition, extended national sovereignty in its coastal waters on 1 August 1947, to the chagrin of the US authorities. Herman Watzinger, Heyerdahl's second-in-command, returned to Peru after the trip with the *Kon-Tiki* and set up an important fishing operation in the coastal waters of the nation, an operation that he worked with for a large part of the rest of his life.

Although Heyerdahl briefly mentioned both the military support and diplomatic support in the *Kon-Tiki* book, he completely left out the central role played by the Norwegian Embassy in Washington. It was the embassy that gave Heyerdahl a permanent base from which he could organize his expedition. Rørholt drafted an informal agreement between the embassy and the expedition on 2 January 1947. Heyerdahl and the people helping him were given a room behind the reception of the military mission of the embassy where Rørholt and Munthe-Kaas worked. They were able to use the telephone of the mission (though paying the bill themselves) and were helped by both the secretary of the embassy, Gerd Vold, and its press counsellor, Hans Olav. They could not use 'c/o Norwegian Embassy' on their letterheads, but were instead to write the address of the building on Massachusetts Avenue shared by the Office of the Defence Attaché and the Norwegian Information Service.[52] An organizational committee for the expedition was also created with Rørholt as its Washington representative and Munthe-Kaas in charge of the finances.[53]

The involvement of the embassy in the creation of a headquarters for the expedition was not uncontroversial in Oslo, which explains why Heyerdahl later did not spell out the connection. The Ministry of Foreign Affairs seemed to have misgivings.[54] Public spending on a private expedition was a delicate issue, especially as Norway was grappling with serious problems of postwar reconstruction. Not even the great Norwegian polar explorer Roald Amundsen had, at the height of his career, been immune from questions when it came to public financing.[55]

On the same day that an agreement between the embassy and the expedition was signed, Munthe-Kaas wrote home to his superiors to defend his move by arguing that it was in the nation's interest to support Heyerdahl.[56] The colonel's cautious tone suggests that he was expecting criticism. Heyerdahl would for his part do all that he could to repay with the popular credit that he was learning to master. Throughout the expedition he was keen to correct the mistake of it being referred to as 'Norwegian-Swedish' (as one of the crew members would be Swedish), or Scandinavian.[57] His endeavour was to lead a Norwegian expedition, for the good of brand Norway.

Heyerdahl's close contacts with the diplomats at the Norwegian Embassy also made it easier for him to gain access to the US Department of State. Foreign Liaison Officer Colonel Graling had suggested that such a connection would be useful, and Munthe-Kaas wrote to the Norwegian ambassador to Washington to help make this meeting possible.[58] According to the diplomatic protocol such a contact had to be made by someone at the civil branch of the embassy. On 17 December Heyerdahl travelled from New York to Washington.[59]

No documentation is left from the meeting with the Department of State. Just what Heyerdahl offered and what the Department of State was willing to give remains unclear. The next time the Department resurfaces in the *Kon-Tiki* paper trail is after the expedition when five of its employees were invited to a cocktail party at the embassy welcoming the crew back to the USA.[60] Two of these had held junior positions in Scandinavia, and only one had some South American connection. The most prominent member of the group was Loy Henderson, director of the Office of Near Eastern and African Affairs.

After Heyerdahl had returned from his expedition the Department of State used his story for the same reasons as everyone else – publicity. First it was Heyerdahl who approached them and asked for a meeting with President Harry S. Truman through the Norwegian Embassy.[61] The request was granted and Truman received the crew in the White House and symbolically accepted a US ensign that had been flown on the raft. This happened during a fifteen-minute meeting starting at noon on 3 October 1947.[62] Truman was thrilled, and he later liked the *Kon-Tiki* book so much that he sent Heyerdahl an appreciatory letter.[63] Soon after he had been granted a photo-op with Truman, the Department of State asked Heyerdahl if they could reproduce an article about the expedition in the magazines *Neue Auslese* and *Heute*, both published by the military government in occupied Germany and Austria.[64] The story of the white culture-bearing race fanning out over the world had travelled in an ironic full circle and was now published in US magazines meant to counter years of Nazi propaganda.

## A Media Event Takes Shape

Soldiers and diplomats made the expedition a distinct possibility, but Heyerdahl's trip would not have been complete unless he also made sure that he had the media on board. His aim was, after all, as he had told Olsen, to create a sensation.[65] The journey across the Pacific was to be a story for a popular mass audience, and this was important both for Heyerdahl's desire to reach fame and for repaying with publicity the aid that he had been receiving. Among the first steps that Heyerdahl took after beginning to plan in earnest for an expedition in November 1946 was to secure a book contract with his Norwegian publisher.[66] But even more important than a Norwegian book was to interest an international press syndicate in the journey. Through the help of the Norwegian journalist Egil Tresselt, Heyerdahl would eventually come into contact with the North American Newspaper Association (NANA).

NANA had the great advantage that it supplied articles to the respectable *New York Times*, close to the Truman administration and far from the yellow press.[67] The general manager of NANA, John Neville Wheeler, was a man well connected in both politics and media who had previously signed up significant writers like F. Scott Fitzgerald and Ernest Hemingway. Heyerdahl also received an offer from the Hearst press that he turned down, since, interestingly enough, he thought its sensationalism would hurt the expedition.[68] Not all publicity was good publicity for Heyerdahl; he seemed keen to avoid the same kind of press coverage that had in the end served to make the turn-of-the-century race to the Poles into a grotesque media circus.

Heyerdahl signed a deal with Wheeler at NANA in the beginning of February 1947. He got $1000 for the exclusive worldwide rights, with the exception of Norway.[69] Soon afterwards a contract was also signed between Heyerdahl and NTB for the Norwegian rights.[70] Heyerdahl was disappointed that none of the money from the contracts was to be paid in advance, but at least he had managed to ensure that his small raft would be in the papers. Now the only problem was how to relay all the articles that he was supposed to write. The days when audiences patiently waited years for news of explorers in the polar seas and tropical jungles were over. The modern media event was based on almost instantaneous gratification.

In the *Kon-Tiki* book, Heyerdahl portrayed himself as reluctantly bringing a radio on board the raft, only agreeing in order that they could send reports and observations of the weather and the like.[71] This is explained in a didactic passage in the book where Heyerdahl first instinctively refuses the idea: the radio would be out of place on their primitive raft and he is only convinced when the scientific-sounding words 'observations' and 'reports' are mentioned. The *Kon-Tiki* could be both primitive and scientific. Heyerdahl was however uninterested in discussing the importance of the role of the radio in creating his publicity sensation. Even in a less public text such as the expedition prospectus written in February 1947, the radio's function on the raft was described as being only to transmit weather observations and as a possible emergency signal.[72]

The centrality of the radio on the *Kon-Tiki* can be illustrated by the fact that Heyerdahl brought four radio sets aboard and no fewer than two radio operators, Haugland and Raaby (see plate 7). One set was specially manufactured by the US company National and was later sold (with due reference to the *Kon-Tiki*) as the 'National NC-173'. The company was tightly linked to the US armed forces, so it is not improbable that the contact was made through the Pentagon. The National set was slow in delivery, and Haugland wrote to his contact Brigadier F. W. Nicholls of the British military intelligence agency MI8 in order to ask for a 'B Mark II' radio that he was used to from his days in the SOE.[73] He eventually got the set, but the issue of radio communication gave rise to a heated conflict between Rørholt and the two radio operators.[74] The US Navy and the US Signal Corps supplied two more sets, one for emergencies (SCR-578) and the other to make contact with aircraft (AN/TRC-7).[75] Haugland and Raaby were unfamiliar with the latter set and were trained in its use by the US Signal Corps at Fort Monmouth, New Jersey, on 6 and 7 February 1947.[76]

The Pentagon was not only instrumental in supplying the radios used on the raft, they also gave Heyerdahl a technological infrastructure. The US Signal Corps requested the aid of the Penn State University Amateur Club to work as an official contact station for the *Kon-Tiki* transmitting on amateur frequencies with the Norwegian call signal LI2B. The traffic to Penn State was primarily directed to the US Army call signal ALMA, but also to the club's own W3YA. All information sent was overseen by the US Army, who required Heyerdahl for some reason to leave out any information about the Penn State involvement.[77] The unofficial official contact station also recorded a number of Heyerdahl's transmissions to be used for radio broadcasts.[78] If the Penn State station outside Harrisburg was not enough, Heyerdahl could still count on the 30 stations of the US Federal Communications Commission, as its chief field engineer, George Turner, had ordered them all to be attentive to LI2B calling.[79]

Heyerdahl turned his prehistoric raft into a modern communications hub with the help primarily of the US Signal Corps. The four radios and the two operators received approximately 370 telegraphic messages during the *Kon-Tiki* trip and they probably sent as many themselves.[80] To this could be added the voice communication. One wonders how Heyerdahl's crew managed to sleep holed up next to busy, noisy equipment, the crackling, distorted voices emanating from the receivers mingling with the mangled piercing beeps of the inbound Morse.

Heyerdahl was to send approximately one article every second day from the raft to the young editor Peter Celliers at NANA who worked with the *Kon-Tiki*. The main aim of the radio communication clearly was to supply articles. This was illustrated when the batteries of the radios started running low during the voyage. NANA became concerned that they would not receive any more articles and started planning to ask the US Army to fly out with a plane from Hawaii and drop a battery. It would, they suggested, make a good story and be feasible as the army would welcome the type of publicity this would bring them.[81] This might have been correct, but NANA showed here that they did not fully understand Heyerdahl's creation. He needed to appear as though he was free and independent, cut off from land and also at risk. The technological dimension of the *Kon-Tiki* was to appear as just an added extra, and could not be made to seem pivotal by such a dramatic action. Heyerdahl was keen to associate technology with positive images. In his account of the voyage he connected the use of the radio to that of the public-serving ham community when describing how the crew radioed a doctor after the raft's arrival in Polynesia for advice on how a boy with an abscess on his head could be treated.[82] Heyerdahl thus even managed to turn the radio communication into a story in itself, another one that concealed a more prosaic truth.

The most important communication conducted over the radio, the one between Heyerdahl and NANA, relayed via amateurs and Penn State, was fraught with problems of a non-technological nature from the very beginning. For the first time Heyerdahl encountered a concept of publicity different from his own, and it came from the professionals in the media industry. Heyerdahl wanted to create a sensation but he did not want sensationalism. If the sensationalism of his adventure was stressed to the extent that his scientific rationale became obstructed, the publicity would backfire. This seemed to have been completely clear to Heyerdahl, but what he would soon find out was that a much thinner line separated good publicity from bad in the media world. What mattered to sell newspapers was publicity, full stop.

NANA might have been more upmarket than the Hearst press, but this did not mean that it was altogether averse to the sensational. Heyerdahl should have known as much from a letter that Wheeler wrote to Rørholt on 23 January, before a deal was signed. Wheeler speculated that the men living in cramped quarters might very well produce some internal rows, as had happened in the expeditions to the Poles, and if any such developed Wheeler wanted to publish it.[83] Heyerdahl got the same demand while on the raft from Celliers, who asked how the morale was on board, implying the usefulness of a juicy conflict story.[84] The expedition's secretary Gerd Vold answered for Heyerdahl saying that if the morale were bad they would never write about it, but instead hope to remember it with a laugh when the journey was over.[85] Celliers was unsatisfied and responded that rows and conflicts between the expedition members would make much better copy than any amount of good spirit, and that when one enters the public world of the media it is necessary to let go of any lingering reservation one might have about self-exposure.[86]

Celliers also became impatient with the slow inflow of articles, adding that Heyerdahl ought to be worried because if he was not in the paper now he would make less money out of the enterprise when he went on lecture tours and wrote books later on.[87] Celliers was not completely averse to the notion that the more 'serious' scientific side of Heyerdahl's expedition was something that could be used to create publicity, even though a row would be better. Many of the articles passed to Celliers were the stuff of popular travel writing, with adjectives such as 'mysterious', 'rough', 'fantastic', 'dangerous' and 'roaring', but the great majority of them were loaded with 'scientific' signifiers. Celliers even asked for more texts of a scientific nature that were based on Heyerdahl's theory of Polynesian migration.[88] The newspapers published articles focused on science and on adventure even-handedly. The conflict around which Heyerdahl had arranged his life was approaching a solution.

In Heyerdahl's view, the *National Geographic Magazine*, with its focus on popular science, appeared as the ideal venue for an adventure that was to be serious as well as sensational. The one-and-a-half-million readership of the yellow-wreath-covered magazine represented a perfect audience for Heyerdahl, and he could never bring himself to accept that they turned his project down. Heyerdahl was furious when Wheeler, after the end of the expedition, sold an article to the *Reader's Digest* as he feared that the *National Geographic* would not want it any more.[89] Heyerdahl argued that it did not make economic sense since it would undercut the market, and that he could sell the story to smaller magazines for the same amount of money. What was more important for Heyerdahl was to gain the right kind of readership for his story; publicity and sensation were not only about numbers but also about the context in which they were achieved.

Wheeler soon became exasperated with what he deemed to be Heyerdahl's unreasonable demands.[90] Heyerdahl had earned his first disaffected business partner. The soldiers and the diplomats had hardly caused any problems, but when it came to the media Heyerdahl encountered a different agenda. The income from NANA could have been greater if there had been more rows, if someone had been lost overboard or even if the raft had sunk. To play with sensation was to play with fire, and Heyerdahl's obligation was not only to himself and his crew. He had taken a mortgage on his own success by offering to provide a good story for so many that he could not afford to do anything other than achieve it.

## The Voyage

Heyerdahl left the USA with Herman Watzinger on 12 January 1947. They were travelling to Ecuador to find balsa logs in the jungle with which they would construct the raft. The first major problem soon presented itself. He had been so preoccupied with the planning and, it seems, so ignorant of the local conditions that he had not realized that the rainy season made travelling to the jungle virtually impossible. Through some good contacts and luck Watzinger and Heyerdahl managed to find transport and enough material with which to build the raft, and they arranged for it to be taken to Peru. Heyerdahl was back in the USA on 7 February and continued with the increasingly hectic preparations. On 13 March he travelled to Lima to supervise the Peruvian Navy personnel who were to build the raft. Heyerdahl's diplomatic networking had paid off. Soon the crew gathered: Hesselberg, Watzinger, Raaby and Haugland. A sixth member was found in Peru, the Swedish anthropologist Bengt Danielsson, who had participated in another South American expedition under the leadership of the Finnish ethnologist Dr Rafael Karsten. Danielsson, aged 25, was the youngest crew member; the oldest, Heyerdahl and Hesselberg, were 32 (see plate 5). The expedition's headquarters in Washington DC was now staffed and run by Gerd Vold alone, as discord between Haugland, Raaby and Rørholt had seen the latter distance himself from the project.

The crew made a journey up into the Andes to see all the terra firma they could before setting sail. After a test run the raft was finally ready to be towed out from the harbour of Callao on Monday 28 April. The crew were to spend 101 days on the small surface made of balsa logs lashed together. When they reached the Tuamotu islands in French Polynesia on 7 August they had drifted 4300 miles on the Humboldt Current. Their passage was to be mostly calm, and without any major incidents. Heyerdahl kept himself exceedingly busy in any case. He wrote numerous articles, exposed thousand of metres of film and began to write what would become the *Kon-Tiki* book.[91] This frantic activity was in a way ironic as one of the dominant themes of the articles, film and book was to be how relaxing it was to float leisurely across the ocean far from the stress of civilization and the rat-race of everyday life (see plate 10).

After a short sojourn on Tuamotu the crew was picked up by a schooner sent out by the French government that also took the *Kon-Tiki* raft in tow. From the capital of French Polynesia, Tahiti, the crew and raft then travelled on board a Norwegian freight ship bound for the USA. They arrived in San Francisco on 28 September and made their way to the east coast. Only a little more than a year had passed since Heyerdahl had come to the USA in the summer of 1946 with his idea of sailing from South America to Polynesia on a raft. A combination of determination and circumstance had brought him close to his goal of making a sensation.

The actual voyage of the raft was instrumental in providing raw material for this story and also media publicity, but at the same time it was only a small step along the way. It was after returning from the Pacific that Heyerdahl would have to begin the painstaking work that would lead him to that great audience he wanted to conquer.

# 3

## From Raft to Brand

### Keeping a Raft Afloat

Heyerdahl quickly learnt the art of generating publicity during the organization and execution of his raft expedition. The *Kon-Tiki* story was to repay not only his backers, but also his own travails. That the story was also ultimately going to be in Heyerdahl's possession, literally, was clear from the very beginning. The written contract-like agreement between the *Kon-Tiki* crew members and Heyerdahl, drafted in early January 1947, states he was to be in charge of all publications and retain the right to write *the* book when the expedition was over.[1] This was not an uncommon procedure when it came to the organization of this kind of expedition. It was the leader, after all, who took the financial risks. The document does however show that the *Kon-Tiki* was clearly thought of as a media event by its participants.

The USA was from the beginning Heyerdahl's preferred market. It was there his story was to be sold. Not only had he tried to settle in the USA, but he had also come back to its shores one year after the war to realize his fanciful idea of a raft expedition. As the *Kon-Tiki* organization was taking shape Heyerdahl searched and found a US firm to syndicate his articles, and during the making of the expedition he also hired a literary agent, Ingeborg Barth, to try to place his book with a US company.[2] Barth failed, however. Heyerdahl had been thinking ahead and negotiated a deal with his old publisher in Norway, but if it had been up to him to decide it seems reasonable to assume that the first *Kon-Tiki* book would have been published in the USA.

In the *Kon-Tiki* expedition's prospectus Heyerdahl claimed that offers received for the publicity rights had been refused since making a profit from such sources would conflict with the scientific nature of the expedition.[3] This was neither true (he had by that time already signed a deal with his Norwegian publisher), nor credible. The prospectus was written in order to make him seem more serious in the eyes of potential backers. In reality, Heyerdahl's problem was that no one in the USA was offering him a good deal for either the book or the film. This remained the case even when Heyerdahl returned to the east coast of the USA in September 1947, a fact that disappointed him greatly.

Heyerdahl created a sensation with his expedition, but it was not big enough for the huge media market in the USA, and, more importantly, the media did not really seem to know what to make of the event. Heyerdahl's press agent claimed in October 1947 that the article sales had not been remarkable.[4] This, however, was probably a comment mostly born out of the conflict over money in which the two had become embroiled. Contrary to Wheeler's assertion, the *Kon-Tiki* did get substantial publicity in the North American press. Extrapolating from the unfortunately incomplete sources, a rough estimate is that Heyerdahl sold around 500 pieces about his voyage to North American newspapers. This was not a small number, but it was evidently not enough.

It had not been easy for the newspapers to know what to do with the *Kon-Tiki*. The prestigious *New York Times*, close to NANA, had taken an interest in the expedition and published 36 of Heyerdahl's approximately 60 articles. This was a confirmation of Heyerdahl's respectability. The copy-editors at the paper had also helped to temper the sensationalism of Heyerdahl and Celliers, changing article titles such as 'Storms, Whales, Porpoises, Unfriendly Sharks, Enliven Days During Kon Tiki Raft's Slow Journey Across Pacific' into 'Raft in High Seas Rides Easy and Dry'.[5] But the *New York Times* did have a problem in defining what Heyerdahl's creation really was, and the articles about the journey would end up in wildly different sections of the paper: foreign news, domestic news, business news, science and education, as well as entertainment news. After the completion of the journey the paper editorialized the feat by the 'Scandinavian scientists' as 'one of the great adventure stories of our time'.[6] Finally Heyerdahl had received exactly the kind of coverage he wanted.

On top of the newspapers, both the *Reader's Digest* and *Life Magazine* published Heyerdahl shortly after the voyage. He still wanted to publish with the *National Geographic Magazine*, as that would give him more scientific credibility. The massive numbers in which both *Reader's Digest* and *Life* were circulated did not seem to signify too much to Heyerdahl. The *Reader's Digest* article was to be reproduced in all of the international editions, a rare feat as its editor, DeWitt Wallace, wrote to Heyerdahl in a congratulatory letter.[7] But Heyerdahl wanted the right kind of sensation, not just huge circulation. Despite his success in getting out his *Kon-Tiki* story it was as though he still had not worked out how to address his audience in the right way.

Heyerdahl briefly returned to Norway in the end of 1947 and did a short lecture tour, but by January 1948 he was back in the USA. Lecturing was now his main strategy to raise publicity around the *Kon-Tiki* and to acquire funds to repay the loans that had enabled him to set sail. The other *Kon-Tiki* crew members toured as well, but mostly in Europe. Heyerdahl had entered an agreement with National Lecture Management that would take him on a tour throughout the USA during the winter and the spring of 1948. The lectures were popular, but in the end the deal proved a financial disaster. Heyerdahl had signed a poor contract, and the problems did not end there. Despite the success of the tour Heyerdahl had still not been able to raise enough interest to sell the book he was going to write and the film that he had shot on the raft. He wrote to his former crew and reported that the publicity that the *Kon-Tiki* had received was still not enough, adding that the USA was a larger country that any of them could have imagined.[8] What would make a success in Norway counted for little in the USA.

In late April 1948 Heyerdahl was forced into a tactical retreat. The *Kon-Tiki* book had to be written before it was too late, even if it meant that Heyerdahl would have to content himself with publishing it in Norway. The dream of making it in the USA had to be put on hold. Heyerdahl travelled back and began writing the book in a chalet outside Lillehammer in the southern Norwegian mountains, moving after some months to another log-cabin in Tydalen, a short distance north. He worked from nine in the morning to eleven in the evening, seven days a week. Every word was crafted by pencil in his square handwriting during the day, and then typed in the evening. The manuscript was eventually finished on 4 August 1948, four days after the publisher's deadline, but in good time to get the book ready for the Christmas rush.[9]

## The Beginnings of a Bestseller

What Heyerdahl had in the spring of 1948 was a story he was desperate to tell, a lot of debts and a contract with Harald Grieg at the Norwegian publishing house Gyldendal that he had signed back in December 1946.[10] When he started writing the eternal question of science and adventure presented itself: how much of each would make for a perfect mix? Acutely conscious that he was writing a book for an imagined mass audience, he was careful not to put the lay reader off with too much of his theory about prehistoric migrations. The first theoretical chapter was reworked, shortened and simplified after the first draft, and he opted for a strategy of dispersing references to the theory throughout the book so as to not weary the reader.[11] Apart from such minor adjustments the text was remarkably similar to Heyerdahl's articles, and anybody who had followed the newspaper reporting of the raft would have recognized all the major events and stories in the book. Heyerdahl did not introduce any new themes or specific occurrences at this stage. He focused his energies on constructing a smooth narrative that would bind together the *Kon-Tiki* story.

Like Rørholt at the Norwegian Embassy or Dr Cohen at the UN, Grieg at the reputable firm of Gyldendal soon became someone who would open doors for Heyerdahl. By June 1948, when Heyerdahl was not even close to finishing his book up in the mountains, Grieg had enticed the largest and most important Swedish publishing firm, Albert Bonniers Förlag, to publish the future *Kon-Tiki* book. Heyerdahl accepted the offer by 10 July.[12] He had now sold his first foreign rights, not to the USA as he had hoped, but it was still a step in the right direction. He had never managed to get this far with his first book about the journey to Fenua Enata.

Grieg soon scored yet another triumph in selling the still-unfinished *Kon-Tiki* in the summer of 1948. Philip Unwin of the British publishing house Allen & Unwin had travelled to Norway on holiday. He knew that he had to do a bit of work, as his uncle and boss Sir Stanley Unwin expected his staff to visit foreign publishers on their holidays.[13] Philip Unwin called on Grieg, publisher of Knut Hamsun and many of the greatest Norwegian writers. He left the office having been persuaded to buy the translation rights to quite a different kind of book than what he probably had in mind when he walked though the doors: the story of a raft journey across the

Pacific that was being written some 500 kilometres north of them by a young adventurer almost completely unknown in Britain. For Heyerdahl it must have begun to seem that the *Kon-Tiki* was much easier to sell in Europe than in the USA.

The Swedish and British deals that Grieg achieved for Heyerdahl were not the only ones that came his way during this period. The articles that Heyerdahl had let the US Department of State use in magazines published by the military government in Germany and Austria had helped to spread interest for the *Kon-Tiki* in the occupied zone. H. M. Brenner from the Austrian branch of the German publisher Ullstein wrote to Heyerdahl in March 1948 and expressed his interest in the German-language rights for a future book, an interest that had been stirred by a January 1948 number of the magazine *Heute*.[14] By this time the German publisher Brockhaus in Leipzig had already contacted Heyerdahl.[15] The possible deal with Brockhaus eventually foundered on the prohibition against German publishers signing foreign authors, something that both parties seemed strangely unaware of until August 1948.[16] Heyerdahl used the offer by Brockhaus, however impossible, to put pressure on Ullstein, a strategy that worked so well that by the end of the summer Brenner offered him a deal without even having seen the manuscript.[17] The contract was agreed upon by 1 October, and the book, *Kon-Tiki: Ein Floss treibt über den Pazifik*, was set to be published in May the following year.[18] The first international edition of the *Kon-Tiki* would sensationally enough be in German and would owe its existence in part to the US military authorities. Heyerdahl could thank his lucky stars that Dr Hans Günther, who had to spend three years and twenty days in an Allied internment camp,[19] had not taken him and his idea of the white Polynesians under his wing back in 1938.

The very first copy of Heyerdahl's book appeared in the Norwegian bookshops on 2 November 1948. The book carried the simple title *Kon-Tiki ekspedisjonen* (The Kon-Tiki Expedition). Grieg showed confidence in Heyerdahl's creation by printing a staggering 10,000 copies in the first run. Norway was a small market still crippled by postwar economic strife. Decades later, in better times, Grieg would usually not print more than 3000 copies of a trade book, so 10,000 was a remarkably large number for a first edition in 1948.[20] Grieg's gamble paid off: the first print run sold out in only fifteen days, and Heyerdahl even had problems procuring copies for the former crew members.[21] In 1925 the Norwegian explorer Roald

Amundsen had managed to sell the same number of copies of *Gjennem luften til 88° Nord* (Our Polar Flight) in six hours,[22] but Amundsen had been at the peak of his career and the economic situation had been better; a relatively unknown Heyerdahl could in 1948 be more than pleased.

Grieg soon ordered a further 7000 copies of the *Kon-Tiki* book from the presses so that they could arrive in time for the Christmas sales. Heyerdahl was receiving the first encouraging news as far as money was concerned. The *Kon-Tiki* had up till then virtually landed him only with expense. With the income from the first print run and from selling some foreign rights there was enough money to pay off the last remaining debts. For Heyerdahl this was a symbolic event. He wrote to Knut Haugland saying that with the enterprise reaching financial solvency the *Kon-Tiki* men could celebrate their expedition finally reaching its destination.[23]

Heyerdahl had written a book that someone was to call 'A Book to Restore One's Faith in 20th-Century Mankind' in part to restore his own finances.[24] The initial success soon made him dare to dream that the *Kon-Tiki* would solve his money worries, and more. Even so, he was not very impressed with the success of the book in Norway. Heyerdahl grumbled over Grieg and Gyldendal, thinking that a better marketing campaign could have sold even more books.[25] It was true that Grieg's approach to advertisement and marketing was old-fashioned.[26] The claim, later repeated many times, that Heyerdahl's book was not a success in Norway is, however, untrue. In less than a month 17,000 copies were out in the market, and Grieg constantly had to return to the printer for more.[27] After a year around 40,000 copies had been sold. A successful fiction book, easier to sell than non-fiction, could in Norway at this time hope for a total sale of around 10,000 copies.[28] In 1952 the famous US publisher E. P. Dutton speculated that a book was an international bestseller if it sold somewhere around 50,000 copies.[29] Heyerdahl's dissatisfaction with the Norwegian sales was only a testament to the scale of his ambition, an ambition that had been further fed by the sale of foreign rights.

## Adam Helms and the Branding of the *Kon-Tiki*

Heyerdahl would soon encounter a man who could match him when it came to achieving sensations. His name was Adam Helms, and he was an entrepreneurial Danish-Swedish publisher and friend of Harald Grieg, who worked at the Swedish publishing house of Forum, a subsidiary to Bonniers that had bought the rights to the *Kon-Tiki* book in July 1948. Helms read the Norwegian edition of the book, probably encouraged by his wife Greta who was Bonniers' sales director, and saw in it such great potential that he tried to make Bonniers let him publish it instead. As they already had five travel books on the way they were willing to negotiate.[30] The executives at Bonniers gave Helms the book on condition that he published at least 10,000 copies.[31] This ensured that Helms would have to put considerable energies into marketing the book; a failure would have been an embarrassment.

When Helms wrote to Grieg to inform him that he had obtained the rights in January 1949, he made it clear that he not only wanted to publish the *Kon-Tiki* and see how it did, he wanted to push it to becoming a success.[32] Grieg was impressed with his friend's enthusiasm and urged Heyerdahl to accept the transfer to Forum as Helms was a first-rate man who personally backed his books far more than the larger and more impersonal Bonniers could.[33] Heyerdahl accepted, but he decided to test Helms's commitment by asking for a considerable increase in the royalty: fifteen percent after 7000 copies instead of staying at ten percent for any number after 3000.[34]

Heyerdahl was writing to Grieg in Oslo concerning the deal with Helms in Stockholm from the southern Swedish city of Malmö. He had spent time in Sweden lecturing during the autumn and winter of 1948, sometimes appearing together with Bengt Danielsson and sometimes alone. What the two had been discovering in Sweden was a spectacular interest in the *Kon-Tiki*. It was the first time lecturing had been easy, profitable and consistently popular.[35] The raft adventure seemed to hold some special attraction for the Swedes. This popularity gave Heyerdahl more reasons to try to strike a good deal with Forum. The eventual contract would include a substantial increase of royalty – but only after the twenty-five-thousandth copy. Helms, despite his belief in the book, thought that this was a sign of hubris. Maybe, in the best-case scenario, a little more than 10,000 copies could be sold he thought, but the prospect of 25,000 sales seemed distant.[36] Heyerdahl, on the other hand, gambled on success, not for the first or the last time, but this occasion would prove to be one of the most rewarding.

Adam Helms was a vibrant jokester with down-to-earth Danish *bonhomie* (see plate 11), in contrast to Grieg whose patrician airs were famous and feared in Norway. Ten years Heyerdahl's senior, Helms hailed from an upper-class Danish family of doctors. In his youth the family's fortune had disappeared, and a rebellious and wild Helms was sent to be trained as a bookseller, a trade then considered to be safe in times of depression. In 1939 Helms met Greta Nilsson, a Swedish woman working for Sandbergs bookshop in Stockholm. The two married and settled in Sweden, where they started working at the import bookshop owned by Bonniers. The couple eventually moved into publishing in Bonniers and helped pioneer the Swedish book club system in the early 1940s. In 1944 Bonniers founded a subsidiary by the name of Forum, run by Helms. Forum was to publish cheap re-editions of the classics on the model of the Everyman Library series that Joseph Malaby Dent had started in Britain in 1906.[37]

Forum was thus a highly specialized publisher, mostly of translations, and Helms had little experience of books like Heyerdahl's. The company had never previously published a travel book. What Helms did have, in contrast to many publishers, was direct experience of the retail end of the industry. He knew how it was to work in a bookshop and how it was to convince customers. When he sat down with the *Kon-Tiki* he was focused on how it could be sold as a thing in itself, rather than just another travel book about the well-worn theme of the South Seas. The bookseller should be in the position to promise something unique to his customer. And what was needed to lend this singularity to Heyerdahl's creation was a tag line, a hook, a trademark that could snare the presumptive readers. Helms realized that the strange-though-easily-pronounced exotic something that was the '*Kon-Tiki*', a raft, a journey, a dream, an adventure, was, in fact, a brand waiting to be developed.

How Helms came to this conclusion is difficult to conjecture. Part of the ideas he would use can be found in the French editor Édouard Théodore-Aubanel's *Comment on lance un nouveau Livre* (How to Launch a New Book) from 1937. Théodore-Aubanel's suggestions overlapped to some extent with Helms's ideas as he underlined the importance of a good catchy title and a cover that would stand out when seen from a shop window, as well as the necessity of targeted marketing.[38] Helms also went further than these ideas and can be considered as a self-taught publishing genius. He would over the years build up an enormous interest in the industry. All through his life he collected everything he could that was written about the publishing world, from printing to selling. On his death in 1980, Helms left a large library of 6000 volumes on publishing, now housed in the University Library of Stockholm.[39]

In a 1952 lecture Helms claimed that it was all quite simple: 'Repeat, repeat, repeat; is the law of all advertisement.'[40] But what his work with the *Kon-Tiki* would prove was far more complex than this, which also suggests that Helms frequently acted on instinct. He realized, as modern marketing literature makes clear, that brands initially need media publicity rather than advertisement. If the brand needed to be repeated anywhere it was by the media itself, and not in paid advertisements from the company trying to sell it. Advertisement maintains the brand, but does not make it.[41] When Helms set out to sell the *Kon-Tiki* he methodically tried to create a media buzz around something that was more than a book, something akin to a little fraction of epic adventure for sale.

The first step in Helms's *Kon-Tiki* campaign was however not to convince the media, but the booksellers. These were fed with material in order to stir excitement over a book that Helms promised would be out of the ordinary. He sent out calendars that counted down to the date of publication, informative circulars and then many advance copies close to the date. A supply of balsa wood was also procured from a firm producing model aircraft, and pieces of the wood were sent out to be displayed in bookshops.[42] This was a stroke of genius that Helms could not have read in any manual. The *Kon-Tiki* was itself to be a fraction of the epic and the little piece of balsa wood a symbol of the raft. This was making physical the very function of brands; to make the consumer feel part of some greater thing through offering a fragment that can be touched, tried and, importantly, bought.

Helms also put a lot of emphasis on the visual dimension of the *Kon-Tiki*. All Swedish booksellers received a three-dimensional ready-made window display that only needed to be assembled.[43] This model featured two stylized waves between which a paper model of the raft was to be placed, and it had a slot for the actual book to be displayed. The book cover itself was designed to be as eye-catching as a poster, as it was Helms's policy always to view potential book covers from the same physical distance as though he were a customer looking through a shop window.[44] Taken together, the display was thus a dynamic juxtaposition of visual messages and forms. All the lines of the composite exhibit led the viewer's eyes straight to the brand itself, 'The *Kon-Tiki* Expedition', which was written in the middle of the display's background.

On Friday 12 August 1949, the day of the *Kon-Tiki* book's publication, the citizens of Stockholm could take part in an extravagant live version of

Helms's window display. In the bookshop of the major department store PUB in the centre of the city another, more realistic, model of the *Kon-Tiki* raft was being displayed together with Erik Hesselberg's humorous drawings and photographs. This 'Kon-Tiki Exhibition', as the newspaper *Svenska Dagbladet* dubbed it, also featured the appearance of Herman Watzinger whose job it was to chat to prospective customers, offering his stories from the journey.[45] The event was duly advertised in the press with the catchy selling line: '*Kon-Tiki* at PUB – a marvellous adventure in modern time …'[46] The press had been invited for a preview and were supplied with visual material. This was only the first in a long series of publicity-generating stunts that Helms carried out for the *Kon-Tiki* once he had laid the groundwork for his campaign by enticing the booksellers.

Helms's correspondence during the *Kon-Tiki* campaign shows that he had realized something of which Heyerdahl himself was not yet aware. Heyerdahl aimed at a broad popular market, but he was concerned that the medium carrying his story would affect it; the *New York Times* was preferable to the Hearst papers, *National Geographic* to *Reader's Digest*. Helms, in contrast, hinged the *Kon-Tiki* on its universality. It was as though the fact that it could be read by almost everybody was more fascinating than the science and the adventure and the South Seas all put together. That everyone could consume the *Kon-Tiki* also made it, with the homeopathic logic of a trademark, eternally divisible but always carrying a trace of that difficult-to-explain surplus that consumption of the same would entail.

To argue that the *Kon-Tiki* book was a universal story Helms had vehemently to deny that it was in some way quite similar to the run-of-the-mill books of exploration mostly read by boys and men. It became very important for Helms to claim that the *Kon-Tiki* was not a travel book and that it was also a book for girls and women of all ages. The *Kon-Tiki* was so universal that it was unique. This was a new angle for Heyerdahl, who had somewhat falteringly tried to claim that it was his anthropological theory that made it special. Now Heyerdahl had met someone who could sell him even better than he could himself, and he was full of appreciation for Helms's work. Here, finally, was the master impresario he had been waiting for.

A couple of days before the Swedish publication Helms wrote to Heyerdahl and said that both he and the Swedish booksellers were now in the grip of *Kon-Tiki* fever.[47] Soon that fever was to be unleashed onto Sweden as a whole through a clever publicity campaign supported by extensive advertisement. The fever Helms was referring to had as much to do with Heyerdahl's book as with the brand Helms had helped to create. Heyerdahl had supported the product and the brand name, but, a brand is also made up by promotion, advertising and presentation, and it is a synthesis of 'physical, aesthetic, rational and emotional' elements, as argued by John M. Murphy.[48] It cannot be reduced to a trademark or a product; the brand is the spirit of what is being marketed. The brand is an amorphous whole that can be described as a not wholly physical *thing*. The fever was thus for the thing that was the *Kon-Tiki*, and not only for that story of a balsa raft in the Pacific Ocean.

## *Kon-Tiki* Fever Spreads

Heyerdahl began another Atlantic crossing on 4 February 1949, this time on the Swedish ocean liner *M/S Gripsholm*. He was beginning to sense a European success. The book had been launched in Norway, and Heyerdahl had delivered popular lectures in Sweden. He had sold the translation rights of his book to Germany, Sweden and Britain, and also to the Netherlands, Denmark and Finland. Yet it was a North American success that Heyerdahl craved most of all, and crossing the merely physical obstacle of the Atlantic was a price that he was more than willing to pay to see this happen.

During his failed US lecture tour a year before he had continued to look for a North American publisher for his book. It was in part for this end that he had been criss-crossing the vast country. Although this tour had left Heyerdahl disappointed, it had not all been in vain. In February 1948 he had lectured in the august surroundings of the University of Chicago Club before an all-male audience. Andrew McNally and Bennet B. Harvey from the Chicago-based publishing house Rand McNally & Company had been there.[49] When they got back to their office Harvey had allegedly exclaimed that he had 'seen some pictures of a knockout trip across the Pacific' that he thought could make an interesting book.[50]

Bennet B. Harvey was indeed so impressed with what he had seen that he lost no time in putting his editor Jane McGuigan on the job of trying to entice Heyerdahl to publish his, still unwritten, book with Rand. McGuigan called the evening of the lecture and inquired if the US rights were for sale.[51] Heyerdahl refused the offer with the forced explanation that he did not want to sell the book before it was written. (This had not stopped him before.) The truth of the matter was that Heyerdahl's aspirations were set higher than a relatively small Chicago publisher of maps and globes with no real experience in either fiction or travel writing. Once again Heyerdahl showed that he would not let his story go to the first bidder.

Rand's interest in the *Kon-Tiki* did not diminish over time, regardless of Heyerdahl's less than enthusiastic response. For his part, Heyerdahl, hedging his bets, cautiously entertained a correspondence with them over the summer and autumn of 1948. On 10 September Heyerdahl sent Rand a copy of the Norwegian edition but told them that, all of a sudden, another publishing house had the first option on the US rights.[52] This might have been a ruse to test the dedication of Rand, and if this was the case it worked. They wrote back assuring him that they were ready to offer liberal terms.[53]

When Heyerdahl arrived in the USA in early 1949 he stayed on the east coast where many of the large publishing houses had their main offices. Rand McNally in Chicago was still not his first choice. Interest from the larger publishers was, however, only lukewarm. Heyerdahl had again hit an invisible wall. He was still only an unknown foreigner. To his former crew members Heyerdahl wrote a woeful letter explaining the problems of enticing someone to take a chance on a nobody like him.[54] This was part of it, but sometimes the problem was that the publishers were simply not very impressed with Heyerdahl's writing. The young novelist William Styron, then working at McGraw-Hill, dismissed the book as 'a long, solemn and tedious Pacific voyage'.[55] Heyerdahl was becoming increasingly nervous. He had to act fast in that most crucial country as he defined it, if he was still to take advantage of any of the publicity his expedition had resulted in two years previously.[56]

Heyerdahl had hopes that the big publisher W. W. Norton in New York, a company with which both Harald Grieg at Gyldendal and Stanley Unwin at Allen & Unwin had good contacts, would make him an offer. Heyerdahl met the editor Storer Lunt at Norton but it took time to work out a deal. Part of the problem was that Heyerdahl was as concerned with getting a perfect contract as with being signed by a good publisher. After his acrimonious experiences with John Wheeler at NANA and the lecture-tour organizer he had built up a healthy fear for being short-changed in the New World. Heyerdahl demanded that Norton publish him in a sizeable first edition, or else there was to be no deal. This was an important point as it would guarantee that the publishers would have to spend money on promotion to cover their costs. If he were published in a small edition he would also easily sink without a trace in the large US media market. But it was difficult to drive a hard bargain as a previously unpublished author who needed to have his book translated. After a while it was clear that Rand in Chicago was the only firm still interested, as they kept on inundating Heyerdahl with calls, telegrams and letters.[57]

Less than a month after his arrival in the USA Heyerdahl gave up his efforts to find a big, respectable publishing house for his book. He travelled to Chicago and met the management of Rand McNally in the same University Club where they had heard him lecture a year before. Heyerdahl himself said that the negotiations lasted for twelve uninterrupted hours before Rand agreed to a first edition of 10,000 copies, the same as Grieg had given him and Helms had promised.[58] An employee at Rand who had been present at the negotiations later claimed that the meeting had taken only six hours, but added that Heyerdahl was a 'shrewd businessman'.[59] He was clearly no longer a novice when it came to selling his story.

Heyerdahl had his misgivings about Rand, but it is interesting to note the similar trajectories of Rand and Forum. Both companies came from specialized fields within publishing and released their first-ever travel book with the *Kon-Tiki*. The work on Heyerdahl's book would also change these companies' futures; both would start publishing more travel literature for larger audiences. Two years later the vice-president of Rand, Bennet B. Harvey, would write to Stanley Unwin at Allen & Unwin to beg for any books about exploration and travel like the *Kon-Tiki*.[60]

After signing the deal with Rand Heyerdahl travelled westwards to Santa Fe where he continued his research on Polynesian migrations in a study overlooking the Los Alamos valley where Oppenheimer and his team had developed the atom bomb during the war.[61] It had been a turbulent time for Heyerdahl both professionally and privately. Liv had tired both of his affairs – Heyerdahl turned out to be as much of a ladies' man as his father – and the fact that he prioritized fame over family, and

she brought him before a court to get a divorce.[62] Heyerdahl travelled
to the USA with his new love, Yvonne Dedekam-Simonsen, ten years
his junior, and they got married in Santa Fe. Heyerdahl now needed to
return to his studies in order to have a claim to even his outsider scientist
status. He had promised a treatise on his theory in the media, so he had to
deliver. The success with the *Kon-Tiki* had also opened up some doors to
more august institutions supporting adventurous science. Heyerdahl had,
for example, given a lecture to the Royal Geographic Society in London
in December 1948, the same society that had sponsored Darwin and the
polar explorers Scott and Shackleton.

Heyerdahl retreated to Santa Fe for the spring, but the voyage of the
*Kon-Tiki* book continued without him. In late April 1949 Allen & Unwin
received the English translation that they had commissioned, which would
also be the basis for the US edition.[63] The British company had received
the galley proofs for the Norwegian edition in September 1948 and had
sent them out to two readers who responded enthusiastically.[64] Stanley and
Philip Unwin were also excited after having read the translation, but this
was not a feeling shared by everyone at the Allen & Unwin office: 'remote
subject, bad title, *and* a translation'; the misgivings were many.[65]

The Unwins had made their name by their eclectic taste. Their
company had published the radical philosophy of Bertrand Russell and
the political musings of Ramsay MacDonald and had introduced the
writings of Mahatma Gandhi to Britain. They had also published J. R. R.
Tolkien's *The Hobbit* and commissioned the work that was to become *The
Lord of the Rings* in the mid-1950s. Now the Unwins wanted to publish the
narration of a Norwegian raft journey over the Pacific, and they would
not let themselves be dissuaded by the worries of their cautious staff. They
had understood that it was in the book's originality that its strength lay
and refused to take out the word *Kon-Tiki* from the title despite criticism
that it might appear foreign to the British reader. Stanley Unwin later
said that they held onto the word as it was 'simple enough for anyone
to pronounce and yet exotic enough to attract'; the word also had the
promise of becoming 'a household name'.[66] The very same observation
would also later be made by Helms who said that Heyerdahl had invented
the 'ideal book title', easy to pronounce and remember and translatable
into all languages.[67] It was as if all of them had heard George Eastman's
explanation of why he had picked the name Kodak for his product: it was
'short, vigorous, incapable of being misspelled' and started with a K.[68]
This K was the 'incisive "K" sound', as Adrian Room has argued, favoured

by the likes of Coca-Cola, Kleenex, Klaxon, Kleer, Kit-Kat and Kotex; denoting not only an exotic tinge but also linking it in English to prestige words like *clear, clean, quick, clever, king* and *queen*.[69] Brands with this kind of phonetic element are also perceived to be easier to recognize and recall.[70] The Unwins did agree to elaborate the title to contain more than the *Kon-Tiki* with its distinct and exotic nature.[71] The translator suggested the subtitle 'By Raft from Peru to Polynesia' but Heyerdahl, carefully managing all his contacts via mail from Santa Fe, objected and asked for something that could have a more popular ring to it.[72] 'By Raft Across the South Seas', suggested Philip Unwin, and Heyerdahl wrote back saying that he agreed.[73] It was not a bad choice since it added more exoticism (the South Seas), at the same time as keeping it descriptive (By Raft Across). The stronger alliteration of the subtitle's two last words also added effect besides being such a widely disseminated symbol of both adventure and sensuality. If there remained any doubts at Allen & Unwin at this time they would soon be dispelled by the publication of the Swedish edition, without subtitle, of the *Kon-Tiki* book.

## The *Kon-Tiki* Crosses the Atlantic

The first foreign edition of Heyerdahl's book appeared in Germany and Austria in the late spring of 1949, but it was with the Swedish edition, published on 12 August of the same year, that the first success outside Norway would come. Helms had managed to create a feeling of anticipation for his product and had pushed the first print run up to 12,000 copies, all of which had been ordered in advance by the booksellers he had bombarded with information.[74] In less than a month 25,000 copies had been sold, the number that even Helms thought unrealistic when he signed the contract. Heyerdahl had by this time returned to Norway but was brought over to Sweden to take part in the publicity campaign. The media frenzy had now gained momentum, and the book continued to do phenomenally well. In one year it had sold the almost incomprehensible number of 100,000 copies in the small Swedish market alone. The *Kon-Tiki* seemed to be on everybody's lips.

Helms celebrated the achievement of the 100,000 sale with one of his customary stunts. A small-scale replica of the *Kon-Tiki* was launched on one of the waterways of Stockholm. There were no crowds to see it but there was a group of journalists present to secure publicity for the *Kon-Tiki* by having it mentioned in the papers, which was what mattered in the end.[75] Heyerdahl had in large part Helms to thank for this spectacular success that not only awarded him a handsome income in royalties but that also meant that more and more publishing houses around the world started to take an interest in his book. Through Helms, Heyerdahl had gained a model for how his book could be sold as something more than just a story about travel, adventure or rebellious science, but rather as a piece of the exotic, the dream of a life beyond the grey everyday. All this was condensed in a word that could be repeated infinitely: 'Kon-Tiki'.

Predictably, following the incredible success of the *Kon-Tiki* book in Sweden, the other foreign publishers who were getting their editions ready turned their eyes on that country. What had happened? Correspondences were initiated between Helms and foreign publishers interested in his ideas. This was testament enough to the originality of his concept. Helms, in his letters, stressed the careful work Forum had devoted to creating an interest in the *Kon-Tiki*, and also how the book's most important selling point was its ability to suit any kind of reader. He also stressed the importance of avoiding labelling it as travel writing.[76] Helms received enthusiastic responses, for example from Allen & Unwin who were fascinated with his focus on the theme of universality rather than travel.[77]

Danish and Finnish translations of the *Kon-Tiki* appeared in 1949, but the next large market to welcome the book was Britain. Allen & Unwin had been so impressed with Helms that they decided to mount a carbon copy of his campaign. Booksellers were sent circulars, and a copy of the window display designed by Forum was distributed to all British bookshops. Journalists were enticed to mention the *Kon-Tiki* and in so doing provide publicity. Twice the normal number of review copies were sent out. A *Kon-Tiki* exhibit like the one in the department store in Stockholm was put up at Harrods in London. Allen & Unwin also brought Heyerdahl over to Britain in the spring of 1950 to join in the campaign.[78]

Advance sales made Stanley Unwin up the first print run to 30,000 copies, launched on 31 March 1950. Wartime restrictions on printing and rationing of paper had recently been lifted in Britain, but the *Kon-Tiki* sold so well that the problem was soon that there was not enough paper on the market to meet the demand for new copies. Stanley Unwin later said that he had seldom published a book that so immediately gained public recognition.[79] The orders were pouring in, and he had to search high and low for paper to buy. In just two months 100,000 copies were printed, and they were selling out as soon as they hit the shops. By December 1950, less than nine months into the book's publication, 220,000 copies had been sold. Stanley Unwin was euphoric and concluded that no other author had ever sold so many copies so quickly in Britain, and that the numbers sold were an absolute record for a travel book and for a translation.[80]

In February 1951 Stanley Unwin visited Norway and expressed his admiration for Heyerdahl. The *Kon-Tiki,* he said, would outlive him; it was a book that 'talks to all people' and not even the Bible had sold so many copies in such a short time.[81] But the *Kon-Tiki* was more than a book. It was a concept, a brand that established itself as a household name in Britain as it had in Sweden. *The Times* parliamentary correspondent likened the ability of the Labour government to survive to 'the six young men' on the *Kon-Tiki.*[82] The Royal Navy's 891 Naval Air Squadron commissioned a badge with a picture of the *Kon-Tiki* head as embossed on the cover of the Allen & Unwin book.[83] Writers of juvenile literature fictionalized Heyerdahl's account, and poets versified it. The *Kon-Tiki* was on the radio, it was preached about in sermons and lectured about in Sunday schools, and companies bought the book to give as inspirational reading to their employees. Success was immediate and immense.

Rand McNally had been as impressed with the Swedish success as Allen & Unwin and wrote to Heyerdahl to ask about Helms's campaign. Heyerdahl told them to get in contact with Helms direct and added more praise to his handling of the Swedish edition of the *Kon-Tiki.*[84] The British success with a clone of Helms's campaign could only have convinced Rand further that he had realized how best to sell the *Kon-Tiki* and they proceeded to mount a Helms-like campaign in the USA. Focus was put on creating the same kind of excitement for the book as had been generated in Sweden and Britain, and the window display was again copied down to the smallest details. Rand also came up with their own ideas, such as supplying booklets containing reviews of the book to the booksellers. For this something more Heyerdahl awarded them his highest praise: their idea was almost as good as Helms's.[85]

Rand had even more ideas on how to promote the *Kon-Tiki,* but they were sometimes too innovative for Heyerdahl. When they asked him to appear on the Bing Crosby radio show he refused, holding that it would compromise his scientific claims. He ended by stating that he by now knew his public; that in other words he knew what publicity would help him and what would harm him.[86] Heyerdahl was still wary of what he perceived to be New World sensationalism, though having *Kon-Tiki* exhibitions in European department stores was not, after all, a much more elevated way to create exposure. Rand let Heyerdahl have his way, and continued without Crosby. They spent more than $21,000 on their Helms-inspired campaign, a campaign that would win them the *Publishers' Weekly* 'Best Ad Campaigns of 1950' award.[87]

The money Rand put into *Kon-Tiki* proved to be a good investment. The company's first success came as soon as April 1950 when the Book-of-the-Month club bought the book, guaranteeing an order of between 200,000 and 250,000 copies.[88] Bennet B. Harvey wrote to Heyerdahl to report about the absolute joy at Rand, and admitted with characteristic frankness that they were as happy for themselves as they were for him.[89] The gamble to go along with Heyerdahl's insistence on a 10,000-copy initial print run had paid off. When the book was released to the bookshops on 5 September 1950 it immediately sold well. It only took five weeks for the *Kon-Tiki* to get to the top of the bestseller list for non-fiction.[90] When it happened Harvey was so ecstatic that he asked Heyerdahl to call him Ben.[91]

The *Kon-Tiki* would go on to be one of the best-selling non-fiction books of 1951 in the USA. Fifteen printings were done of the book in its first eighteen months.[92] It stayed on the *New York Times'* non-fiction bestseller list for 33 weeks, almost a record.[93] It reached the fifth place in the *Publishers' Weekly* annual bestseller list of 1950 (though it was only published in September), and sold 128,848 copies during 1950 excluding book-club sales.[94] This meant that Heyerdahl was selling almost as many copies as Hemingway was with his new book *Across the River and Into the Trees*.[95] In one full year the *Kon-Tiki* sold around 600,000 copies overall.[96] Just how phenomenal this figure was is illustrated by the fact that as late as 1989 no non-fiction book written by an author hitherto unpublished in the USA sold more than 100,000 copies in a single year.[97]

## The *Kon-Tiki* Pandemic

Adam Helms sold the *Kon-Tiki* as the universal story accessible to all and made it into a brand that quickly spread across Western Europe and North America. There were editions published in South America and Asia during the early 1950s, but the majority of the over two million copies of the book were sold in the West. This had also been Heyerdahl's focus. The *Kon-Tiki* finally crossed the Atlantic with the help of Helms's ideas on how to make it into something more than just a book. These criss-crossings helped Heyerdahl appear as neither Old nor New World, but as some kind of representative of an Atlantic spirit that could manifest itself with equal ease in Stockholm, London or Chicago.

This success did entail new challenges for Heyerdahl. His *Kon-Tiki* became ubiquitous, which was good for selling books but could be easily used by others to sell whatever they wanted. This worried Heyerdahl, and he wrote to Rand in the autumn of 1950 to ask them to try to copyright the word 'Kon-Tiki'. He stated that the name had already been used, without his permission, to name merchandise that he had nothing to do with such as neckties and underwear. He added that there should be no problem in protecting the name, if it was not too late, since the spelling of the Peruvian deity 'Kon-Tiki', as opposed to Con Tici and Con Ticci, had been his invention, aimed at providing a distinctive name for his raft.[98]

Heyerdahl had been aware enough of the functions and use of brands and trademarks to adopt an original spelling, as the marketing textbooks of today say: 'If you want to build a brand, you must focus your branding efforts on owning a word in the prospect's mind. A word that nobody else owns.'[99] But even though he was aware of the need to create this *word*, he missed out on legally protecting it. At the end of the day this would not matter very much. The very success of Heyerdahl's appropriation of the pre-Columbian god indicated that he did not, contrary to marketing wisdom, have to worry about the legal protection. He might have disliked others making money from his creation, but at the same time he was gaining unprecedented publicity for his own product which could, now marketable as 'authentic', sell more and more. Heyerdahl was living in close symbiosis with the liberal capitalist market that was one of the defining features of the postwar Atlantic world he had made his own.

As the *Kon-Tiki* moved to conquer all of Europe and North America in the early 1950s the question started to arise of how the media phenomenon of the *Kon-Tiki* would fare in a market that was neither Western nor capitalist. The logic of Helms's reasoning was that the book was universal, and therefore sellable everywhere. Even behind the Iron Curtain that had descended across Europe after the war. Heyerdahl had already negotiated with a Czech publishing house in 1949 but claimed the following year that the contract had been cancelled by the communist authorities, implying political censorship.[100] He also negotiated with a Hungarian company around the same time. But the publication of the book in the USA and Western Europe soon made Heyerdahl concentrate fully on his self-defined home market rather than trying to break through communist suspicion.

Snorre Evensberget, an editor and friend of Heyerdahl, later claimed that Josef Stalin forbade the publication of the book because of a 1947 photograph of the crew handing a US ensign from the *Kon-Tiki* raft to Harry S. Truman outside of the West Wing of the White House.[101] The photograph appeared in the US and Swedish editions, though not, for example, in the Norwegian, British or French. This image was the visual representation of the very close relationship between the *Kon-Tiki* and the new superpower. If Stalin and his censors wanted incriminating evidence on Heyerdahl being too 'Western', this would have been a good illustration.

The only communist country that published the *Kon-Tiki* was, symptomatically, Tito's more Western-leaning Yugoslavia where different language editions came out in 1951 and 1952. By May 1955 Heyerdahl had seen his book translated into 33 languages, but he had not signed any contracts in countries under the domination of the USSR. That this situation, challenging his universality, was beginning to irritate him becomes clear when he stated that he did not even expect any major financial return, just as long as he got published.[102] He did not have to wait long: the same year the first USSR edition was published in a staggering initial print run of 50,000 copies. Heyerdahl went from being banned to publishing his largest first edition ever. As the USSR routinely did not follow copyright conventions Heyerdahl would get, as he predicted, little money. What was more important was the signal from Moscow, two years after the death of Stalin, that the *Kon-Tiki* was allowed. Soon the book was published all over the Eastern bloc.

The *Kon-Tiki* fever in eastern Europe and the Soviet Union was to a large extent similar to the one in the West, and by this time a certain way of selling the *Kon-Tiki* as a brand had already been well defined. The *Kon-Tiki* trademark was also widely copied here and used for selling just about everything. Heyerdahl positioned himself very actively in the late 1940s and early 1950s as someone belonging to an Atlantic world, and his book in itself was very openly a Norwegian enterprise sponsored by the might of the US armed forces. The *Kon-Tiki* phenomenon was however made, through a complex set of interactions and by effacing parts of the story, to appear universal.

# 4

## The Seamless Craft of Writing Legend

### The Book behind the Fever

The *Kon-Tiki* fever of the late 1940s and early 1950s was so remarkable that it was, and is, easy to forget the content of Heyerdahl's book. *Kon-Tiki* ended up becoming little more than a by-word for some pleasant elsewhere. This could be an exotic place or just an 'anywhere but here'. In May 1951 *Time Magazine* could report that when the deposed president of Panama feigned disinterest in his indictment in the country's national assembly, it was the pages of Heyerdahl's book that he flipped through.[1] The exotic qualities of the story did serve to remove *Kon-Tiki* from its time, something that led to a number of curious outcomes. Heyerdahl's theory of a noble white race taking root in an Atlantic world that had just defeated Nazi Germany was one problematic example. Another was the fact that the story of an expedition that allegorically followed the US Navy out into the disputed waters of the Pacific became a major success in the USSR.

A slightly deeper reading of the *Kon-Tiki* success could interpret it as a reaction to a postwar fatigue and malaise in the West. The 'elsewhere' was an attractive place for a reason. The 1950s brought a return to order and conformity after the chaos of the war. Sociological works like David Riesman's *The Lonely Crowd* from 1950 and William Whyte Jr's *The Organization Man* of 1956 lamented the moral stagnation and alienation of the modern bourgeois society. Novels like Sloan Wilson's *The Man in the Gray Flannel Suit*, published in 1955, fictionalized the same fears.

In Western Europe the philosophical vogue surrounding existentialism poked its probing finger into the side of the newly settled postwar order. The economy turned around surprisingly quickly in the 1950s, but there remained many other good reasons to worry.

One can perceive the *Kon-Tiki* phenomenon as another challenge to the conservatism of the 1950s, this time aided by a massive media apparatus. In this sense the *Kon-Tiki* was not any different from other adventurous voyages of the era, the first ascent of the Everest or the underwater explorations of Jacques-Yves Cousteau – events, ultimately, that acted more as invitations for daydreaming on the train from suburbia than as instigations to real escapes. This type of masculine adventure on the model of the old journey of discovery could be a challenge to cultural conservatism and postwar domesticity, but at the same time it was perfectly possible to read them as supporting the same. None of this, however, explains the universality of Heyerdahl's creation. They are all further illustrations of it. This is why it is important to qualify that universality that Helms and his colleagues spoke of with such rapture.

From only a cursory look at the *Kon-Tiki* book it is clear that it is about travel. This was also something that Heyerdahl's publishers knew, though they were keen to avoid it being labelled as such. It made sense to sell the *Kon-Tiki* as being something more in order to increase the readership, but, ironically, it made equal sense for it to be about voyaging for the very same reason. The travel narrative is ideal as it makes it easy for the form and content to appear inseparable. The narration of themes such as manly adventure and inventive science can rely on a clear and given structure in order to become even more pronounced. For travel is more than a genre; it is a universal story in itself. It is the most fundamental idea in Christianity, a religion built on the notion of exile from Paradise.[2] Everyone can identify with travel. Life is a journey, as the hackneyed metaphor goes.

Travel supplies a structure to a story rather than demanding a story to explain and justify its form. The three elements of departure, journeying and return are so basic that they go to the very heart of what a story is. The barest plot that a story can have is one position that shifts to another.[3] This is, at the most elemental level, the very nature of a story of travel. The protagonist quits one place and arrives at a new one. The foundational texts of our literature, from the Mesopotamian epic of *Gilgamesh* via

Homer's *Odyssey* to Virginia Woolf's *To the Lighthouse*, are all about travel and the changing of place. The use of travel as a plot is perhaps the most common way of writing a text that contains the minimum amount of obstruction for the reader.

The literature that overtly deals with travel in a non-fiction form, such as the *Kon-Tiki*, has often been labelled as heterogeneous and difficult to group into a genre. Since so much can be counted as travel the consensus has become that these texts display a staggering variety of forms.[4] This is true for the motifs, symbols and tropes of travel in literature, but it is hardly the case when it comes to the structure of non-fiction travel books.[5] The stories of travellers may differ, but not the plot that travelling provides. Few genres are as homogenous as travel literature. Travelling as a structure conceals itself, like an invisible scaffolding round an elegant building. The plot of Heyerdahl's book was not exceptional in any way. It followed to the letter the formula of how a travel book should look. This was also why it could appear to be something else.

From the evolution of the modern travel genre in the eighteenth century, and often withstanding twentieth-century attempts at redefinition, the structures of travel books share a simple base. They begin with the 'fitting out' when the traveller prepares him- or herself for the journey and continue with the departure in which the protagonist has to sever ties with his or her environment and assume the role of the traveller. Many times the next step is a smaller 'test travel', or 'expedition within the expedition', which functions as an insurance to the reader that the traveller knows what he or she is doing. Then comes the initiation of the actual journey with preliminary trials. When the traveller has overcome these first problems he or she enters, or fails to enter, the moment of 'passage'.[6] This midpoint between departure and destination is a potentially timeless period in which the traveller becomes one with his or her travel and environment; this is broken up by the arrival in which the traveller is either reluctantly brought out of a successful passage or delivered from a failed one, in order to dissociate him- or herself from the role as a traveller and either re-establish the pre-departure equilibrium or reach a new one.

The circularity of this structure reinforces the role of what comes between departure and arrival. Both of these can be left out, but the period in the middle is impossible to ignore. A departure followed by an arrival would not be travel as such, but merely a change of place that does not promise the rewards and challenges of the passage.[7] It is only when the traveller is in this stage that he or she can reflect on the promise of travelling.[8] The failure to reach passage, inversely, leads to despondency, and travel becomes hard work, *travail*, but a passage that is achieved leads the traveller to feel at one with his or her movement.

The differences between a failed and a successful passage are not merely of scholastic interest. Travel narratives that contain a successful passage in the sense that the journey gives rise to a feeling of timelessness further conceal their very structure. The passage takes the reader to a romantic realm safeguarded from the gaps and dissonance of the real world. The reader is swept along in descriptions that are often harmonious and that focus on the beautiful in nature. The effect is to communicate a sensation of effortless narrative development, a moment of minimal resistance, both for the traveller and for the reader. The journey appears to unfold itself. What happens on a general level in the travel narrative, the plot giving birth to the story, here happens in a concentrated and romantic form. Travel is seemingly transcended, and motion paradoxically suspended. An analogy would be the creation of a sensation of drifting, which was a recurrent theme in the *Kon-Tiki*.

Heyerdahl's *Kon-Tiki* was a classic travel narrative even to the level of including such structural details as an expedition within the expedition. The text was divided into six distinct parts: a theoretical introduction to the reasons for the endeavour, and the narration of the organization and 'fitting out' of the expedition; an 'expedition within the expedition' in the Ecuadorean Andes to find balsa trees and transport the logs down to the Peruvian Pacific coast where they were put together as the *Kon-Tiki* raft; the setting out on the raft, learning to handle it and becoming accustomed to the new environment; the substantial expedition across the Pacific Ocean in which the drifting on the Humboldt Current is described as a successful passage; the dramatic landfall that signals the end of that passage; the final concluding sojourn in the destination, Polynesia.

The important departure and arrival 'scenes' in the *Kon-Tiki* were extremely clear, something that also served to mask the structure of the narration. The raft is towed out from the coast by a tugboat of the Peruvian Navy and then all ties to land are broken. The expeditionaries are at the mercy of wind and current. Like parachutists they have jumped from safety, and now only need to find out if the raft floats, and then follow it where it goes.[9] The arrival is equally unequivocal. As they approach the reef of the atoll group of Raroia in French Polynesia, the crew realize that they have no way of steering around the reef, and that the only thing they can do is to prepare themselves for becoming shipwrecked.[10] It will be impossible to use the raft again after arriving, and they prepare to abandon it once they have been stranded on the reef to seek security on an island in the lagoon. Again, just like the parachutists they know that they are to land, and there is precious little to do more than to hang on and hope that all will go as well as possible.

The correspondence between form and content expressed in the passage of the journey is as strong in Heyerdahl's book as is the focus on departure and arrival. He and the crew are described entering the passage in the first two paragraphs of the fifth chapter, entitled 'Halfway'. They are now, in form as well as in action, in the middle of the journey: weeks pass without them seeing any ship while drifting, and they experience intense feelings of 'peace and freedom'. Nature cleanses both their minds and bodies and they start adapting to the harmonious sea. They no longer live the false life of modern man, a life that belongs in the place from where they departed.[11]

Drifting in the middle of the sea is for Heyerdahl timeless, harmonious and beautiful. It does not take long for him to link these attributes to the 'pre-modern man' whose voyage he is supposedly reproducing. The travel into history and the life of the historic man merge as Heyerdahl's story develop. Heyerdahl both impersonates primitive man and explains the superiority of a primitive existence over modern technological society. It is as though he has forgotten that the primitive he wants to be was a mysterious white culture-bearing race that spread civilization around the world. Instead Heyerdahl merges the timelessness of the passage with the historylessness of the native, the primitive, the non-Western.

Heyerdahl skilfully interconnected the story of travel for spiritual completeness and the completeness of pre-technological man in a message of the superiority of nature over culture. The crew came to feel at home in the sea and realized that primitive men had known more about man's true spirit than scientists could figure out with their unfeeling technology. Life before modernity had been more intense and contained more joys. Above all, it was an existence in which time did not matter, only the daily tasks. The crew are 'swallowed up in the absolute common measure of history'.[12]

The physical environment they encounter out in the Humboldt Current that lent them timelessness is full of fish, and fishing is a topic to which Heyerdahl devoted considerable space in his book. The abundance of fish as food serves the important function of reassuring the reader that the expedition could go on forever. Again it is the primitive way in which Heyerdahl travels that ensures his access to nature. He states that while motorboats would scare away the fish, he and his crew sit just next to the surface of the water, drifting by noiselessly.[13] This makes the life of the crew safe, as it would be impossible for them to starve.[14]

That Heyerdahl was very well aware of what he was achieving with his passage is evident from a correspondence with his US publisher. When the editors at Rand wanted to indicate the time-spans of the chapters in their edition he disapproved. He knew that a realistic time presented chronologically would interfere with the structural timelessness that he was striving for. He responded by stressing that he wanted to communicate the feeling of drifting outside time.[15]

Heyerdahl was thus at some levels conscious of what he tried to create with his plot, and his way of going about this was through avoiding a realistic style that risked making the plot of his story obtuse and bare. He wanted a well-rounded, uncomplicated and classical narration that would not refer to its own creation. It was as though he wanted to write out the writing of the text. In addition to this Heyerdahl also sought with his plot to cleanse the story of the more problematic aspects that would limit its universality. The most poignant example of this is the location of the departure and arrival. Heyerdahl never saw the *Kon-Tiki* as a Norwegian story for a Norwegian audience alone. He needed to have more options open in order to be sure of an international success. What he did was, carefully and creatively, to locate departure and arrival in halfway houses that would be as accessible to European as US audiences. The departure takes place in the dockyard in Callao, and the home-coming is situated as the crew leaves Tahiti on a Norwegian ship, though bound for the USA and the 'twentieth century'.[16]

## Epic Seamlessness

It is improbable that Heyerdahl consciously studied how to write the appropriate plot in order to perfect his travel narration. The biographers of Heyerdahl attest to his lack of interest in literature. There were however other sources that could lend inspiration. If there was one type of text that Heyerdahl had read an abundance of it was the legends of the people of Polynesia and the Americas that he made to fit his theory of prehistoric migration. This knowledge he would use to good effect.

The *Kon-Tiki* voyage was supposedly based on a myth, and it was written like a legend. The legendary aspect of the *Kon-Tiki* added another layer to the potential of the narration for becoming a universal story. Myths and legends are the type of stories that lose the least in translations over cultures, languages and time.[17] They are stories without origins in a constant evolution that at their best can hold true for people living in very different cultures at different times. The King Kong of Hollywood can replace Homer's Cyclops, but the fight against the monsters remains the same. It was this kind of story that Heyerdahl sought, probably without too much reflection, to align himself to.

One book that Heyerdahl would most probably not have read was the German literary scholar Erich Auerbach's tome *Mimesis: The Representation of Reality in Western Literature*, published in 1946 at the same time as the *Kon-Tiki* expedition was being planned. But Heyerdahl still followed to the letter Auerbach's definition of what a legend should contain when he sat down to write his book. Legends do not anchor themselves too firmly in descriptions of time and place. The legend also outlines the actions and motives of a few men who are unwavering in their determination. What distinguished the legend from other literature for Auerbach was that it read 'far too smoothly'; anything that could cause friction, 'everything unresolved, truncated, and uncertain', was removed as it only confused the clear succession of events and the simple characterization of the actors.[18]

Writing the legend was to write a two-dimensional world, a world without ambiguities or doubts or attempts to look at a story from a psychological perspective. This simplicity permeated the pages of the *Kon-Tiki* book. Heyerdahl had written to his publisher in order to convince the editors to keep out clear references to the outside world in order to reproduce a sense of drifting. He had himself repeatedly stylized and simplified events, condensing several visits to the Pentagon and to the UN into singular occasions. He was also careful to limit references to the world of the late 1940s that was the setting for his efforts in order for the book to appear above politics and the mere quotidian. The men on Heyerdahl's raft were also clearly outlined: Bengt was cast as the absent-minded scholar,

Erik the bohemian painter, Knut and Torstein the hardy commandos and Herman the inventive young engineer. For himself Heyerdahl preserved the role of the paternal leader.

The lack of character development in the *Kon-Tiki* should not be seen as Heyerdahl's literary failure but as his success in creating a legend. Just as with Odysseus it was important that he was unchanged when he returned to Ithaca.[19] This need for the story to be neatly circular and simple is essential in creating the mythical figure. The story creates hurdles that the hero overcomes in order to show his greatness, but it needs to do this without changing him. Heyerdahl is convinced of his theory; he needs to prove it and sails across the Pacific for this end.

The mythological narrative with its unchanging hero can be contrasted to its alternative where the story is a quest that leads from ignorance to knowledge and where events do not only call for action but also contemplation and interpretation.[20] In such a story Heyerdahl would have had a hypothesis that he tried to prove by seriously considering what spoke for and against it, something that he did not do. Heyerdahl always claimed that the *Kon-Tiki* was a quest for the truth as to the origins of the Polynesian people and culture. He tried to appear as the detective or the rebel scientist that would uncover the solution to the mystery of the Polynesians by weighing the evidence. However, what he did in the *Kon-Tiki* book was, at most, to prove his theory for others, namely the conceited scientists, and not for himself. There is no real quest to find out just who Kon-Tiki had been, no whodunit when it came to the settling of Polynesia and no actual weighing of evidence. The conclusion of the *Kon-Tiki* book, that a white pre-Inca king populated Polynesia, is established before the actual voyage.

Heyerdahl wrote a legend at the same time as he made it appear a story of scientific mystery, much as he wrote a travel book however much Helms claimed that it was not. He did it because both the travel narrative and the mythological story were the most translatable, the easiest to communicate. Writing in one mode at the same time as pretending to write in another is in Heyerdahl's case not a sign of failure, but an attempt to mask the narration. Heyerdahl had a good grasp of what he was doing, even though it was probably in part instinctual; he did not slip and stumble his way around different narrative forms that would have created dissonances and discontinuities. If, for example, he had really raised the scientific question in his book, if he had reflected on any doubt of his own, if he had started to discuss the possible implications his journey might have on him, his crew and his readers – if he had done any of these things he would have altered the narrative substantially and *Kon-Tiki* would not have been so appealing.

Part of the explanation of why the mythological form came so easily to Heyerdahl was his familiarity with prehistoric legend, but there are also interesting similarities between Heyerdahl's techniques and those to be found among the mythmakers of Hollywood. Though Heyerdahl was not a well-read man, he was not averse to cinema. As a child he had been fascinated by *Tarzan* and he included several references to Walt Disney in the *Kon-Tiki* book. Heyerdahl even took his *Kon-Tiki* crew to see a film about Polynesia featuring Dorothy Lamour, probably *Rainbow Island*, as part of their preparations.[21] The influence of Hollywood is also present in an easily overlooked detail from the very first lines of the *Kon-Tiki* book itself when Heyerdahl for a second begins from the middle; he is in 'an odd situation' drifting in the Pacific on a raft and wondering how it all came to this.[22]

Heyerdahl technically begins his story in the middle, from the passage, and then switches the narration back to the beginning when his crew didactically explains why he is on the raft. The rest of the story is then narrated chronologically. The calm and even mock-heroic tone of Heyerdahl makes this opening seem quite unremarkable and it does not stand out in any way in relationship to the rest of the text. It is however exceedingly rare for travel narratives to start in this way, now as in the time of Heyerdahl. Heyerdahl chose to start his story in the middle of the action, whereas most travel narratives would have begun with an explanatory foreword or preface, or simply from the chronological starting point. What Heyerdahl had done was to make a Hollywood beginning, and he would go on to use the exact same beginning in his two other straightforward travel books about the *Ra* expedition in 1970 and the *Tigris* in 1979.

In *How to Write Photoplays* from 1920, John Emerson and Anita Loos explained that filmic narration must start 'with the story itself and not with the history of the case which leads up to the story'.[23] In the words of David Bordwell, a scholar of cinema, the opening of classical Hollywood films contains a 'preliminary exposition' that 'plunges us into an already-moving flow of cause and effect' where the characters can gradually assume the responsibility for furthering the story.[24] This is exactly what happens in the first two pages of Heyerdahl's book; it is Bengt, Erik, Herman, Knut and Torstein, his 'five companions', whom he asks where he is and why he is there. They can tell him that they are 850 sea miles out from Peru, with 3500 miles left to the closest island and '15,000 feet above the bottom of the sea and a few fathoms below the moon.'[25] In other words: in the middle of the Pacific and the middle of the story. However, they can not tell him why they are there; questioned about it Bengt replies that Heyerdahl knows that better than they do, which helps the author to switch the narration 'back', in the sense of a flashback, to the chronological beginning of how he got the idea for the journey, back to the beginning of a perfectly linear and strong narration that henceforth evolves from start to finish.

The effect of this 'preliminary exposition' is to allow for a point of entry from which the narration can gradually make itself invisible. After giving the spectator vital information for the understanding of the story the narration will become less selfconscious and omniscient as the characters assume the burden of carrying the story forward. This shift gives the illusion that the narration 'vanishes', and is vital for Hollywood's style of continuity.[26] In other words, this effect is at the foundation of the 'seamlessness' of the classical Hollywood style, that 'excessively obvious cinema' as Bordwell has called it in one of the chapter titles of his book *The Classical Hollywood Cinema*. Form negates itself in an artful way for the benefit of the story.

Apart from the technique of opening with a strong narration, Hollywood cinema complied with the demands of the mythological narrative with which Heyerdahl was already familiar. According to Bordwell, classical Hollywood cinema aspired to conceal its own structures with techniques that aimed at establishing a narration that could appear as universal, using stories that transcended geography and politics in order to maximize audiences. The structure was to be made 'invisible' in other words.[27] This kind of film, like the story in the *Kon-Tiki* book, sets up obstacles against which the protagonist must test his strength, and which he also overcomes by the end.[28] Stressing the character's motivation for his actions creates an illusion of realism.[29] In the narration nothing is allowed to slip and form discontinuities and dissonances. If gaps arise, they have to be filled before the end of the narration for the sake of continuity. Heyerdahl's narrative is a perfect example of this with its repetition of the obstacle-struggle-solution theme; whether it is getting money for the expedition, finding balsa for the raft or making it over a coral reef; but also in the larger questions of the theory behind the voyage. It was with the help of this logic that Heyerdahl did his bit to contribute to the purported universality around which Helms would make such a spectacular marketing campaign.

## Racism, Sexism and Universality

The mythological structure that Heyerdahl created for his *Kon-Tiki* book was mirrored by a story that performed the task of myth; mediating between conflicting themes and making them come together in one. There were three such important mediations in the *Kon-Tiki*. In the first, the unheroic science of laboratories was contrasted with the hardy adventures of the explorer. The second saw a detached desire for the exotic contrasted with the more radical wish to encounter the true primitive. In the final one the terrifying and sublime sea that devoured men was opposed to the calm and beautiful sea that gave life rather than taking it. These three themes will be explored in detail in the last three chapters of this book.

Beyond the more immediately recognizable sets of opposite themes of the *Kon-Tiki* narration there were also those that Heyerdahl left unmediated and that were constitutive to his story without ever being addressed or overcome. Whiteness was almost always favoured over the non-white, and the masculine over the feminine. These were topics that Heyerdahl so took for granted that he could just inscribe them in the text and count on them becoming as invisible as his structure based on travel and myth. The point here is not to chastise Heyerdahl for concealing that he wrote a travel book in which he mythologized himself and white men, while letting his publishers claim that it was a universal story, one that 'even' women could read. Racism and sexism in the time when Heyerdahl wrote, as they still are today, were almost universal stories. At the same time it is necessary not to perpetuate the invisibility of these themes.

The fact that racism and sexism can be seen as part of universal stories does not mean that they are, and were, the only way to see the world. In the postwar West women were actively dislodged from the emancipation that had accompanied the militarization of men, and part of the military activity at the end of the Second World War was redirected to fighting colonial subjects for whom the war had often entailed a momentary liberation from their masters. In this context cultural texts were needed to perform and strengthen sexist and racist presuppositions. Heyerdahl was not only repeating what was part of Western culture; he was also unconsciously working towards re-establishing a masculine vision of white supremacy that the war had challenged. There were many stories of travel at the time that took an opposite approach and actively sought to question, in particular, racism. A great number of other voices in the West also called out for a rejection of the concept of race and of racism in the 1940s and 1950s. The famous British-American anthropologist Ashley Montagu called arguments built on race 'man's most dangerous myth' in a book with the same title from 1942. Heyerdahl, on the other hand, did not divert from the colonial script he had been following on Fatuiva in the 1930s. That he had no qualms in continuing to use the idea of a white master race whose origins can be traced to Spanish chroniclers of the colonization of the Americas and to the writings of pseudoscientists like Arthur de Gobineau, who argued for the superiority of the white race in the mid-nineteenth century, can only reinforce the same image. Heyerdahl was not simply an innocent child of his time.

The *Kon-Tiki* book made repeated references and allusions to an 'old vanished civilized race' of 'white and bearded men' who had 'taught Aztecs, Mayas and Incas their amazing culture in America', and then, under the leadership of their king and god Kon-Tiki, vanished from the western shores of the American continent.[30] There is no attempt to conceal the Caucasian origin of this people as the 'wandering teachers of men of an early civilized race' most likely had come 'from across the Atlantic'.[31] The Swedish and Norwegian editions also included a map of the Americas in which an arrow pointed from the east towards Mesoamerica with the inscription 'White Race?' Why this map was omitted from later editions like the British, French and US is not clear, but the text with the same meaning was left intact.

Right at the beginning of the *Kon-Tiki* Heyerdahl sets up his objective as being to solve the mysteries of the Pacific by finding a 'rational solution' to the question of the identity of the old Polynesian mythic hero Tiki.[32] Heyerdahl then swiftly moves on to present his hypothesis. He argues that a race of white people had arrived in Mesoamerica from somewhere across the Atlantic. Here they started the Aztec and Maya civilizations, after which they moved south, down towards the Andes, where they initiated a pre-Inca culture. They were then expelled from their headquarters at Tiwanaku (Tiahuanaco) on the shores of Lake Titicaca by another tribe from the Coquimbo valley (in present-day Chile) under the leadership of the chief Cari.[33] The leader and god, Virakocha or Kon-Tiki, and his closest men managed to escape down to the Pacific coast and disappeared overseas. Kon-Tiki, synonymous with the Polynesian deity Tiki, reached Polynesia around 500 AD and was thus the first to settle these islands. A later immigration came to Polynesia in 1100 from the northwestern coast of the American continent. These people arrived first in Hawaii and then moved southwards, mixing their blood with the race of Kon-Tiki along the way. Later, more immigration had taken place from the east.[34] This was the solution to the enigma of the origin of the Polynesians that Heyerdahl presented as his own. It is perhaps more correct to label it as rather wild conclusions drawn from various Spanish chroniclers like Juan de Betanzos and Pedro Cieza de León and more recent pseudoscientific theories.

Heyerdahl claimed in the *Kon-Tiki* book that no one had previously looked for the origins of the Polynesians in the Americas.[35] This was not the truth – as Heyerdahl would have been well aware; the Spanish friar Joaquín Martínez de Zúñiga had done this as early as 1803.[36] The link between Tiwanaku and whiteness had also been argued before. Heyerdahl told Hesselberg to copy the face of a Tiwanaku sculpture, 'the bearded one' (see back cover), reproduced in an article by the US archaeologist W. C. Bennett, 'representing' Kon-Tiki and paint it on the raft's sail.[37] It was from Tiwanaku and Lake Titicaca, Heyerdahl argued, that the priest and king Kon-Tiki of the sun-worshipping, white-skinned and bearded race had led his closest companions to the sea to escape their enemies. The raft would now re-create how this escape had continued out into the Pacific.

An Austrian expatriate engineer in Bolivia, Arthur Posnansky, had excavated Tiwanaku in the first decade of the twentieth century and came up with 'proof' of an ancient and mysterious race. This had excited, among others, Edmund Kiss, a Nordicist and writer of fanciful novels. Kiss concluded that Posnansky's race could be no other than the Aryan master race, and travelled to the site in 1928. When he returned to his native Germany he popularized the idea of a blond Nordic people having lived in Tiwanaku long before the Incas. In 1939 Heinrich Himmler, the poultry-farmer turned head of the powerful Nazi SS, commissioned through his 'research institute', the Ahnenerbe, a large expedition to Tiwanaku under the leadership of Kiss. Twenty experts were to stay in South America for a year to prove that the site had been the home of an ancient Nordic race. The outbreak of the Second World War led to the indefinite postponement of the expedition.[38]

There were a number of physical characteristics that Heyerdahl used to describe his itinerant people from the shores of Lake Titicaca: they were white, bearded and tall.[39] In the monochromatic universe of Heyerdahl, people were either white or brown, and the indigenous peoples of South America were most definitely brown, or derogatorily 'swarthy', as were the present-day Polynesians. As is usual in racist pseudoscience the implication was that these physical traits translated into psychological characteristics. Brown people were not only beardless but also inferior and plebeian. The whites were the bearded culture-bearing patricians. In Polynesia this had been especially clear when the 'first' Europeans arrived there after the conquest of America; according to Heyerdahl they encountered two groups of natives, one almost white that descended from the first chiefs, the second brown with 'flat pulpy noses'.[40] There was no doubt which of the groups was the more important. The very idea that culture belonged to the white race could only reinforce this conclusion. This the Spanish chroniclers of the conquest of the Americas had argued through reporting, self-servingly, supposed 'indigenous' folktales of white culture-heroes, tales which anthropologists could tell Heyerdahl should be used with a grain of salt.[41] The same concept had been put in plain text by de Gobineau in 1855 in his fourth volume *Essai sur l'inégalité des races humaines* (An Essay on the Inequality of the Human Races) where the author stated that the high civilizations of the Americas had been so advanced that a white race simply must have travelled there to get them started.[42] Native Americans were too inferior to have constructed advanced civilizations by themselves.

The idea of race that Heyerdahl used implied that strength came through purity. De Gobineau's main thesis was that the mixing of races would produce an inferior one, which was part of the reason why his ideas later became important in Nazi Germany. Heyerdahl also appears to have had a fear of 'miscegenation', or the mixing of races. He could, after all, have carried present-day Polynesians or South Americans on his raft, but it seemed that these people were no longer white enough. Heyerdahl had to rely on a Scandinavian crew that, one is led to assume, had better preserved its racial purity. When Heyerdahl described racial mixes directly in his *Kon-Tiki* it was in negative terms. In one passage, observing a gathering of 'sinister-looking individuals' in Ecuador he describes them as being an 'unpleasant mixture' of Spanish, Indian and Negro blood.[43]

The white patrician race was distinguished not only by its physical features but also by its sagacity. Like most theorists of race, Heyerdahl in reality saw evolution as Lamarckian and not Darwinian. Not only physical traits were inherited, but also social and cultural ones. Heyerdahl referred to his mysterious white race as an itinerant, 'wandering', race of 'the white teachers'.[44] Heyerdahl argued, uncritically following Spanish chroniclers of the colonial era, that this 'peaceable race' of 'mysterious white men' had helped the brown people of the Americas and Polynesia to construct advanced civilizations.[45] And Heyerdahl did not seem to doubt for one moment that the brown people indeed needed this help. When he describes Quito in the *Kon-Tiki* book he notices Indians 'hunched up along the adobe walls dozing in the hot sun', just like the Mexicans he must have seen in Westerns.[46] Heyerdahl's brown people are a function of their environment, an environment that seems to suppress them. When he reaches the Andean *altiplano* in search of balsa logs he reflects that the natives seem to have 'grown up out of the earth itself' which made them as much part of the landscape as the grass growing on the 'cliff and scree'. Heyerdahl also likened them to wild animals and children, almost unable to articulate speech but with more aptitude for laughter.[47]

Andean people, according to Heyerdahl, would have needed the help of the peaceful, wise instructors who migrated from the north if they were to establish advanced civilizations and empires. Was it, one wonders, the same unimpressive nature of the brown people that made it so inconceivable for Heyerdahl that the Polynesians had come from the west, from Australia and Melanesia, where in his view only primitive black people lived, or from further west, the Asian coast, whose cultures had, according to him, at times sunken deeper into the Stone Age than almost any other place on earth?[48]

Being themselves very white, and most conspicuously bearded, the crew of the *Kon-Tiki* itself played their part perfectly in Heyerdahl's reconstruction of the colonizing westward journey of his mythic white race.

This is accentuated most forcefully when their whiteness can be contrasted to others' brown-ness. When building the raft in the naval dockyard in Callao it was as though Heyerdahl and his Scandinavian crew has stepped firmly into the shoes of the vanished white race. As he described it, 'Six fair-skinned Northerners' worked alongside 'brown naval ratings with Inca blood'.[49] One does not have to speculate who taught whom how to build the raft. That Heyerdahl is a teacher is similarly clear when they arrive in Polynesia and he starts lecturing what he calls the 'intelligent' though 'uneducated' natives on the history of the settling of their lands.[50]

After this impromptu lecture the bearded white crew deploy their sagacity and technology to cure the indigenous brown population of their ailments. First a small boy with an abscess on his head is saved from death by virtue of the crew's superior technology. They radio a doctor in Los Angeles for instructions, and then proceed with some surgery, after which penicillin and plasma are used. When their magic powers had been proved for the brown people, a steady supply of patients was secured for 'Dr. Knut and Dr. Herman' to deal with, and when the medicine ran out they treated the natives with porridge, something that worked especially well on 'hysterical women'.[51]

It is only on the raft itself, away from the chattering and effeminate natives, surrounded by the sea, that the colour scale of Heyerdahl becomes muddled. Here, under the Pacific sun, the crew itself seems to have become brown for a moment as Heyerdahl described them as 'half-naked, brown-skinned and bearded, with stripes of salt down their backs', twice during the voyage.[52] Possibly this is the result of their whiteness no longer being able to shine clearly against the brown-ness of the natives in Peru and Polynesia, or maybe it is just a logical slip by Heyerdahl; in any case it only lasts as long as they are isolated on the raft.

Heyerdahl and his men do not spend the time on the raft in complete isolation: they are joined by a seventh crew member, Lorita.[53] She is a parrot from Peru, and one of the very few females portrayed in Heyerdahl's book. The bird is stereotyped as the effeminate native: a chattering buffoon whose favourite pastime is to bite off the wire of the radio's aerial in some anti-technological impulse. At times she is caged, which clearly shows who is her master, and after a while starts talking Spanish with a Norwegian accent. Later she is able to sound 'Torstein's favourite ejaculations in full-blooded Norwegian'.[54] That this native of Peru would have been incapable of making the voyage by herself is forcefully illustrated when one night she is released from her shackles and swept away by a wave. She needs the protection of her bearded male masters. In this instance the men can even be bronzed, as the binary is moved from colour to gender, in contrast to the more complex situation on land.

The sexist and patriarchical language of Heyerdahl is evident right from the beginning of the *Kon-Tiki* book and far more pernicious than in the story of the parrot. In Heyerdahl's epiphany on Fatuiva it is the approving 'roar of the breakers' that responds instead of his wife to his statement about the similarities between Polynesian and South American stone monoliths.[55] The only reported speech, quoted sentence, by a woman in the entire book is a line from a letter by Heyerdahl's mother who wishes them well before departure.[56] Apart from this, the white nurturing mother, the female sex is at very best capable of more or less unintelligible chatter and verbal ejaculations like those of the parrot. When the crew greet the inhabitants of a village in Raroia where they land, the native men are able to 'mumble' the traditional greeting 'io-ora-na', whereas the young women greet 'coquettishly and shyly' and apparently mutely while the older women simply 'babbled and cackled' before proceeding to point at the beards and white skin of the crew.[57]

The categories of gender seamlessly shift to the categories of race in the *Kon-Tiki* as the 'brown' South Americans and Polynesians are portrayed as effeminate and talkative. The pointing to the markers of the crew's whiteness by the old women on Raroia is in no way coincidental, and highlights this identification between race and gender. At one point Heyerdahl's beard even saves him from the effeminate primitive. During an aborted attempt to paddle the *Kon-Tiki* ashore the crew is helped by a group of Polynesians. As night falls the native men become scared of drifting out to sea and decide to leave. Heyerdahl recounts the goodbye when the native leader with tear-soaked eyes kisses him tenderly, something that makes Heyerdahl 'thank Providence' for his beard.[58] The brown Polynesian men behave almost like women; they are ruled by sentiment, they cry and they kiss – feminine in all but body. This transsexuality is deeply threatening to Heyerdahl who is saved by the most concrete marker of his unquestionable white masculinity: his beard.

Marianna Torgovnick in her book *Gone Primitive* (1990) correctly identified the tendency for a conflation of gendered and racial discourses in Western representations of the 'primitive'.[59] The tropes used for the one (women) are easily deployed on the other (primitives) – and vice versa one might add. This results in 'Global politics, the dance of the colonizer and colonized' becoming 'sexual politics, the dance of male and female.'[60] The *Kon-Tiki* is a good illustration of this. In the colonial voyage of Heyerdahl whiteness and masculinity were direct markers of superiority, whereas brownness and femininity belonged to the vanquished, the chattering and sentimental that had to give way to the articulated and the rational. Heyerdahl had now unhinged femininity from the rationality of his mother and placed it firmly it the realm of the irrational.

It is interesting to compare Heyerdahl's treatment of the effeminate natives in the *Kon-Tiki* book with that present in his first book from 1938 about the time on Fatuiva. Although the similarities are many, there are some interesting discrepancies. The natives in the 1930s might have been like animals, women and children, but on the whole they were more articulate than the South Americans and Polynesians in the *Kon-Tiki* book. They were furthermore always scheming against Heyerdahl, which also gives the impression that they were imbued with more rational thinking and cunning compared with those of ten years later.

From 1938 to 1948, Heyerdahl's natives regressed, which can be ascribed to his increasing interest in pseudoscientific racist theories. This kind of argument presupposed a clear centre and a periphery in human development. A white race had stood for all the major advances in human civilization as it moved around the world, implying that non-white people were too uncreative to have done this themselves. Heyerdahl subscribed to a so-called diffusionist discourse in which the core (almost always white) was represented as being inventive, rational, theoretical, disciplined, adult, sane, scientific and capable of progress.[61] The periphery, in contrast, was imitative, irrational, spontaneous, child-like, insane, believing in sorcery and stagnant.[62] By the 1920s theories that postulated that there had been one single origin to all the world's civilizations, so-called hyper-diffusionism, started to gain currency through the writing of the likes of the Australian anatomist Grafton Elliot Smith.[63] Smith and his fellow diffusionist the British anthropologist William James Perry argued that a group of sun-worshipping demi-gods from Egypt was responsible for all civilizations.[64] What separated Heyerdahl from Smith and Perry was his strong insistence on race, especially on the superiority of the white one. This description of the exalted white race had more in common with a biological racism theorized by the likes of de Gobineau and Hans Günther.[65] There was little new or original in Heyerdahl's theory, and much that was troublesome.[66]

The development of diffusionism was tightly linked to the German auto-identification with the Aryan 'race' which had sprung from the nineteenth-century argument that a white master race, the Aryans, had managed to preserve racial purity through enslaving people of darker complexion. They had moved from somewhere in Asia in the east to Germany in the west establishing complex civilizations as they went. The belief in the Aryan background to the 'Germanic race' (to the extent that it was even sometimes argued that Aryan culture first originated in the north before migrating to Asia and then back) also became one of the main tenets of Nazi ideology, an illustration of which was their use of the Hindu swastika symbol. The main proponents of this theory were Gustaf Kossina, Alfred Rosenberg, Hans Reinerth and Hans Günther, from the last of whom Heyerdahl had tried to obtain support before the war.

Diffusionism was a theory linked to the Nazi project, but it worked perfectly well also after the demise of the Third Reich, something that Heyerdahl's *Kon-Tiki* illustrated. The period from 1938 to 1948 in which Heyerdahl 'discovered' and articulated his diffusionism also saw a general resurgence of this kind of philosophy in Western society. Diffusionism, outside Germany and Italy, had declined in the interwar period, mostly due to the colonial project having reached a precarious equilibrium after the violent movements of the nineteenth century. The war led to a weakening of the old colonial powers of Europe and an acceleration of colonial liberation. Almost as a response to this development, diffusionism was 're-born' in the shape of modernization theory in the late 1940s and 1950s. Colonies might become independent, but the argument that they all needed liberal capitalist economic structures to develop (modernize) led back to the colonial mindset embedded in diffusionism. A Third World in need of the West was created. The World Bank, 'almost by fiat' as the critic of this discourse of development Arturo Escobar has argued, turned poverty into the defining feature of the non-West by macro-economic indicators.[67] The starkness of this poverty thus defined meant that poor nations needed to emulate the rich in order to overcome their backwardness. Yet again the 'primitives' were the dark, poor, passive and uninventive peripheries that needed the help of the white West and its modern technologies to make progress.[68]

The white race of the *Kon-Tiki*, technologically advanced culture-bearers, was nothing but a historic parallel to modernization theory. Judging from how the South Americans and Polynesians in Heyerdahl's book were described, the peripheries of the world still seemed to need the help of the core just as much as they had at the time of king Kon-Tiki.

Colonies were beginning to liberate themselves in Africa, the Middle East and Asia, but the old masters tried to ensure a place for themselves in the new political and economic orders by arguing that the old colonial subjects could not develop without the West that had previously ruled them. Colonialism was challenged in the postwar period, but the figure of the superior white man was reinforced, in part thanks to stories such as the *Kon-Tiki*. Heyerdahl made an unflinching link between whiteness and civilization. This was not a link that was, or is even now, challenged, perhaps thanks to the fact that Heyerdahl was ostensibly talking about the past (re-creating the past). By using an allegorical story Heyerdahl could avoid crude racism and direct colonial discourse and instead weave his ideas into both his epic structure and mythic story.

In the late 1940s the Allied forces occupying Germany and Austria interned men like Hans Günther for putting their theories of a white master race at the service of the Third Reich. Heyerdahl was indeed fortunate to have found backing in 1946 in the USA rather than in 1938 in Germany. But as the US and British support of Heyerdahl showed, it was not so much what was said that was important, but in what context the message of white supremacy was delivered. The lack of criticism of Heyerdahl to this day for his racism shows how deeply ingrained these concepts remain.[69] It is not true, as the anthropologist Graham E. L. Holton argued in an article entitled 'Heyerdahl's Kon Tiki Theory and the Denial of the Indigenous Past' (2004), that Heyerdahl's language 'was bound to draw criticism' as the memories of the horrific slaughter that a belief in a white master race had led to in Nazi-occupied Europe was still so fresh in people's minds.[70] On the contrary, Heyerdahl's message was never questioned, apart from one review in a scholarly journal of one of his more scientific works in 1953 that stated that it was hard to 'avoid reading racism' in Heyerdahl.[71] His project remains still to this day largely unchallenged.

The silence in relation to Heyerdahl's sexism was, and has been, even more monolithic than that regarding the racism in his writings. Only Heyerdahl's biographer Ragnar Kvam Jr touched upon the subject in 2005, but then in relation to Heyerdahl's private life. At the time of the publication of the *Kon-Tiki* book the publishers made a lot out of the purported appeal of the book to women. But these claims, although possibly true, do not arise from any lack of sexism in the *Kon-Tiki*. A good example is Stanley Unwin's assertion that 'Those who prophesied that women would not like it have been confounded, because the BBC have serialised it in "Woman's Hour"."[72] This serialization, broadcast in the summer of 1950, was however faithful to the book and contained nothing that could possibly be construed as specifically appealing to a female audience, such as female characters and so on, in contrast to the typical stories in the 'Woman's Hour' programme.[73]

The lack of criticism of the *Kon-Tiki* today for its racism and sexism does not mean that its historical context is unimportant. More than anything it shows that conceptualizations of core versus periphery – both when it comes to a global scale (imagined 'race' and 'ethnicity') and to gender – have changed depressingly little. But it also illustrates how Heyerdahl managed to inscribe himself in a mythic realm seemingly immune to these issues.

Heyerdahl did, from the moment of his break-through, succeed in making 'invisible' both the construction of his epic plot as well as the racist and sexist premises of his story. Heyerdahl's writing appeared to have the ability of erasing itself, taking on the guise of being a naïve and unmanipulated account of an eccentric journey. But there was nothing in either the making of the expedition or the writing of the legend about it that was the outcome of a spontaneous creation. Just as the *Kon-Tiki* was consciously made into a brand it was also made, in the book, to conceal its own production. This illustrates that it is exactly the apparent simplicity and transparency of the *Kon-Tiki* book that made it into a complex cultural text. It is important to re-create the process through which a media event was created around this text not only to understand it, but also to point out the disturbing stories, like racism and sexism, that have a tendency to be present as the invisible aspects of the universal.

# 5

## To Review a Classic

### The New-born Classic

The most intense *Kon-Tiki* moment was between 1949 and 1953. In these years Heyerdahl's book sold in enormous numbers. The *Kon-Tiki* name became a widely spread buzz word that came to represent an image of carefree yet exciting adventure in the South Seas. As such, the *Kon-Tiki* travelled from a Europe characterized by bombed-out, gritty cities like Berlin and Rotterdam to the well-tended lawns of US suburbia. The Atlantic Western world, whether in ruins or not, was to a great extent the epicentre of the phenomenon. By 1953 the *Kon-Tiki* had sold 910,000 copies in Britain and Canada; 562,000 in the USA; 230,000 in France; 220,000 in Sweden; and 170,000 in Germany and Austria. After these countries there was a considerable drop down to the 70,000 copies in Norway and the 32,300 in Denmark. The South American editions together amounted to little more than 40,000 copies, just a bit more than the Danish figure.[1] South America at the time was home to over 110 million people, Denmark just over four million.

In order to understand the success of the *Kon-Tiki* book it is necessary to look not only at the marketing of it as well as its structure and content, but also to try to form a picture of how the book was appreciated by its millions of readers. This is a difficult task, made none the easier by the decades separating us today from this first reading of the *Kon-Tiki*. One way to start understanding the reaction to Heyerdahl's book is to look at how it was received in the press. Critics are not ordinary readers, but they represent a middle station between the producers, whose motives have been discussed, and the ordinary consumers whose reactions are so difficult to generalize. The critics are also interesting to study as they themselves contributed to giving *Kon-Tiki* much of its publicity and helped to shape the readership and its possible reactions.

This chapter will focus on the reception of the book in some of the main countries of the *Kon-Tiki* success such as Sweden, Britain and the USA. In doing this it should be remembered that Heyerdahl and the *Kon-Tiki* came almost from nowhere. Heyerdahl was unknown and his raft journey had been mainly unreported and largely forgotten by the time the book came out, especially in Europe. The lack of coverage in Europe was not surprising. The winter of 1947 had been the continent's most severe since 1880. Reconstruction after the war had stalled and by the summer there was a mood of 'impending disaster', as Tony Judt has put it.[2] Many were too busy trying to survive; reading about a balsa raft in the Pacific was not a top priority. The expedition in 1947 probably received, in Europe, greatest coverage in Norway, followed by Sweden. In Britain there was almost no mention of the expedition in 1947. Of the major papers only the *Manchester Guardian* ran a couple of articles. The French situation was similar: only *Le Figaro* and *Le Monde* had a few articles in 1947. The US media coverage had been better but the US edition of the *Kon-Tiki* was published over three years after the expedition so it was difficult for Heyerdahl to rely on any public memory of his feat.

The lapse of time between the *Kon-Tiki* expedition and the book meant that Heyerdahl failed to capitalize on the little coverage the expedition had given him. This was the price he paid for not managing to place his book before his journey or immediately afterwards in a country like the USA. Looking at other successful adventures and travel books of the period we can see that Heyerdahl's speed in getting out his product was not impressive. The French mountaineer Maurice Herzog climbed Annapurna in the Himalaya in 1950, and in 1951 he published his book *Annapurna premier 8.000* in France. By 1952 his book had been published in both Britain and the USA. Herzog's countryman Alain Bombard sailed a rubber dinghy over the Atlantic in 1952, publishing *Naufragé volontaire* (The Voyage of the *Hérétique*) in France and Britain in 1953. The following year a US edition came out. The most impressive was however the leader of the successful British Everest expedition of 1953, John Hunt, author of *The Ascent of Everest*, who published in both Britain and France the same year as the expedition. The US edition was published one year later.

Heyerdahl got a second chance to create a media sensation with his *Kon-Tiki* through the book. This time he was more successful. The accolades rained over Heyerdahl's narration. Most critics were lavish in their praise, and almost everybody recommended the book as a good read. Heyerdahl's publishers could rub their hands at the great publicity that the reviewers gave the book; they could not have written more enticing blurbs themselves. The *Kon-Tiki* fever spread quickly from publishers to booksellers to newspapers around Europe and North America. As has been mentioned before, there was no one who questioned Heyerdahl over his pseudoscientific racist theory. Reviewers focused for the most part on the concept of universality with which the book was promoted.

A recurrent theme in the *Kon-Tiki* reviews was that the book was a classic in the making, and this even before the book had reached a success that could qualify such judgements. This trend began in Sweden. The tabloid *Expressen* stated in 1949 that Heyerdahl's book had 'all the potential to become a classic adventure book'.[3] Other critics were even firmer on this point; the book was going to 'be a classic', pronounced the paper *Arbetet*.[4] The concept of the classic went well with the universality of the *Kon-Tiki*. A classic was utterly translatable and would stand the test of time. Classics were books that had become more than just texts; they had acquired some mythic standing in themselves. This larger than life attribute was also repeatedly stressed in the Swedish reviews. *Aftonbladet* ended its overwhelming review with the grand conclusion that: 'This book is the big, real, adventure in print.'[5]

That the *Kon-Tiki* was a classic in the making was repeated in the British reviews the following spring. S. Barrington Gates called the book, in the respectable *Times Literary Supplement*, a 'superb adventure story which all the world may, and probably will, read'.[6] Others followed suit by praising the book as an 'extraordinary adventure' that was among 'the finest stories of adventurous travel' published in a long time, or simply 'one of the best adventure books ever written'.[7] Peter Quennell, himself among the most famous British travel-writers, said that he had liked the book 'more than any other book of adventure that I have read for many years'.[8] The translatability of this classic adventure was also stressed in Britain, where the author and journalist Arthur Ransome prophesied that 'men of every nation' would rejoice in the 'high-spirited, gallant and modest-minded' story of Heyerdahl.[9]

If Heyerdahl and his publishers were pleased with the kind of publicity the reviewers in European countries like Sweden and Britain were producing, they would soon be overjoyed with the US critics. Heyerdahl had fought hard to get his book published in the USA, but when he did the response was overwhelming. The critics lavished on it strong adjectives like 'incredible', 'thrilling' and 'fabulous'. Van Allen Bradley of the *Chicago Daily News* even stated that Heyerdahl's 'magnificent tale of adventure' was beyond description; 'superlatives seem wholly inadequate in the face of its grandeur.'[10] Joseph Henry Jackson said in the *San Francisco Chronicle* that Heyerdahl's 'great epic of the sea' would 'keep almost any reader utterly fascinated from beginning to end.'[11]

It was rare to find any dismissal of Heyerdahl for being too directed towards a popular audience. Overall there was no difference in the tone of the reviews in tabloids and more prestigious journals or papers. The sole exception was France where only *Paris-Match* and *Carrefour* reviewed the book, favourably, but where the highbrow literary magazines made no mention of it. The US situation where the major publications endorsed Heyerdahl was much more common. There one could read about the book in the pages of magazines like *The Atlantic* that called it the 'most audacious story of seafaring since the war', and 'an astonishing adventure for readers of every age.'[12] *The New Yorker* was also enthusiastic about the book and *Time Magazine* highly recommended it even though the language of the review was a bit more tempered.

For a book so aggressively marketed and so extensively reviewed it was overall remarkable that so few of the comments concerning it were negative. The only slight exception to this wall-to-wall praise was a reaction by the Swedish-speaking academic establishment. They reacted mostly against the image of Heyerdahl as a *bona fide* scholar that had started to appear in connection with the discussions around the *Kon-Tiki* and they dismissed the diffusionist theory that Heyerdahl proposed. One of the first dissenting critics was the botanist Carl Skottsberg. Mentioning his own research in the Pacific Skottsberg tried systematically to oppose Heyerdahl's theory of pre-Columbian migration in an article of 26 November 1949 in *Göteborgs Handels- och Sjöfartstidning*.[13] Stig Rydén, who had participated in archaeological excavations at Tiwanaku, Bolivia, followed up this critique in the same paper one month later.[14] This debate eventually spread to another paper, *Aftonbladet*, in February 1950, and to *Svenska Dagbladet* in June 1950. Both Heyerdahl and his friend Olof Selling, professor of botany at the Museum of Natural History in Stockholm, would meet this criticism in the same papers. Selling would also introduce Heyerdahl to the Royal Swedish Society for Anthropology and Geography. Heyerdahl rewarded Selling amply for his support in 1951 when, through Helms, he anonymously donated a sum of money to fund an exhibition at Selling's museum.[15]

While some Swedish scientists rejected Heyerdahl the scientist they were in their writings still in awe of Heyerdahl the adventurer. Skottsberg mused that the *Kon-Tiki* had been a 'singular' feat, 'a grand chronicle' that 'offered many inspiring and funny moments' though maybe belonging more to the world of sport than science.[16] At no point did he or his colleagues suggest that the book itself was not worth reading; they only begged to take issue with Heyerdahl's science. That they did so in the public media arena that Heyerdahl had chosen was perhaps not a good strategy if they wanted to discredit him in the eyes of the wider public. As most normal readers would have too little knowledge of the complicated scientific discussion in any case the intervention of the scientists risked simply reinforcing Heyerdahl's image of them as obscure and conceited.

Heyerdahl was so unanimously approved in the media that he was not even attacked from any political quarter. Newspapers and magazines with very different political leanings all supported Heyerdahl. In a Europe that was nervous about US intervention, especially in areas of culture, Heyerdahl's alignment to the US armed forces raised no questions. He had managed to sail his *Kon-Tiki* into a world so mythical and removed from the concerns of the day that he could appear as entirely apolitical.

## Proud Science and Common Sense

Many scientists specializing in Polynesia greeted the *Kon-Tiki* voyage with incredulity. The Maori scholar Sir Peter Buck, aka Te Rangi Hiroa, had already in a 1949 interview in *The Auckland Star* 'thrown back his head with laughter' at the mention of the *Kon-Tiki*, adding: 'A nice adventure [...] But you don't seriously expect anybody to call that a scientific expedition?'[17] He was wrong: discussions of science were at the very heart of the reviews of the *Kon-Tiki* book. Heyerdahl's project of casting himself in the role of the academic outcast, the scholarly rebel, had been successful. The detail in the *Kon-Tiki* book that was most often referred to was Heyerdahl's meeting with the disdainful unnamed scientist, Spinden, who allegedly rejected his thesis without having read his argument. Richard Hughes in the *Observer* illustrated perfectly the drama created by this meeting when he referred in the opening lines of his review to Heyerdahl as 'a young anthropologist that no one would listen to'.[18]

The defiance of the young scientific rebel Heyerdahl in the face of the scientific dogma contributed importantly to the greatness of the *Kon-Tiki* book, according to its reviewers. The critics rejoiced that Heyerdahl had been able to 'prove' his theory for the disbelieving academics by physically carrying out his suggested prehistoric migration. The daring of Heyerdahl and his crew led them to win the argument against the enfeebled and book-learned 'experts'. The most 'powerful appeal' of the book was, according to Harry Gilroy in the *New York Times,* that Heyerdahl's idea had so strong a 'value' for the crew that they were 'willing to stake their lives upon its validity'.[19]

The non-scientific critics accepted Heyerdahl's wish for his book to be understood as a scientific adventure, and no review was without a reference to the purpose, the theory, of the *Kon-Tiki* expedition. But although the theory was made clear, it is also evident that it was the adventure that was the most important element. The science simply vouched for the purity of the enterprise. Although the theory was often discussed in detail, many reviewers pointed out that any deeper appreciation and understanding of it was not a prerequisite for enjoying the book. Peter Quennell put it directly when he stated: 'You need not feel even the mildest interest in anthropology, archaeology, or the theory of a cultural link between Polynesia and South America to appreciate this extraordinary account of how a wild idea gradually developed into a well-organised, well-equipped, and well-led expedition'.[20] This argument was followed by, among others, Sir John Squire: 'Mr. Heyerdahl brings a good deal of linguistic and ethnological evidence in support of his theory. But many readers are not interested in such things, and they will be fully satisfied to find the book one of the finest stories of adventurous travel which has appeared for many years.'[21]

That adventure through travel was the key to the book, and that the *Kon-Tiki* as a whole was about these two themes more than anything else, was similarly stressed by the Swedish reviewers. 'However captivating the ethnologic speculations are, they are in any case not as important as exciting adventure', as *Morgon-Tidningen* put succinctly.[22] Let the scientific truth be 'whatever it may', *Sundsvalls Tidning* argued, 'for the general public [the book is] this autumn's most exciting tale of adventure'.[23] The critics were consciously trying to lift the book from the scientific realm, outside the specialist world of probability and evidence in which most readers of the *Kon-Tiki* would likely find little interest.

In general, the British and Swedish reviewers took a more critical stance towards Heyerdahl's theory itself and employed a more sceptical tone than those in the USA for whom the successful conclusion of the trip was often taken to indicate the real validity of his argument – which was going a step further than Heyerdahl himself, who claimed no more than it proved only the possibility of his being right. There was not the same interest in separating Heyerdahl's work from 'true' science. Symptomatic of this was Fredrick Laws in the *News Chronicle* thinking it wise to point out that the experts 'still doubt the theory behind the expedition'.[24] The reviewer in *Arbetet* even thought that it was 'of course […] impossible for a layman to say anything in this scientific debate'.[25] Similar caveats were prominent in both British and Swedish reviews; though Heyerdahl the underdog excited interest with his scientific challenge, it did not appear well advised to throw expert opinion completely overboard.

This cautious language was rarer in the USA where one could read bombastic pronouncements like those of Sterling North in the *Buffalo Courier-Express* who claimed that now 'Proud "science" must again bow to an older "discipline" – courage and common sense.'[26] Common sense, it seemed, was different on the two sides of the Atlantic: in the USA the sensory indication or first impression could be trusted, while in Britain and Sweden there was more doubt as to whether that which was apparent was also true, and possibly there was more faith in the opinion of experts.

The discussion of the science, itself mostly centred on the underdog-challenger theme, thus dominated the digested versions of Heyerdahl's book that appeared in its reviews. This is a strong indication that science, in a certain conception, was central to the *Kon-Tiki* story, for Heyerdahl as well as for its readers. But the focus on the courageous outsider also ensured that there would be no conflict between science and adventure. An illusion of entwinement was created, whereas in reality the science became a function of the adventure rather than merging with it. The step, in any case, from science to adventure was never great, as the critics showed. From discussions of Heyerdahl's theory the reviews could easily pass into recounting snippets of dramatic stories such as storms and the man-overboard drama. In turn these stories, with their focus on danger, served to reinforce the image of a courageous and foolhardy young scholar risking everything for his theory. This double function of the underdog theme is well represented in a review in the Swedish scout magazine *Totem*: 'It [the book] is a remarkably captivating narration of a young man's overcoming of the resistance that conservatism, narrow-mindedness, and formalism can muster. But Heyerdahl and his comrades also had the forces of nature to overcome.'[27]

The reviewers made Heyerdahl into a sort of mirror image of the kind of weak man typically berated in 1950s cultural discourse. Heyerdahl had in the view of the critics avoided succumbing to the oppression of a wife or a boring job; his wartime experience did not seem to have traumatized him; he was not locked into a corporation with a crushing routine. Heyerdahl was everything that the man in the grey flannel suit was not. Conservative science had to stand in for the oppressive structure in Heyerdahl's account, but the reviewers focused for the most part not on the implication of science itself but on Heyerdahl's exploits; conservative science remained a practical foe that could in reality be substituted by an oppressive home, a dull job and gruesome routine. Implicitly the reviewers suggested that Heyerdahl managed to reconquer a certain masculinity that had been lost after the war.

When they linked the *Kon-Tiki* to other images in order to give the prospective reader an indication of the nature of the book, the critics focused in most cases more on the theme of adventure and the masculine coming-of-age story than on the challenge to science, even though it was the science that had been stressed in their reviews. Heyerdahl would probably have been happiest compared to a classic scientific challenger like Columbus or Galileo, but this was not very common. A rare exception was Robert H. Prall's review in the *Herald Post* of El Paso, Texas, which claimed that Heyerdahl, the 'Hero of Pacific Crossing', was a 'new Columbus'.[28]

The maritime theme of the *Kon-Tiki* was stressed repeatedly by reviewers, and there was no doubt that Heyerdahl's travels belonged to a long line of tales of the sea. The *Kon-Tiki* was called a 'Sea Adventure' (*Morgon-Tidningen, Minneapolis Sunday Tribune, Boston Sunday Globe* and *Chicago Time*), 'Sea Exploit' (*Chicago Daily News, Helsingborgsposten, Arbetet*), 'Sea Voyage' (*Cleveland Press*), 'Sea Tale' (*The Pittsburgh Press*), 'Epic of the Sea' (*Richmond Times*), 'Pacific Saga' (*Sacramento Times*) and 'New Sea Classic' (*New York Post*). This image was in turn strengthened by the references critics provided to help the reader connect the *Kon-Tiki* story with others. The single most important such story was that of the Vikings. Many reviewers evidently considered the 'Norse' qualities of Heyerdahl, his crew and the expedition as key to understanding it.

The Viking references to Heyerdahl can be dated back to the subtitle of the 1947 *Life Magazine* article about the *Kon-Tiki* which read: 'Cruise of the Kon-Tiki: Modern Vikings Sail 101 Days Across the Open Pacific'.[29] Although it is unlikely that the *Life* article subtitle stuck in the head of critics who reviewed the book several years afterwards, there was something in the story itself which made the idea of 'Modern Vikings' an appealing one. Vikings were after all, manly men from the North who travelled the seas and wrote about it. Or, as Joel Fine concluded when talking about the *Kon-Tiki* in the *Oakland Tribune*: 'From earliest times, Norsemen have been great navigators and have left in their wake stirring sagas of the sea.'[30] The critic of *The Times* even claimed that Heyerdahl had a 'Viking touch'.[31] But what exactly did it mean to be like a Viking, apart from the obvious fact of braving open seas in flimsy vessels and writing sagas about it?

For most critics Vikings symbolized audacity and ingenuity in the face of danger. The *Kon-Tiki* was described by Van Allen Bradley as 'the incredible odyssey of these latter-day Vikings'.[32] Alice Dixon Bond argued that the secret behind the voyage's completion was the 'firm faith and ingenious efforts of six stalwart and indomitable young Vikings'.[33] Lewis Gannett in the *Herald Tribune* claimed that the book had 'Viking gallantry, a salt-sea tang, a warm South Seas rhythm', something he rightly described as a rather 'rare combination'.[34] Wilton M. Krogman in the *Chicago Sunday Tribune* added co-operation and triumphant human spirit to the qualities of the crew, and this human spirit was potentially what Harry Gilroy alluded to when in the *New York Times* he claimed that Heyerdahl was 'a man with the heart of a Leif Ericson and the merry story-telling gift of an Ernie Pyle'.[35] An anonymous reviewer in the Swedish *Helsingborgsposten* even claimed, linking the Vikings to the story of science, that it was the mere fact of Heyerdahl being Norwegian that made him challenge scientific dogma with a practical counter-example.[36]

This identification of 'Norse-ness' with audacity and practicality was however easier to understand than Raymond Mortimer's claim in the *Sunday Times* that the book had 'Viking simplicity and freshness of narrative'.[37] Mortimer was probably referring to the Norse sagas and was trying to get at Heyerdahl's apparently unsophisticated and rough literary style, in which Peter Quennell had detected 'a certain back-slapping heartiness'.[38] The same style made James A. Michener, author of *Tales of the South Pacific* (1946), react against the 'wooden' portrayal of the crew and conclude that even though Heyerdahl was a 'superb adventurer' he was not a 'great writer'.[39] But the unsophisticated simplicity identified as a negative thing by some reviewers was for the most part interpreted as something that contributed to making the *Kon-Tiki* read like a saga. Saga was also a word used to describe Heyerdahl's style, together with epic, simple, clear, heroic, thrilling and honest. One of the most common characterizations was the somewhat curious word 'clean'. For the *Newsweek* reviewer the *Kon-Tiki* was 'a clean, thrilling, honest story'.[40] Heyerdahl's narrative was streamlined, devoid of unnecessary introspection, focused on action and morally uncomplicated; in short, a bit like both the Vikings and their sagas.

During the Victorian period the Vikings had been crafted into a model of manly heroics by writers like Thomas Carlyle in *On Heroes and Hero Worship* (1841). The Viking was to signal determined masculinity rather than wanton violence – as had been his previous image. How this heroic upgrade of the Vikings happened is outside this book's scope, but it is fascinating that in 1979 Wyatt Blassingame published a children's book in the USA about Heyerdahl entitled *Viking Scientist*, a curious combination of images. But in the early 1950s when the *Kon-Tiki* book sailed around the world the Viking-ness or Norse quality of Heyerdahl's text linked it strongly to another story that had arisen out of recent history.

The second most important reference encountered in the *Kon-Tiki* reviews was to the Norwegian resistance against Nazi Germany during the Second World War, and the image of Viking intrepidity and the fight against the occupation easily blended into each other. Heyerdahl had tried to capitalize on his connection to the story of the Norwegian resistance when constructing his expedition in 1946 by, for example, including war heroes in his crew, and this paid off greatly in terms of respect, acceptance and credibility gained, both during the planning of the expedition and the selling of the book.

The *Kon-Tiki* was often seen as a continuation of the manly Norwegian resistance, as in Harry Gilroy's *New York Times* review where he argued that the courage that Heyerdahl's crew showed in putting their lives on the line for an idea could have been developed 'during the fight on behalf of human freedom against the ancient sanguinary witchcraft of German fascism'.[41] What this kind of review did was not only to equate the courage of the *Kon-Tiki* men with the Norwegian resistance of the war, but it also indirectly linked the 'idea' of the Polynesians' origins to the 'idea' of national freedom and sovereignty. In both cases the Norwegians displayed a thorough conviction that they were in the right, and they were ready to die to demonstrate this. The implication of this metaphor was further to castigate the 'experts'; not only were they bookish cowards, they were also irrational and shady. If the tenacity of the Norwegian resistance was transferred to Heyerdahl, the dogmatic power of the 'scientists' could be figuratively linked to that of an effeminate Nazi oppressor.

The notion that Heyerdahl and his crew were all that his opposition was not was further reinforced by the reviewers mentioning that he (and sometimes his crew) had been parachutists during the war. The image of parachuting underlined the boldness of Heyerdahl; in cutting all ties with land and casting off on a flimsy raft which he could not be certain would support him, he contrasted with the arm-chair 'experts' who theorized from the safety of their studies. According to the *Atlantic* review, Heyerdahl 'at the first opportunity after the war, in 1947 [...] gathered together a ship's company of six Scandinavians; war veterans, explorers, and a meteorologist – men who had learned to operate radio in the Resistance, parachutists who were not afraid of the unknown.'[42] Now Heyerdahl had hurled himself into the enemy camp with his theory; just as his voyage itself was like a jump, a malfunctioning raft would be like a parachute that refused to deploy (at least in the story), and they would be lost. The *Kon-Tiki* was thus raised to epic simplicity; to the level of life or death.

As the parachute of the resistance fighter came to be paralleled to the raft of the modern Viking anthropologist, the method of Heyerdahl was also linked to the war itself. His bravery, tenacity and uncompromising approach was commented on by Alfred Stanford in the *New York Herald Tribune*: 'After the war, in 1947, with five other casually gathered comrades, similarly schooled by war in the idea of direct action and freed from ordinary fears, Heyerdahl talked himself and them into the idea of an expedition.'[43] Stanford's characterization of the Second World War sounds like that of someone who has received only the mythic media image of the war, the image that would lead to the production of films like *Edge of Darkness* (1943) with Errol Flynn and *The Heroes of Telemark* (1965) with Kirk Douglas about the war in Norway. And if Heyerdahl had to improvise his raft to beat his opponents, this was another image of the 'ambusher' – taking on a powerful and static machine (be it the Nazis or the scientific community) with the weapon of surprise.

Heyerdahl tried consciously to link the *Kon-Tiki* to the Norwegian wartime resistance, and he did include three cursory references to the Vikings, but there were other stories that were much more important in

his book. He referred to a bearded white culture-bearing race coming with
civilization to the New World many more times than he talked about the
war. But whereas the reviewers were happy to comment on the Second
World War none of them chose to remark on the theory of the white
race. Heyerdahl's blue-eyed 'folk' were mentioned in various reviews, but
this legend was in no way challenged. The 'whiteness' of the crew in raw
nature was only used to link them to positive heroes. Heyerdahl's rough
and ready literary style blinded the reviewers with Viking whiteness.

## Raft of Redemption

The *Kon-Tiki* reviews clearly show how the book was read as being a work
of and for its time as well as a timeless classic or saga. Heyerdahl's tale
was compared to the story of Odysseus and Jason's quest for the Golden
Fleece, as well as to more contemporary adventures like those of T. E.
Lawrence, Joshua Slocum and Fridtjof Nansen. The *Kon-Tiki* was even
likened to fictional adventures such as *Robinson Crusoe, Moby Dick* and the
works of Jules Verne, Joseph Conrad and Ernest Hemingway. Heyerdahl's
style was said to be both like the 'merry story-telling gift' of the US war
reporter Ernie Pyle and something much more gothic that could have
been 'devised by Jules Verne and written by Conan Doyle'.[44]

The characteristics that the reviewers found in the *Kon-Tiki*, courage
and manly intrepidity, coupled with their appreciation of the story as one
rooted in its time yet still able to overcome it, led to powerful conclusions.
Many argued that the book was valuable in more profound ways than being
simply an entertaining read. A moral message was found in Heyerdahl's
text, a message bordering on the messianic. And the success of the book
itself would only further contribute to this assessment, as Alfred Stanford
claimed in his *Herald Tribune* review: 'Originally published in Norway, it
has quickly spread through the world in some twelve languages with the
speed of a small classic being born and the suggestion that it contains a
strong medicine for modern man.'[45]

One of the most articulated suggestions of what that 'medicine' could
be was found in a review in the *Newark News* by Bill Robinson. He argued
that Heyerdahl's book helped shift the readers' attention away from the
sordid present that was written about in 'tomes on Russia, homosexuality,
and the ills of civilisation' and instead heralded a return to the 'elemental

truths' that were 'grandeur, beauty, and simplicity'.[46] These very factors made it into an anti-decadent text. 'Simple' suggested 'pure', and in the dichotomy of Robinson's review Communism, homosexuality and a modern civilization gone astray signalled the impure. Edward Shanks in the *Daily Graphic* was even more triumphalist when it came to the ability of the *Kon-Tiki* to communicate a higher moral ground: 'Who says that Western man is growing decadent? Anyone who does should read these astonishing pages for his correction.'[47]

The *Kon-Tiki* was read as an epic not only because its language was like that of a saga, but also because the content itself held 'higher truths'. It was a classic, conservative and timeless remedy to contemporary decadence as expressed in deceitful Communism, transgressive homosexuality and enfeebled modernity as a whole, unable to hold principled beliefs and unwilling to display courage, individuality and masculinity. Sean Fielding in his review, appropriately entitled 'Hope for Humans', in the highbrow New York magazine *Tatler* gave the following reason for calling the *Kon-Tiki* an epic: 'in an age when the dignity of man is dwarfed by the onrush of eerie half-knowledge, when much of the human spirit lies mangled and bleeding under the tramp of godless armies, and even the stars seem to lose their eternal beneficence, this book comes as a high trumpet call and also a blam.'[48]

Fielding's review is important in that it described the messianic connection to the epic through clear religious references. It is not only the image of communist armies that trample on the human spirit that is linked to religion by being 'godless', but more importantly it is the book, the *Kon-Tiki*, that 'comes as a high trumpet call', a passage soaked in religious connotation. Fielding's trumpet call is hard to interpret as anything but a praise of God; 'Praise him with the sound of the trumpet' (Psalm 150:3). But the trumpet is also a promise that we shall be redeemed: 'the trumpet shall sound, and the dead shall be raised incorruptible, and we shall be changed' (1 Corinthians 15:52). Stanley Unwin had in 1951 claimed that not even the Bible had sold so many copies in such a short time as the *Kon-Tiki* had.[49] This was an exaggerated comment, but in some ways it pointed towards the religious values that were so easily ascribed to the *Kon-Tiki*.

It was the epic timelessness and stress on courage and masculinity that lent the *Kon-Tiki* its redemptive qualities. The contemporary world seemed for many critics to be devoid of such stories. It was, in short, decadent. 'If you have been depressed by all the novels and films about cruelty, madness and despair', wrote Raymond Mortimer in the *Sunday*

*Times*, 'let me recommend a new book that is more cheerful than fiction.'
And that book was of course Heyerdahl's *Kon-Tiki*. Mortimer commented
that recently (meaning in the war), 'men have had to use all their resources
of enterprise and courage against their fellow man', but now along came
Heyerdahl and adopted the 'captivating virtues' of martial life in order
to face the elements.[50]

Mortimer's idea was that the elements formed a pure backdrop to
the enacting of that which was worth celebrating in the human spirit.
Only when the background was as basic and uncomplicated as the
elements themselves could that which is important in the story form
an easily delineated foreground of action. This was a romantic notion
that argued that the most important story was man's (as in the male)
encounter with nature, rather than with other men. The human drama
in anything but a small group surrounded by nature was too complicated
and muddled to yield moral lessons, since it would have to take place in
a civilization that was by definition decadent. For people with a romantic
penchant, the Second World War could not but reinforce this conception.
Not even the most sophisticated propaganda could maintain romantic
myths about the war, as its sheer scale served to undermine its potential
for creating small-scale heroics. Mortimer's comment is evidence that
this was the case even in Britain, a country that when it came to literature
thrived on heroic and nationalistic myths from the war to a greater extent
than the USA.[51]

The *Kon-Tiki* was for some, like Mortimer, a blessing in that it showed
a return to romantic adventure that had miraculously survived the
onslaught of mass warfare. Harrison Smith in the *Washington Post* thought
it 'natural' that there had been a dearth of adventure during the war: 'Great
adventure stories are less likely to emerge from the mechanized mass wars
and revolutions that have swept over the world during this century than
from courageous and hardy men who risk their lives against the forces
of nature.'[52] This negation of heroic potential in war is worth noticing
as it runs counter to what would characterize representations of war in
popular culture for so much of the postwar period. It was the elements of
nature and not the culture of war that made the great adventures possible
for the generation that had just survived the Second World War.

Some reviewers focused less on the proper staging of the human drama
in order to achieve epic adventure than they did on the redemptive virtues
that the *Kon-Tiki* contained. Peter Quennell in the *Daily Mail* was one of

the reviewers to focus on the inalienable goodness of the characteristics displayed by Heyerdahl and his crew: 'I have enjoyed "The Kon-Tiki Expedition" more than any other book of adventure that I have read for many years. It is a book to restore one's faith in 20th-century mankind. These young Scandinavians were genuinely "men of good will", alert, courageous, disinterested, and "intellectually inquisitive".'[53]

From the first three characteristics that Quennell lists one could draw the conclusion that for being 'men of good will' restoring 'one's faith in 20th-century mankind' it was enough to live up to the Scout credo. This conception could go both with a Christian and a romantic reading, but what upsets the picture is Quennell's reference to them as being 'intellectually inquisitive'. If one adds the reference to Scandinavia, as opposed to any 'Viking-ness', it is possible to postulate that Quennell was implying that the man of good will was also a humanist and a good democrat. But naturally Quennell could simply have meant that Heyerdahl was in this way different from the ideal man of Nazism, Communism or any other twentieth-century experience that was certainly not considered as hope-inducing by the mainstream in the postwar West. There is, however, an interesting hint in the direction of the notion of political progressiveness in Quennell's words. Maybe it was just Heyerdahl's urge to prove himself right that inspired Quennell, but it seems possible that the anti-hierarchical leadership and self-professed intellectual agility and openness portrayed in the *Kon-Tiki* could have played a part.

Quennell's notion of the story's hopefulness being based on the crew being 'intellectually inquisitive' was mirrored on a much more practical level by H. M. Tomlinson in *John O'London's Weekly* who emphasized the dexterity of the crew. Tomlinson thus situated the redemptive, hopeful qualities of the *Kon-Tiki* neither in the peaceful use of human resources, nor in the inherent qualities of these resources themselves, but rather in the particular application of them: 'The cheerful nonchalance of the crew of this temerarious outfit, when matters were at their worst [...] and their invention and dexterity when extricating themselves from an apparently hopeless situation, is enough to give one fresh hope of mankind.' Tomlinson ended his review by saying that 'If only our statesmen could show the same good humour while cunningly turning doomsday into a May morning!'[54]

The deftness and humour that Tomlinson read in the *Kon-Tiki*, together with Quennell's focus on the 'good will' of the crew, represent two common interpretations of the hopefulness of Heyerdahl's story. There was, however, one review that took the interpretation to a new level and articulated another (like the story of the white race) invisible theme of the *Kon-Tiki*: the frontier. The hardiness, intrepidity, masculinity, messianic religiosity, democracy and communion with nature all met in this concept. And this was a story that was not exclusively a North American one. Heyerdahl would have grown up with stories of cowboys and Indians and the great promise of the West, as would any European at the turn of the century in the wake of the mass emigrations to the USA. When Heyerdahl and in his crew shout 'Westward ho!' in the *Kon-Tiki* book[55] he is not consciously trying to appeal to a US market, but repeats a mantra inscribed in a shared Western popular culture.

Georges Carousso in the *Brooklyn Eagle Sun* tried to inscribe a transcendental value in the very direction 'West', arguing that 'the march was always to the West' ever since the first cavemen started exploring their world. Carousso claimed that the drive westward brought man over the North American continent until the Pacific was reached. This was the apparent end of the frontier, and man 'felt cheated, because there was no further "Westering" left for him'. But the wait was finally over as Heyerdahl had delivered 'a book that tears down the barrier and opens the West once more to exploration. But a different West. The Pacific Ocean itself.'[56]

What Heyerdahl redeemed according to Carousso was the frontier, something that reintroduced the hope that the US mission to spread westwards, as articulated in the concept of 'manifest destiny', could continue. Carousso's high-pitched language does not contradict the fact that he was in part right in his argument. That man was programmed to go west must however be seen as a particular North American interpretation of the general development of civilization. In 1856 de Gobineau's US translator H. Hotz had claimed the same when he stated, 'It is a familiar saying that *civilization travels westward*.'[57] Carousso was however correct in arguing that Heyerdahl did participate in opening up the Pacific frontier to the west as a new US project. This conclusion Carousso divined without even knowing, one would assume, the complicated level of support that Heyerdahl had from US authorities for carrying out a conscious frontier project in the Pacific at the time. Heyerdahl had thus not only redeemed man through adventure, he had also resuscitated one of man's most epic projects: the frontier.

## Singular Universality

Heyerdahl and his publishers succeeded beyond their expectations in making the *Kon-Tiki* into what seemed like a universal story with a large scope for accommodating various interpretations and readings. If we are to believe the reviewers of the book, the creation was singularly universal, to the point of being, in their eyes, a classic and a legend in the making at the very moment of its publication. None of the critics tried to examine the narrative itself in order to understand how this had come about, apart from the vague references to the clarity of the prose linked to the Viking sagas. What they did was to turn to themselves, reading the *Kon-Tiki* through their emotional response to it. As a consequence of the book's ability to move the reviewers to such a significant degree it was reported to be unique, and of universal appeal.

One outcome of the emotional reading of the *Kon-Tiki* was that the reviews neglected to place it in a specific genre. No taxonomies were put forward beyond the vague categories of the text as an epic or an adventure. The previous chapter demonstrated that the *Kon-Tiki* in many ways was a typical travel narrative. Only a few critics such as Frederick Laws in *News Chronicle* and Sir John Squire in the *Illustrated London News* explicitly called the *Kon-Tiki* a travel book.[58] The majority of critics stuck to the nebulous category of 'adventure' and did not even mention travel. 'Adventure' was, significantly, a universal term itself; it could feature as a component of a number of genres. Travel, in contrast, was a term that resolutely inserted the *Kon-Tiki* into a literary trajectory that was too constricting. It had been for this reason that Helms was so concerned about the fact that the *Kon-Tiki* should not be called a travel book.

Sometimes the critics tried to read Heyerdahl through the figures of famous travellers such as the sailor Joshua Slocum, Heyerdahl's childhood polar hero Fridtjof Nansen or the British desert explorer and man of letters Charles Montagu Doughty. However, most of the authors mentioned in conjunction with Heyerdahl were firmly rooted in the realm of fiction, from Homer to Hemingway. These authors wrote texts centred on travel, but not, for the most part, travel books. They contained masculine heroic adventure, albeit in fictional form. The main reason that Heyerdahl could be perceived as carrying a redemptive message was that he had physically performed the feats of adventure fiction in real life. At least this was what

Heyerdahl claimed, and the critics believed him. Heyerdahl was not treated as yet another travel-writer; he was heralded as the embodiment of legendary stories.

Helms's concept of universality was not only accepted, it was also greatly expanded. Most significantly this came through references to Vikings and the Norwegian experience of war. These were in part specific stories born out of the possibility of connecting Heyerdahl to them through his character, but most of the time they were read as universal and unquestionable assertions of white masculine heroics. Naturally these were in essence not universal categories. They were deeply rooted in a specific trajectory of the creation of Western masculinity, but the important fact is that the critics presented them as being universal.

That they, mostly white men, missed out on Heyerdahl's racism and sexism is not so surprising, but that practically none of them understood that the epic nature of Heyerdahl's *Kon-Tiki* lay not only in the voyage but also in the way the narrative was constructed is more baffling. It is unrealistic to expect that critics at the time should all have dissected Heyerdahl's narrative in search of the techniques that made it attractive, but that no one did is extraordinary. The wave of approval that greeted a travel book about a raft journey across the Pacific written by an unknown Norwegian adventurer in the late 1940s and early 1950s was of almost unheard-of proportions. It seemed that Heyerdahl, and his publishers, had got it just right. Heyerdahl, the master narrator, the creator, the bricoleur, of the legendary narrative had been joined by a host of fellow mythographers that pushed the *Kon-Tiki* into the postwar imaginary. But the tactics they employed, constructing a legend that was made into a brand, were going to prove to be specific for the medium of written text. A radically different tactic was needed when making and selling the film.

# 6

# The *Kon-Tiki* Film and the Return to Realism

## Visualizing the *Kon-Tiki*

Heyerdahl never considered the *Kon-Tiki* book as the only vessel that would carry his story to a greater audience. The book was to be followed by a film. He spent as much time and effort making this film as he did with the book, and it also eventually became a spectacular media event in its own right. The story of how the *Kon-Tiki* film came into being is however largely unknown, and its success proved a much more ephemeral phenomenon than the book's. Whereas millions of copies of the *Kon-Tiki* book took up, and still take up, place in people's homes and in bookshops the film quickly passed into a less accessible area of lived experience. This transience is unfortunate, because the making and reception of the *Kon-Tiki* film not only tell us more about Heyerdahl's sensation, but also speak of the important impositions and demands different media and generic conventions put on the same story.

Heyerdahl was convinced from the very beginning that the *Kon-Tiki* needed to be documented visually. Film and photographic equipment were among the first things he requested from the Pentagon, and the US Army Signal Corps later supplied them.[1] His future book needed photos, and a film was necessary for lecture tours, for newsreels, and for a documentary that could be screened in cinemas. In dealing with the visual side of narration Heyerdahl however proved himself more of a novice than when it came to writing. The one thing he was convinced of was that the *Kon-Tiki* had to be an illustrated epic saga. When the book was published he was always adamant that it should include a lot of illustrations, as he believed these to be of key importance for selling the book to a large public.[2]

The various editions of the *Kon-Tiki* book came to include many photographs and maps. In flipping through these first editions it is possible to form an image of how Heyerdahl approached the visual dimension of his journey. There were three illustrations that appear in all the important first editions. The first one is of Heyerdahl steering a provisional raft made of the balsa logs that would become the *Kon-Tiki* down a river in Ecuador. The second picture shows the construction of the final raft in the harbour of Callao (see plate 4). The third is of the raft at sea with hoisted sails and a man on the mast (see plate 6). The images reinforced the linear and seamless narrative, showing the first phase of the journey, the making of the raft and the raft itself as it traverses the ocean.

The visual material in the *Kon-Tiki* book gives reason to believe that it was Heyerdahl's intention to make a future film much in the same way as he had constructed his textual narrative. There was going to be continuity, seamlessness, chronology and an attempt to conceal the means and ways of the production of the narration itself. In all three pictures the observer is placed outside the story. This is particularly clear in the last picture in which the raft is seen from the viewpoint of someone at sea. The viewer is enthralled with the suggestive shape of the raft and the wave engulfing it, and does not stop to think that it must have been a shot taken by someone who had headed out from the raft in a rubber dinghy. The effect is like that of a classic Hollywood film when the story covers the plot and the artifice that has created it, just as Heyerdahl's book in which he managed to make the story appear timeless and epic.

It is necessary to use the photographs in the *Kon-Tiki* book in order to guess how Heyerdahl had envisaged making his film, because in the end it is possible to claim that he never got to make it. The film project was marred by mishaps and minor catastrophes from the very start. Heyerdahl had been given 64 rolls of film, both colour and black and white, but shortly before the departure from Peru in 1947 someone stole most of the colour film.[3] When the crew returned to the USA after the expedition it was found out that half of the 8000 feet of exposed film had been ruined by dampness.[4] Out of three hours and forty minutes' worth of film, only one hour and fifty minutes was of any potential use. Almost all of this was black and white and of low quality as it was filmed from a shaky 16mm camera on a rolling raft by inexperienced cameramen.

Heyerdahl screened the raw material shot on the raft before a group of Hollywood film executives in 1947, and they were not impressed. An offer was made to cut it all down to a ten-minute newsreel feature, for which Heyerdahl was offered a meagre $100.[5] He refused. With some help he prepared a simple lecture film from the material in the autumn of 1947 and put the plans to make a more substantial one on hold.

*Kon-Tiki* crew member Knut Haugland returned to Norway after the expedition to see his own wartime story filmed. Haugland had participated in the sabotage raid against the Nazi heavy-water production facility at Rjukan in occupied Norway, an event that would be turned into the film *Operation Swallow: The Battle for Heavy Water* that premiered in 1948. This film was a Norwegian-French co-production, directed by the Norwegian Titus Vibe-Müller under the supervision of the French director Jean Dréville.[6] It was a curious, though at the time not uncommon, mix of documentary and fiction that had already featured in the 1946 French occupation drama *Battle of the Rail* directed by René Clémants.[7] Archival footage was put next to re-enacted scenes, in which many of the original participants in the event (though not Haugland) played themselves.

In March 1948 the Norwegian financial backers of the heavy-water film contacted Haugland and suggested that a feature film should be made about the *Kon-Tiki*. They seem to have had the same concept in mind, in which the crew was to re-enact scenes from the voyage. Heyerdahl was thrilled at hearing this news, and claimed in a letter to the crew, surprisingly, to have many offers from Hollywood that he was now happy to turn down. He was excited at the possibility of a non-sensationalist and un-Hollywood-like Norwegian-French co-production, stating that he would not do a film at all it if was not to be a good one.[8] It is reasonable to assume that Heyerdahl's desire to make a 'European' as opposed to a 'Hollywood' film was simply the result of his failure in the USA. He had encountered the same problems in finding backing for his film in his promised land as he had in securing a book publisher.

When Heyerdahl got a more detailed proposal from the men behind the Norwegian *Kon-Tiki* film he could no longer claim that there would be such a big difference between a European film and a US one. The Norwegian filmmakers had something very close to a classic Hollywood production in mind. The film was to start romantically with Heyerdahl and Liv on their South Sea voyage, to be followed by a scene of Heyerdahl at war, then the expedition itself. In short, the film would be a biographical picture, as one of the suggested producers, Salve Staubo, who had made radios with Haugland during the war, told Heyerdahl.[9] It would be a seamless narration that even filled the gap of the war and added a romantic twist with the initial honeymoon of the young couple. If anything, it was Hollywood that seemed to be the inspiration.

The Norwegian *Kon-Tiki* film was never made. It is possible to imagine a number of reasons for the project falling apart. Heyerdahl got conflicting advice from his former crew. Herman Watzinger wrote to Heyerdahl in April 1948, weary of all the sensationalist publicity the *Kon-Tiki* had accumulated, and urged him to return to his scientific work instead of doing a film.[10] Bengt Danielsson was for the film, but only if there were guarantees that it would be a good one, which seems to suggest that he shared Watzinger's concerns.[11] There is no record of how much Heyerdahl listened to his friends; he was used to making decisions independently. The most probable reason for the film never happening is that the Norwegian financiers suffered huge economic losses with the heavy-water film and that a planned British investment that Staubo had hoped for never materialized.[12] It is also possible that, after the separation from Liv, Heyerdahl was not so happy about the focus Staubo would put on the Polynesian voyage of the late 1930s.

## Olle Nordemar and the *Kon-Tiki* Film

The trajectories of the *Kon-Tiki* book and film show some fascinating similarities. Heyerdahl tried to ensure that both would emerge in the USA early on, but found that he had to fall back on Norwegian contacts in the end. After the Norwegian beginnings the eventual success came through the products passing through Sweden where they were changed by skilled entrepreneurs like Adam Helms and made fit for an international market. After the Norwegian project failed, Heyerdahl would have to wait for the Swedish film producer Olle Nordemar at Artfilm to transform his amateur footage into something that could be screened for a large audience.

Nordemar had been to one of Heyerdahl's lectures in Sweden and had become captivated by the film material.[13] He offered Heyerdahl a deal for making a documentary film that was accepted by the early autumn of 1949.[14] Heyerdahl gave up the idea of any type of dramatization of his

1. Heyerdahl and his wife-to-be Liv Torp in the Norwegian mountains preparing for their return to nature on a Polynesian island. © Kon-Tiki Museum, Oslo

2. Heyerdahl and Liv Torp bathing in a river on Fatuiva, an image encapsulating the island's most Eden-like aspect. © Kon-Tiki Museum, Oslo

3. King Heyerdahl of Fatuiva. The crown was part of Heyerdahl's collection of Polynesian artefacts. © Kon-Tiki Museum, Oslo

4. The *Kon-Tiki* under construction in the dockyard of the Peruvian Navy in Callao, with the help of sailors. © Kon-Tiki Museum, Oslo

5. The crew of the *Kon-Tiki*: (l. to r.) Knut Haugland, Bengt Danielsson, Thor Heyerdahl, Erik Hesselberg, Torstein Raaby, Herman Watzinger. Heyerdahl and Hesselberg are the oldest at 32 years old; Danielsson, the youngest, is only 25.
© Kon-Tiki Museum, Oslo

6. The *Kon-Tiki* on the open seas. This was an image that was to serve as the model for many of the covers for different editions of the *Kon-Tiki* book. © Kon-Tiki Museum, Oslo

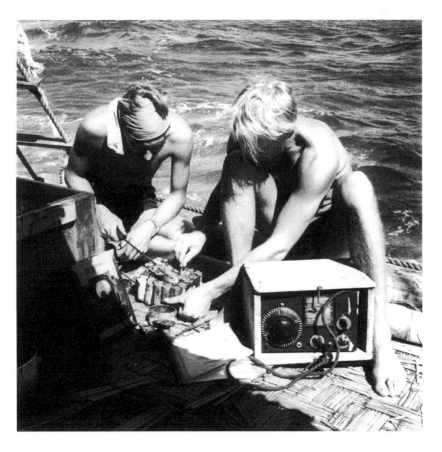

7. Haugland and Raaby doing maintenance work on one of the four radio sets on board the *Kon-Tiki*. © Kon-Tiki Museum, Oslo

8. Heyerdahl with one of the countless sharks that he and his crew caught during their Pacific crossing.
© Kon-Tiki Museum, Oslo

9. Map showing Heyerdahl's journeys of experimental archaeolo the footsteps of a vanished itinerant
© Kon-Tiki Museum,

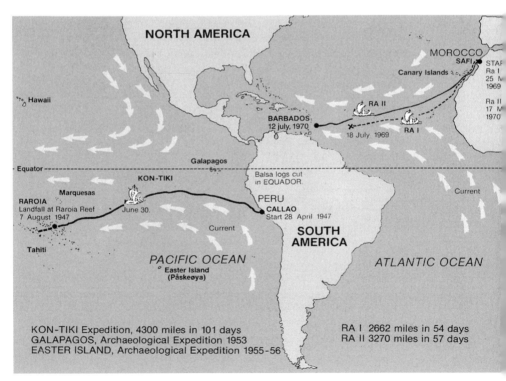

NORTH AMERICA

MOROCCO
SAFI STAR
Canary Islands Ra I
25 M
1969

RA II

BARBADOS
12 july, 1970

Ra II
17 M
1970

Hawaii

18 July 1969
RA I

Equator

Galapagos

Balsa logs cut
in EQUADOR.

KON-TIKI

Current

Marquesas

PERU

RAROIA
Landfall at Raroia Reef
7 August 1947

June 30.

CALLAO
Start 28 April 1947

Current

SOUTH
AMERICA

Tahiti

PACIFIC OCEAN

Easter Island
(Påskeøya)

ATLANTIC OCEAN

KON-TIKI Expedition, 4300 miles in 101 days
GALAPAGOS, Archaeological Expedition 1953
EASTER ISLAND, Archaeological Expedition 1955-56

RA I 2662 miles in 54 days
RA II 3270 miles in 57 days

10. Hesselberg plays guitar for Raaby on the raft, an image of the *Kon-Tiki* as an idyll far from the rat-race of the modern world. © Kon-Tiki Museum, Oslo

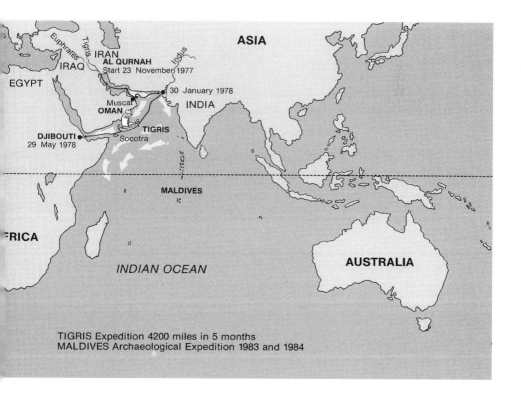

11. A group of Swedish booksellers and Adam Helms (standing) on an excursion, 3 September 1950. Sales of the *Kon-Tiki* book had just passed the 100,000 mark; Göran Wall tugs at Helms's sleeve, who, as the caption runs, 'claims that the *Kon-Tiki* can be seen on the horizon'.

© Adam Helms Collection, Stockholm University Library

12. Hesselberg's stylized drawing of a *monolito* from Tiwanaku, Bolivia, was adopted as the *Kon-Tiki* trademark. Here it is seen as the 'Leo the Lion' image at the beginning of Nordemar's film. © Norwegian Broadcasting Corporation.

13. Heyerdahl the scientist and Heyerdahl the adventurer: contrasting aspects of the hero used to introduce him in the film. © Norwegian Broadcasting Corporation.

14. A *Kon-Tiki* crew member, probably Heyerdahl, signals to a native vessel in the film, using the flags of Norway and the Explorers Club of New York. © Norwegian Broadcasting Corporation.

15. The Kon-Tiki Museum on Bygdøy in Oslo. Here the *Kon-Tiki* raft lies in state, alongside the reed-boat *Ra II*. The museum has received generations of visitors from throughout the world and continues to be a popular tourist attraction.

© Axel Andersson

film and entrusted Nordemar with the material. Maybe he was tired of trying to sell it and had in any case all but given up. Another possibility is that he instinctively saw in Nordemar an energetic entrepreneurial mind that could do for his film what Helms had done for his book in Sweden earlier that year. Both Heyerdahl and Nordemar were young, 35 years old, when they started working on the film, and both were eager to make names for themselves in their respective careers.

What had enticed Nordemar to offer Heyerdahl a deal was that he saw the film's potential in precisely the technical imperfections that had made it so difficult to sell; the amateurishness gave it a real and fresh feel.[15] The material was also a perfect way for Nordemar to test an optical printer that he had just acquired from the USA, capable of enlarging 16mm film to the 35mm necessary for cinema projection. Heyerdahl was more than impressed with how his previously worthless material was salvaged by Nordemar and made into a great film, as he stated in a letter to Philip Unwin in December 1949.[16] Embellishing the lecture film was also a much cheaper and faster way to produce the long overdue picture. The issue of time was particularly important for Heyerdahl who needed to get the film out quickly to coincide with, and capitalize on, the success of the book in Sweden and the imminent book launches in Britain and the USA.

Nordemar was suggesting a very different film from Staubo: the imperfections of the raw material would be retained to create realism, instead of using dramatizations to fill in the gaps. Nordemar's inspiration did not come from a Swedish or European way of making film, but paradoxically it originated in the same Hollywood by which Staubo appears to have been inspired. The young Swedish filmmaker had been able to go to the USA during the spring and summer of 1945, and through a family contact he found work with the US Office of War Information (OWI), a liaison body between the US government and the film industry that had been set up in 1942. He also saw the big studios and the right people during his six-month stint in Hollywood and elsewhere. He was introduced to Sol Lesser at RKO Pictures, as well as Walt Disney, and met weekly with Ingrid Bergman and Fritz Lang to discuss film.[17] He had waited two years for this journey so difficult to arrange in wartime, and when he finally got to the USA he was intent on learning as much as possible.[18]

Leonard Clairmont, the Hollywood correspondent for the Swedish magazine *Film Journalen*, remarked that a 'tornado' had left town when Nordemar returned to Sweden.[19] In contrast to most Swedish filmmakers visiting Hollywood, Nordemar had, according to Clairmont, worked day and night to learn what he could rather than just hobnobbing with the stars. 'It has been a fantastic journey and a fantastically tiring half-year,' said Nordemar to a journalist on his arrival back at Bromma airport in Stockholm on 29 July 1945.[20] He returned promising the first full-length Swedish colour film, but his visit had not only been linked to learning about technical innovations. More than anything, Nordemar's interest was in the military films that Hollywood was producing for the OWI and the Departments of War and the Navy.[21] It was these films that would later give him inspiration for his *Kon-Tiki* documentary. Nordemar had himself made films with military subjects previously, and now he came to a Hollywood where even Walt Disney was involved in their production. Nordemar's and Heyerdahl's US experiences were connected in that they both had insights into the public relations departments of the Pentagon. The US Army Signal Corps, the same body that had furnished Heyerdahl with his cameras, had also many times shot the films that the OWI was producing.

Nordemar's interest in the war documentary was logical as this was not only an area that consumed a lot of Hollywood's energies at the time, but also where most artistic innovations were to be found. The war saw a period of 'high renaissance', as cultural historian Thomas Doherty has called it, for the American documentary.[22] More filmmakers than ever were making documentaries that reached vast audiences as the genre experienced an Indian summer before television and the moral crisis of the film industry under McCarthy would leave virtually only Disney in the documentary market of the 1950s.[23] There were 'morale-boosting films' like Frank Capra's hugely influential *Why We Fight* series (1942–4), in which Capra 'pillaged old newsreels, documentaries, and Hollywood movies' and merged these 'into a seamless cinematic web' in order to convince the soldier and citizen of the necessity of US involvement in the war.[24] There was also the combat report film, usually shot by the US Signal Corps. These films, often filmed in 16mm and later blown up to 35mm like the *Kon-Tiki* footage, threw overboard Hollywood standards of perfection and showed the duress of battle with the poignant realism of first-hand reports.[25]

Nordemar's *Kon-Tiki* film would turn out to be a curious mix of *Why We Fight* and the combat report style of films such as the 1945 *To the Shores of Iwo Jima*. It is evident that Nordemar realized that the war had prepared audiences for new levels of realism that could now be used in films that did not deal with the topic of the war itself. In contrast to the US film executives who had turned down Heyerdahl's film in 1947, Nordemar seems to have been convinced that the cinematic language of the war, rather than an anomaly and a momentary disruption of the smooth Hollywood studio 'tradition of quality', was something that was there to stay. His assumption was, as the success of the *Kon-Tiki* film would show, correct.

When Nordemar sat down to watch Heyerdahl's amateurish film for the first time he must have made the connection to the footage taken under fire: 'obstructed, jerky, out of focus, off-kilter, up close, and jagged'.[26] In short, authentic and realistic. He did not add any re-enacted scenes as in the Norwegian proposal, or any romantic honeymoon biographical drama to keep it all together. Additions such as these would have detracted from the authentic feel of the material, at the same time introducing two different film techniques which would have been difficult to combine while preserving the impact of the original. Nordemar did shoot an introductory studio scene with Heyerdahl and the crew explaining their voyage, but this scene was much more like the serious studio sequences of the *Why We Fight* series, didactic and schoolroom-like, than Hollywood proper (see plates 12 and 13). As in Capra's series, music and narrative score were also added, and stills filled in where the original film was too badly damaged. Maps were included in the narration of the film, showing the progress of the raft with big arrows, just as the movements of armies had been displayed in so many of the war documentaries and newsreels from both sides in the conflict.

Nordemar showed some of Helms's genius for publicity creation when he chose to premier the *Kon-Tiki* at the Grand Theatre in Stockholm on Friday 13 January 1950. A month and a day later Heyerdahl himself could bring the film to the more humble surroundings of the Munken Theatre in his native Larvik, for the Norwegian opening. Unlike the book, the film was released in Sweden first, an illustration of the fact that Nordemar had been even more important in its conception than Helms had been for the book. But Scandinavia was only the first step for Nordemar and Heyerdahl who both had their eyes set on a release in the USA.

Britain was selected as the logical stepping-stone to break into the English-speaking market leading to a US contract. Nordemar managed to place the *Kon-Tiki* film in the programme of the Edinburgh Film Festival in the summer of 1950 where the film was shown twice, on 27 August and 6 September, to public acclaim.[27] He subsequently received an offer to have the film released immediately in London, but rejected it because he did not think it good enough.[28] Nordemar did not find any better options later, and the *Kon-Tiki* did not come to Britain except for limited screenings such as for the New London Film Society.[29] The distribution difficulty was not even overcome when Anthony Eden, the British foreign secretary, was impressed with the film after seeing it at a private viewing at the Hollywood home of the actor Douglas Fairbanks Jr, who for some unstated reason had a copy.[30] The general British audience had to wait.

In the end Nordemar did not need to use Britain to reach the USA; his own contacts there would prove enough to make the breakthrough. A discussion about the *Kon-Tiki* was initiated with Sol Lesser at RKO in the USA. Lesser was an important producer who had made his fame from the early 1940s Tarzan films starring Johnny Weissmuller. When Nordemar had visited Hollywood during the war Lesser had also helped him out.[31] After intensive but successful negotiations by phone and telegram Nordemar went back to Hollywood in October 1950. Just before leaving he wrote to Heyerdahl saying that Lesser and RKO wanted to distribute the film on a fifty-fifty basis in the Western hemisphere. This according to Nordemar was a phenomenal deal; no other documentary had ever received such an offer. Lesser was willing to offer $50,000 for the rights.[32] That was a staggering sum, especially since it was the first time Lesser at RKO had imported a foreign film.[33] He was taking a substantial risk. One month later Nordemar wrote with more information on the proposed deal to Heyerdahl, adding that RKO would also pay for the promotion and the copying of the film for a cost estimated at $100,000. The idea was to make 200 copies and have the film open in 50 theatres at the same time.[34] Nordemar pointed out the uniqueness of the deal, which would have been good for many feature films, let alone for a documentary. Heyerdahl could not possibly have wished for anything better.

To close the deal the *Kon-Tiki* film was screened in New York in November 1950. Besides RKO executives some hundred 'movie critics, literary figures and science writers attended the private prevue [*sic*] of the movie,' as one newspaper reported, all to create excitement around the film but also to help the sales of the *Kon-Tiki* book in the USA.[35] Heyerdahl was due to appear as befitted the important occasion, but he fell ill with pneumonia upon arrival in New York and had to be rushed to hospital instead. This did not seem to affect the negotiation for the film rights, and on 8 January 1951 Heyerdahl received a telegram informing him that RKO was buying not only the rights for the Western hemisphere, but for the entire world.[36]

As the deal with RKO was signed Heyerdahl must have realized how fortunate it was that Nordemar and no one else had made his film, and he now embraced the realistic and anti-classic-Hollywood-style agenda that his film had come to embody. Just after the US première he commented to Kate Cameron in *Sunday News*, 'It is a great satisfaction to me to find that the people at RKO were willing to release my picture just as it was made and let it stand on its own merits, as an amateur production. I was afraid [...] that someone in authority would suggest putting some Hollywood touches on it.'[37] Of course, some years before it was Heyerdahl himself who had contemplated those Hollywood touches.

The 'swank' US première, as the internal RKO magazine put it, took place on April Fool's Day 1951 in the Sutton Theater in New York.[38] The idea of opening the film on April Fool's Day was probably inspired by Nordemar's publicity gimmick of letting the Stockholm world première happen on a Friday the thirteenth. Heyerdahl was again in New York and was involved in an intense promotion schedule on television and radio for the film. The documentary played at the Sutton for an amazing six months, and was then released simultaneously in 21 New York theatres in October the following year. The film also did well in the rest of the country. A year later it had grossed three million dollars.[39] As late as 1948 Barney Balaban, president of Paramount, had predicted that no feature film at the time would manage to make total profits of over three million. This decreed, in what was to be known as 'Balaban's Law', that no film should be allowed to cost more than a million and a half in production as it would only break even at the box-office if it made twice its costs.[40] The *Kon-Tiki* film, indeed, the expedition as a whole, had cost a fraction of that amount, but it made three million in the USA alone. Neither Hitchcock's *Spellbound* (1945) nor *Notorious* (1946) reached the same box-office figures.[41] That the *Kon-Tiki* was a documentary and not a feature film, and that it was made by an unknown director, made its success historic.

By October 1951 RKO finally released the film in Britain. The Italian release came in March 1952 and a month later the French, and so on across Europe and the world. The film was a spectacular commercial success and in 1952 it won an Academy Award as the best documentary of 1951. By that time it had not only won mass audiences and revenues, but somewhere between 30 and 40 other international film prizes, and

Lesser could bombastically claim that it was the most decorated film in the world.[42] Four years earlier Heyerdahl had been offered $100 for his 'worthless' film. As if symbolically to appropriate the successful *Kon-Tiki* documentary as an 'American' story, Sol Lesser handed over the Oscar to Heyerdahl on 4 July: Independence Day. Heyerdahl seemed to have had a much easier time with Lesser than with Nordemar, and Lesser constantly stressed the 'Norwegian' nature of the documentary. The relationship to Nordemar had deteriorated over financial squabbles. But had it not been for Nordemar and his study trip to Hollywood the *Kon-Tiki* film would not have been done in the way it was, nor would it have reached the promised land of the USA to which Heyerdahl was trying to return.

## The *Kon-Tiki* Documentary Meets its Audience

Nordemar's intuition had been to leave the *Kon-Tiki* film with all its gaps. Apart from the studio sequence in the beginning that he had added, the hour-long documentary simply showed Heyerdahl's jerky material. The most dramatic incidents in the book – the storms that the crew encountered and the moment when a crew member fell overboard – were left out as they were not reconstructed. The result was that most of the film dealt with the rather uneventful quotidian life on board the raft rather than the journey's most spectacular episodes.

When the *Kon-Tiki* film was reviewed in the media it was exactly Nordemar's reluctance to fill the gaps in the narration that was praised. Many film critics said that this reinforced the realistic impact, and that it was fortuitous that no studio sequences of the adventure were added in the production. The review of Dilys Powell in the *Sunday Times* was a good example of this. She was pleased to see that the crew had not lowered themselves to 're-enact their adventures' with 'faces frozen in the hero's traditional embarrassment'. They had not been replaced by 'professional actors in a romanticised version of the facts' either. More than anything she was pleased that the film did not end in a tender meeting of lovers – something that was 'almost unique' in cinema.[43]

The title of Powell's review called Nordemar's film a 'Home Made Epic'. This was a fascinating concept in itself, but even more so when compared to the role of the epic narration in the *Kon-Tiki* book. In the latter it was the seamlessness and the gap-filling that had created the legend, the epic. In the case of the film the inverse strategy seemed to produce a similar result. The cinematic medium imposed its own visual logic on the *Kon-Tiki* phenomenon.

Put simply, the missing parts of the film, like storm sequences, equalled authenticity for the reviewers because if the crew had been able to film these events then they could not have been so dangerous. The absence of certain scenes, as the film's narrator disclosed that they had happened, brought something positive in that it confirmed that they had been for real. The Swedish critic Nils Beyer wrote in *Morgon-Tidningen* that 'the very absence of the storm pictures becomes more telling than if they somehow could have been magically inserted afterwards. The film in question is an authentic one.'[44] The *Dagens Nyheter* critic likewise claimed that 'even the gaps in the film […] increase its feeling of authenticity'.[45] The *Manchester Guardian* reviewer raved over the power of gaps, lacunae, to 'make the record the more authentic'. From this position it was a short step to contrast the *Kon-Tiki* with the classic Hollywood style: 'Perhaps the professionals of Hollywood will retell this tale in their own fashion: they will be able to produce nothing as impressive as this simple record.'[46] Many European reviewers found similar opportunities to attack Hollywood through *Kon-Tiki*, thereby making the expedition a curious weapon in the culture wars that raged across the Atlantic.

The assertion that the lacunae in the *Kon-Tiki* film made it more realistic was often accompanied by the complementary conclusion that the gaps were suggestive because what was missing had to be imagined. *The Times* reviewer said that 'the great thing about the most dramatic moments is that they never actually are seen,' and though a reconstruction of them no doubt would have been 'sensational', leaving them as they were was even more 'vivid and illuminating to the imagination'.[47] The same sentiment was echoed in the *Observer*, where C. A. Lejeune said that the film had 'the power of stimulating imagination to fill in the necessary gaps in the narrative.'[48]

The authenticity and suggestive potential of the *Kon-Tiki* film were often likened to those of an amateur film, as if the documentary were a 'Home Made Epic'. Heyerdahl and Nordemar had themselves played on this theme and presented an image of the shooting mainly as recording a vacation with a simple camera: 'the result is proportionate to the problems encountered by amateur photographers working onboard a rolling raft in the open seas,' as the introductory text in the film stated. The intention was to hide the fact that the voyage was in fact inseparable from the recording of it and that one would not have happened without the other. What Heyerdahl, through Nordemar, instead tried to create was an atmosphere in which the spectator felt casually invited onto the raft.

The *Kon-Tiki* documentary was called an 'amateur film' (*Dagens Nyheter*), 'a rather primitive amateur film' (*Aftonbladet*), 'pure amateur film' (*Filmjournalen*), 'an amateur cine-camera jollity' (*Daily Herald*) and 'the sort of record people with ciné cameras make of their holidays' (*Daily Mail*). Heyerdahl was even said to be 'nothing but an amateur who had wanted to shoot some images as a souvenir'.[49] The apparent amateurishness could not only be contrasted with the technical perfection of feature films, but also with that of other documentaries. Eleanor Wintour in *Time & Tide* hailed the film's 'simplicity and sincerity which makes a refreshing change from the sophisticated, professional documentary to which we are accustomed'.[50]

Heyerdahl had the ability to appear to be the very person that people wanted, and his story the story that was needed. In connection with his book he was made out to be the brave scientist simply writing down his story and ending up in creating a saga. When it came to the film he was simply an amateur creating the anti-Hollywood narrative. The Frenchman André Bazin, one of the most famous film critics of all time, even claimed that the crew had filmed 'without thinking too much of its commercial value'.[51] This was clearly a projection of Bazin's own desire and bore little relationship to the facts. In reality Heyerdahl had been more than aware of what he was doing when he brought cameras on board the raft. We do not even know whether the reason for the absence in the film of certain moments, like the storms, was due to the fact that they had not been shot or if this footage was among the portion of the raw material that was destroyed by humidity.

What is clear was that Heyerdahl had again been lucky in that the first Norwegian project to make a *Kon-Tiki* film had failed. This was the case especially among the European reviewers who revelled in the film's lack of artifice. The reviewer in *Göteborgs-Posten* claimed that the film lacked all that usually 'makes a film into a piece of art' like 'dramatic thrill, a coherent plot, a psychological development', and, predictably, 'a love story'. What was left was 'something that the audience is not spoiled with and therefore understands to appreciate; authenticity, the fascinating stamp of reality'.[52] Dilys Powell in the *Sunday Times* said that the 'lack of art' made the film captivating as it allowed the audience to see the action through the eyes of the explorer as no director had been present to arrange 'the crew in manly proletarian gestures' which made the film more real than the purportedly realist contemporary cinema.[53]

The sensation of seeing a world through the recording eye of the camera was so strong for the *Kon-Tiki* reviewers that some, mostly French, referred to the childhood of cinema to explain the effect. Both Jean Nary, in *Franc-Tireur*, and Jean-Louis Tallenay, in *Cahiers du Cinéma*, compared seeing *Kon-Tiki* to the experience that the audience of Lumière brothers' 1885 *L'Arrivée du train en gare* must have had. Nary argued that with the *Kon-Tiki* 'cinema found its way back to its original simplicity', and this simplicity was discussed by Bazin who argued that it lent the film a 'deeply moving sincerity'.[54]

The Lumières' audience had discovered that unexpected realistic images projected in unlikely settings could be not only fantastic but also frightening. When the train pulled into the station in the film the audience recoiled as though the locomotive would hit them. The *Kon-Tiki* film seems to have been experienced with the same physicality. With the bulk of the film shot from the raft or one of the two rubber dinghies it rolled as inevitably as the sea, the horizon being in constant movement. Lejeune remarked in the *Observer* that these pictures 'put a considerable strain on the spectators' eyes, and invite a certain queasiness of the stomach' but insisted that the film 'gains a hundred-fold from their indisputable authenticity'.[55] *The Times* reviewer described similar discomfort, and made the same link to realism: 'the perpetual rise and fall of photographic waves, convey to an audience a faint, a very faint yet an authentic, impression of what life on the raft must have been like.'[56] The *Kon-Tiki* film even caused some of its viewers to throw up out of seasickness, lending the ultimate reality to a real both fascinating and disgusting.

The *Kon-Tiki* was not the only film that made the audience think back to the origins of cinema in the postwar period. Italian neo-realism also relied on gritty and jagged images to convey a sense of authenticity. Implausible as it might now seem, the *Kon-Tiki* was linked with such neo-realist classics as Roberto Rossellini's *Roma, Città Aperta* (1945). The French journal for educational film, *Image et Son*, claimed that it was the achievement of realism through technical imperfection that united *Kon-Tiki* and neo-realism.[57] In the films of the neo-realists there were strong expressionistic links between form and content. To capture the feeling of a chaotic Rome Rossellini had filmed with a mobile camera in the streets. This same performativity was present in the way that Heyerdahl's primitivist project was reflected in his primitive technique. Jean-Jacques Gautier in *Le Figaro* noted this effect when he pointed out that the technical primitivism of the cinematography was significantly in accord with the 'prehistoric aspect of the raft'.[58]

The sometimes forced celebrations of Heyerdahl's film as gap-filling, anti-Hollywood, authentic, amateurish, performative and physical all focused on the film's structure rather than its content. Linking it to such a self-conscious arthouse genre as neo-realism was a natural outcome of this focus on form. This was the opposite approach to that taken by reviewers of the book, where the focus on the analysis had been laid squarely on content. Why this was is difficult to say, but cinema criticism was aware of the technical nature of its particular medium, and thus more inclined to look at how the film had been constructed. The film was also usually appearing in the cinemas after the book had been released, and functioned as an accompaniment to the content of the book.

The exception to this fascination with the structure of the *Kon-Tiki* film was found in the US reviews. It was in Europe that the film was hailed for its brave form, interpreted as portraying a heightened sense of the real. In the USA there was not the same longing to find films that could embody all that which Hollywood was perceived to lack. There Nordemar's film was interesting as a complement, fascinating despite its technical problems, not because of them. It was the adventurous and scientific content rather than the realistic structure that drew most applause. At the most, reviewers like Jim O'Connor in the *New York Journal* identified a certain physicality in the film, excitedly commenting that 'you can feel' the raft and 'you can see the sea'.[59]

The few US voices that did comment on the realism in *Kon-Tiki* discussed how this made it different from the classic Hollywood style. The *Honolulu Advertiser* claimed that 'unlike most Hollywood productions [the film was] strictly unglamorous but highly realistic'.[60] *Time Magazine* spoke of the *Kon-Tiki* film as something beyond Hollywood's ability to fictionalize.[61] A more interesting analysis was to be found in the literary magazine *Saturday Review of Literature*. Arthur Knight's review spoke of how the *Kon-Tiki* helped to wash off the negative connotations of the 'classroom and research' that had become fettered to the concept of the documentary. Furthermore, Knight proceeded to discuss how the themes of 'the real and the authentic' were entering the thinking of Hollywood.[62] For Knight this development was only positive. This was also a more fitting analysis of the film than seeing it just as a complement to the book or as part of the protracted ideological battle for and against the classic Hollywood style. As usual, Heyerdahl was neither Old World nor New, but had in his dealings, and his good luck, managed to create something that worked on both sides of the Atlantic.

## *Kon-Tiki* and Postwar Realism

It was symptomatic that the *Kon-Tiki* became a favourite film for the influential film critic André Bazin, who was to be not only the father of the New Wave in French cinema but also the champion of Italian neo-realism. Bazin's tastes however did not add up to an instinctive hatred of Hollywood that was so often part of the US-French cultural wars in the 1940s and 1950s. What concerned Bazin more than ideological posturing was realism. Good cinema was that which captured the essence of the real, regardless of where it came from. A longer discussion of the *Kon-Tiki* was included in Bazin's posthumously published writings *Qu'est-ce que le cinéma?* (What is Cinema?). Here he sought to insert the *Kon-Tiki* into a historical trajectory of realism in documentary film.

This film genre took shape, according to Bazin, in the 1920s when Robert Flaherty made films like *Nanook of the North* and *Moana* that relied more on journalistic and realistic shots than symbolic ones. This realism was challenged in the 1930s when documentaries became more and more figurative and sensationalist. Now it was no longer enough simply to film a lion hunt; at the very least, as Bazin put it, a porter had to be eaten by a lion as well.[63] After the war there was a return to the original realism of the 1920s. This was due to audiences now being able to see Hollywood films that were so spectacular that they did not need artifice in the documentary genre; also there was a craving for authenticity which made it difficult to re-stage events. All this meant that the documentary film of travel in exotic countries started becoming much more about psychology than action.[64]

If danger was only dangerous for real, if it was too dangerous to film, then it made sense that dangerous travel resulted in very little film. Bazin came to the paradoxical conclusion that the *Kon-Tiki* was 'one of the most beautiful films', but that it did not exist. Only some ruinous traces could be seen, but these were suggestive enough to create a psychological realism.[65] For Bazin, an example of how not to do it was the British film *Scott of the Antarctic* (1948), which had mixed authentic footage from Antarctica with re-enacted scenes filmed on glaciers in Norway and Switzerland as well as in a studio (a concept like that Staubo probably had in mind for the *Kon-Tiki*). There re-enactment was absurd for Bazin; the real could not be imitated; one could not re-create 'risk, adventure, death' in a documentary though illusions.[66]

Bazin's history of documentary realism could easily be translated as being valid for cinema as a whole. The end of the Second World War brought a longing for realist films. Neo-realism came from Italy with a revolutionary force and seemed to question the accepted notions of what film was. Film historian Robert Sklar has pointed out that Hollywood film in the 1930s started to rely more and more on studio shots so that the environment could be controlled and moulded into looking real on the screen. This studio work would result in the films of the period starting to look so real that they paradoxically ended up looking too real, or even surreal.[67] A Hollywood way of filming feature films made even the real 'appear as phoney', whereas contemporary scholars observed that European filmmakers who, like Nordemar, often had a background in documentary film, ended up making films where 'even phoney situations seem real'.[68]

A good example of the surreal realism of the 1930s is Frank Capra's *Lost Horizon* (1937). In order to reproduce a Himalayan mountain scene Capra rented a cold-storage warehouse with near-realistic temperatures so that he could be sure that the actors' breaths would turn into vapour. In *Dirigible* (1931) he had made the mistake of trying to produce the same effect by having his actors put dry ice in their mouths, which resulted in one of them losing five teeth and part of his jawbone.[69] Now Capra made freezing mountains in a refrigerated warehouse instead. And this was not done because the alternative was impossible; Capra could have bussed his crew to a cold mountainous site for no greater cost. The film about Scott, as Bazin noted, had similarly ended up costing as much as the original expedition. But the type of technology and directing preferred necessitated that the filmmaker was in control of nature; and in order to achieve this he had to re-create it. The production of reality, however, was becoming so complex and so contrived that the films began to look staged.

Frank Capra is an interesting director as he had started experimenting with a much more realistic filmic language during the war itself. Italian neo-realism did not appear in a vacuum. Hollywood produced a number of gritty films about the fighting, the kind of films of which Nordemar gained first-hand experience from during his time in the USA in 1945. Comparing Capra's *Lost Horizon* with the wartime *Why We Fight* series that he produced for General George C. Marshall, the US Army Chief of Staff, is an instructive exercise. Capra did not film much of the series himself, but edited newsreel footage, army films and even feature films into 'the single most powerful nonfiction film achievement in the war effort', as it has been called.[70] The cinematic language of *Why We Fight* was something like Hollywood meets Leni Riefenstahl through Orson Welles, but the images Capra dared to use were light-years from the technical perfection of his earlier films. A typical and favoured shot in the films is a dirty, crying child next to a village torched by Nazis (alternatively by the Italians or Japanese), filmed in passing with an unstable camera on gritty black and white 16mm film. The grittier the film the more real the sequence, and the more heinous the crime.

Capra used realism to stand in for the world of the Axis; it was almost as though the enemies and their victims had to appear in 16mm and the heroes in 35. When the US war effort was discussed Capra often switched from grainy images to a highly pedagogic and symbolic language. The first film in the series, *Prelude to Battle* (1942), begins with a quotation from Vice President Henry A. Wallace: 'There is a fight between a free world and a slave world.' Wallace's words serve as an introduction to a didactic separation of an animated globe into two spheres; one western and one eastern. In the film the eastern is folded out of a model of the western, like the dirty flip side of a coin. The eastern hemisphere, the 'slave world', is shown to be in the shade as opposed to the western, the 'free world', which is illuminated. The east represented 'gangsterism'; the west freedom, democracy and peace. Symbolical images also dominate the portrayal of the west – Bibles, statues, victory 'V's superimposed on the Liberty Bells – whereas when the east under the domination of the Axis is portrayed the medium is realistic combat photography.

The involvement of the USA in the war would become more problematic and traumatic when it stopped being about rounding up gangsters and turned into direct encounters in the war zones. As the war moved on, realism would also come to portray the battle on the ground regardless of foe or enemy. In the final years of the war, realism ended up in the combat report that traced the advance across the Pacific. In films like *To the Shores of Iwo Jima* from the last year of the war, filmed with shaky 16mm, the utter tragedy and human cost of combat became the overshadowing tragic plot.[71] Realism was taking over the classic seamless Hollywood narrative and coming up with something at times subversively real. And the grittiness of realism was self-perpetuating as the aesthetics changed and the more flawed the film, the more duress could be assumed of the cameraman, the more real the film would thus seem: it was a 'new screen aesthetic' that, in the words of Thomas Doherty, 'not only permitted technical flaws in photography but showcased them as verification of fidelity to reality'.[72] This was the exact same way Nordemar would make the *Kon-Tiki* film.

The postwar realist aesthetics of which *Kon-Tiki* was one of the most brilliant examples was not long-lived. It was documentary films that first discovered that approaching reality by filming it realistically could easily become politically subversive, especially if the topic was something more directly relating to politics than exotic travel. This was the case especially in the USA, where the Red Scare and McCarthyism, abetted by the growth of television, put the documentary film in a political straitjacket by enforcing censorship and slashing funding.[73] The documentary that remained was mostly escapist, toothless and infantile, like the portrayals of wild nature in the *True-Life Adventure* series (1948–60) of Walt Disney. Even Flaherty, the great celebrator of primitive life in harmony with nature, let himself be convinced by Standard Oil to make *Louisiana Story* in 1948. It was a film centred on how man and machine could come to a happy concord in the Bayou. This work of Flaherty, and the Disney films, could not bear the burden of realism, and ended up as staunchly conservative dramas affirming simple values of family and subservience.

The *Kon-Tiki* film was to become one of the few, and certainly the most successful, documentary of postwar realism for the simple fact that it was experienced as completely apolitical. Heyerdahl's journey had already been labelled as an epic, a saga. The story was made to appear as detached from contemporary events and to belong to some timeless world of adventure and heroic deeds. Yet the *Kon-Tiki* was an Atlantic story with Norwegians co-operating with the Pentagon to create an allegorical tale of a white race advancing into the Pacific. It was in other words nothing but political. Both

Heyerdahl and Nordemar made a brilliant job of rendering the politics invisible, using realist aesthetics in a completely safe way that neutralized the subversive potential of simply showing how something was.

Apart from *Kon-Tiki*, the new realism could soon only be found in feature films, which had an easier task in appearing to be disconnected from a political context. And if they were political, like the films of Italian neo-realism, the questions posed by these films were directed mostly towards Italian society. This is why film companies like RKO, owned by the arch-conservative Howard Hughes, could buy the world rights for not only the *Kon-Tiki* but also neo-realist films. Sometimes, however, political censorship was necessary, as in Roberto Rossellini's 1950 film *Stromboli*, bought by RKO. The originally open ending features Ingrid Bergman's character on the volcano screaming the ambiguous 'My god! Oh merciful God!' In the new RKO version she walks back to the village and a reassuring voice-over tells us, 'Out of her terror and her suffering, Karin had found a great need for God. And she knew now that only in her return to the village could she hope for peace.'[74]

Sol Lesser and Howard Hughes at RKO did not have to make any interventions in the *Kon-Tiki* film. Heyerdahl and Nordemar had managed to bring realism out of its political dimension. They had secured a massive Hollywood contract at the same time as they rode on the wave of a realism that was popular and appreciated in both the USA and Europe. This was a complicated manoeuvre that Heyerdahl would not have been able to do by himself; Olle Nordemar became for Heyerdahl an intermediary who, like Bjørn Rørholt opening the doors to the Pentagon, or Adam Helms inventing a path-breaking campaign, could help him make the Atlantic into his entrepreneurial space. The *Kon-Tiki* film was made with cameras and an optical printer from the USA, in Sweden by a Swede and a Norwegian, and managed to become not only the anti-Hollywood product that Europeans craved but could also appear apolitical and realistic for the US market. The film was the ultimate proof that Heyerdahl had, with some help, managed to tap into an Atlantic universal. A saga-like book and a shaky amateur film about a prehistoric raft had become an legend in the atomic-age West and would soon spread to the rest of the world.

# 7

# A Lone Hero of Adventurous Science

## Science and Adventure in the Realm of the Popular

Heyerdahl set out to create a sensation that would contain both science and adventure. The popular verdict told him that he had succeeded. The book was largely considered to contain more science than the film, but there were almost no attempts in the early 1950s to question either the science or the adventure of the *Kon-Tiki* in the popular press. What did it mean to be a scientific adventurer in the Atomic Age? The terms 'science' and 'adventure' were in no way easily combined, and Heyerdahl made an art of overcoming the conflict that they presented. In order to do this he needed to relate to each concept individually, as well as creating a story in which they could merge. He had to return, once again, to the logic of legend through which he had created his life, beginning with that evening prayer in Larvik.

In Heyerdahl's world, science had been made into something stagnant and stationary, over-specialized, removed from nature, exclusive and effeminate. The modern scientist of the twentieth century was impotent and had lost the ability to dare new thoughts and attempt new conclusions. The scientific establishment was more interested in safeguarding its existing privileges than in questioning its old dogmas. The adventurer was for Heyerdahl a similarly useless figure. It was someone who went down Niagara falls in a barrel, who leapt into danger pointlessly. The adventurer embraced masculinity and daring for nothing but base personal fame. These were the conceptual parameters that Heyerdahl had already begun to create in his youth and experimented with during his first voyage to Polynesia. The *Kon-Tiki* would give him the chance of finally reconciling the two notions with an adventurous voyage that also contained a clear scientific purpose.

In between the dogmatic scientist and the daring adventurer Heyerdahl found the stereotype of the lone genius of science. The lone genius challenged the scientific orthodoxy by viewing science as a 'horse race' where one can come first and defeat all opposition.[1] In the popular conception of this is an embattled figure fighting bad science dominated by power, money and superstition. These battles against scientific orthodoxy often assume the shape of being one of human dignity and freedom against an unfair monopoly of knowledge by an establishment. The 'lone genius' quickly turns into the seeker of truths beyond privileges and power structures.

For Heyerdahl it was as though his search for a scientific establishment to be against had started in 1938 when he discontinued his academic career. It took some time for him to define his project: he was to argue that Polynesia had been settled from the western coast of the Americas rather than from eastern Asia as was commonly believed. This was a thing that could be easily grasped by an audience, but at the same time in no way affected normal people's lives. To make it all the more clear, Heyerdahl often claimed, somewhat disingenuously and in order to be more like a Columbus or a Darwin, that he alone had come up with this theory.

More problematic than Heyerdahl's claim to originality was that the lone genius of science model that he had decided to adopt for the most part fails to grasp what real scientific work is about; it puts too much emphasis on the individual; it does not take into account the role of scientific discourse; it is short-sighted; and it fails to leave space for a necessary openness and circulation of ideas within the scientific community.[2] Instead of proper scientific method it focuses on individual physical action. This is why the opponents are portrayed as a faceless, stagnant mass. Heyerdahl cast the scientists who disagreed with him in the role of the Catholic Church that had opposed Galileo, and it was easy then to extrapolate from this that they were cowards and remote from normal people with common sense.

That Heyerdahl presented the opposition to him as a faceless mass of scientific orthodoxy was unfair to actual scientists, like Dr Herbert Spinden, who had probably given him as much help as he could have expected. Heyerdahl, lacking any scientific qualifications, had after all approached them in order to propound a not particularly original thesis. There was, however, something symptomatic of the times in Heyerdahl's insistence on making his opposition into a shady mass. In the late 1940s and early 1950s the West was in the grip of two connected threats. The first was the Faustian spectre of the nuclear technology that had first been unleashed in 1945 on the Japanese cities of Hiroshima and Nagasaki. The second was the one posed by Communism in the nervous atmosphere of the nascent Cold War. These fears soon merged. The capacity of the USSR to deploy an atom bomb was confirmed in August 1949, an event that caused speculation over nuclear espionage and amoral Western scientists selling themselves to the communists. This in turn led to famous spy trials like that of Ethel and Julius Rosenberg who were executed in the USA in 1953.

The nuclear scientists fitted perfectly into the mould of the scientist as an amoral initiator of uncontrollable events in a lineage *From Faust to Strangelove*, as Roslynn D. Haynes put it in her 1994 book. Not only had they invented a radically dangerous technology that like Frankenstein's monster menaced the world, but they had also committed an error even greater than Frankenstein's by letting the knowledge fall into the hands of the communists. Fear of anonymous technology on the loose reached its climax in an additional threat: the one from outer space. The postwar UFO craze spread like a wildfire from the USA to Europe in the summer of 1947 as the *Kon-Tiki* drifted across the Pacific.

The cultural response in the West for dealing with the threats of Communism, nuclear science and visitors from outer space coalesced in the early 1950s into collective allegorical traumas in science fiction films.[3] It was in these films that the charismatic lone genius on which Heyerdahl modelled himself made one of its most compelling appearances. The science fiction film often included a moral rebel scientist, as Susan Sontag argued, who clamoured for the attention of the authorities, which were frustratingly slow to recognize the threat of a faceless enemy.[4] This figure neatly illustrated how the lone genius relied on direct action, which he seemed to have much more capacity to use than either the sluggish authorities or the aliens. A classic enemy from outer space thinks strategically, schemes rationally and acts en masse. The lone genius is commonsensical and reacts quickly and courageously on a hunch; by his swiftness he defeats the aliens who are ultimately slowed down by their rationality.

# An Adventurous Science

Scientists did not usually get a good press in popular culture, and the role of the scientist was problematic and ambiguous in the postwar atomic period. Heyerdahl had to be careful. He described himself as a lone travelling genius to show that he was not part of the scientific establishment. But to invoke an adventurous science was itself problematic. The tragicomic circus that had surrounded the races to the North and South Poles around the end of the nineteenth century and the beginning of the twentieth had made it tricky to invoke science and adventure in the same breath. This had been 'horse race' science at its best, when coming first had been all that mattered, and real scientific work had been neglected. The most famous example was the almost simultaneous claims by two US explorers, Frederick Cook and Robert Peary, to have reached the North Pole in 1909; the fight over who got there first turned into a soap opera of recriminations in the press that later moved into the courts. The scientific value of these expeditions stood in such stark contrast to the importance ascribed to reaching a nebulous point on the map that it soon started to become clear that this was not about science at all, but about the same kind of individual or national prestige otherwise contested in wars or on the sports field.

The public became increasingly weary of the 'scientific' nature of the expeditions to the Poles, and the scientific establishments often reacted firmly by trying to sever the links between science and adventure.[5] The Cook-Peary media circus over the conquest of the North Pole had been bad enough, but the 1911 race to the South Pole made the situation even worse. The Norwegian explorer Roald Amundsen had been on his way to conquer what Cook and Peary squabbled over, but upon hearing the news he turned south. Amundsen had few, if any, scientific pretensions, in contrast to his contender for the remaining Pole, the British sailor and scientist Robert Scott. Scott reached the Pole shortly after Amundsen and perished on the return journey. Unlike Amundsen, Scott had headed a massive scientific expedition that was to remain in and around Antarctica for years. Scott had, however, been forced to use the allure of the Pole as 'bait for public support' in order to raise funds.[6] The Scott-Amundsen story, like the ongoing legal battles between Cook and Peary, was bad news for adventurous science.

The race to the Poles was a watershed, as it illustrated that the figurative race of the lone genius to prove his idea was difficult to combine with a literal race replete with real rivals. The latter just made it seem like sport, which de-legitimized the 'firsts' for the scientific establishments. It did not stop adventurers from attempting to be first to climb a mountain, to bike around the world, to swim across bodies of water. But from now on that activity was to be something other than science. Scientists who still travelled had to downplay the dangerousness of their work, and take pains to separate it from the popular realm that was the milieu of adventurers. Scientific travel became more scientific, more rational, and more institutionalized.[7] The notion of physical adventure was censored from science, and scientists started talking about their scientific travelling and explorations as 'fieldwork', a concept that denied the movement and adventure still involved in this effort. The stress on individuality through media coverage of adventurous science also helped to push the scientists to stress groups and collectives over individuals. The two concepts essential to the lone genius, individuality and action, were increasingly shunned.

Scientists in the early twentieth century did not physically stop travelling, but they presented their movements as relocation to some other place where they did science, as a not too dramatic shift between 'lab' and 'field'. The consequence of this split between science and adventure that was the effect of the way in which science had been used in sensationalist media had the curious side effect of liberating the adventurers. In contrast to Heyerdahl, many no longer felt any pressure to claim that they performed their adventure in the service of mankind or human knowledge. When the British alpinist George Mallory was asked in 1923 why he wanted to climb Mount Everest, legend has it that he came up with the revolutionary answer 'because it is there.'[8] A similar response was given some time later by the Danish Arctic explorer Peter Freuchen: 'adventure is not an act in the line of duty. It is not something done for science, either. Adventure is a strange experience for its own sake.'[9] There was no why, no reason and no greater good outside its own story of human perseverance. Mallory himself proceeded to perform his adventure, and died in June 1924 in a tweed suit almost within reach of the fabled mountain's summit.

The uncoupling of science from adventure was a major departure in the Western tradition of travel. In Christianity, as Mary Campbell has said, the 'sacred territory is located emphatically Elsewhere'.[10] The search for knowledge became linked to pilgrimages, such as the one to the Holy

Land. But travelling went hand in hand with curiosity, and as much as Christianity was a religion of displacement it was also, as illustrated by Eve's error, a creed with a problematic relationship to the physical search for knowledge. Curiosity, *curiositas,* was declared a sin by St Augustine in the fourth century. In the thirteenth century St Thomas Aquinas still upheld this castigation of curiosity as an illicit desire to gain 'experience through the flesh'.[11] It would take until the scientific revolution of the early Renaissance before curiosity was held to be a virtue, at least if that curiosity was directed towards a rational undertaking. Knowledge of good and evil still belonged to God, but man could in an amoral (as in neutral) way observe the world in order to understand it, as Francis Bacon decreed in the sixteenth century. The traveller could thus become a hero during the Renaissance, but only in so far as he sacrificed tall stories for a more serious application of reason.[12]

The eighteenth century saw reason not only being applied to nature, but also actively produced by travelling scientists.[13] The botanist Carl Linnaeus created a system in which all the planet's various species had to be found and extracted from their surroundings, perceived as arbitrary, and be placed in a newly constructed system with new 'secular European' names.[14] The whole world had to be catalogued and brought to order. It did not take long, according to historian Mary Louise Pratt, before nature started talking back. Romanticism came with its cult of the mystic and sublime. It too had its own scientists, like Alexander von Humboldt who through his famous travels to South America between 1799 and 1804 demonstrated that nature was no longer as 'accessible, collectible, recognizable, categorizable' as it had been for Linnaeus, but was rather a spectacle of 'dramatic, extraordinary nature' that risked 'overwhelming human knowledge and understanding'.[15] This is why the Romantic scientists like Humboldt had to adopt a scientific voice that was often more detached and god-like than his predecessors.[16]

To put it simply, both 'rational' and 'romantic' science necessitated travel and exploration. As long as there were more species to be discovered, and more majestic nature that one had to stand firm against, then the application of reason to the world was in large part an outdoors activity. It would not cease to be this after the Earth's last unknown land masses were explored as the nineteenth century turned into the twentieth, but the race to the Poles put a dent into the image of the travelling scientist as a hero who had been in existence since the Renaissance. The adventurers and the scientists began to part ways, and the former did not have to engage with the difficult question of how best to study nature and for what end. Heyerdahl decided to revisit adventurous scientific travel with his *Kon-Tiki* against the grain of the times, and now using the lone hero's rejection as the excuse for travelling. This also meant that he in the end had to ponder over the issue of nature. Was it more rational than mystic and spectacular? True to his mythic reflex Heyerdahl would answer both at the same time. The irrational primitive he wrote of, for example, had once been a civilized white race. And the sublime sea was not only dangerous but also welcoming, nurturing and controllable.

## Adventure and Science in Postwar Travel Literature

Heyerdahl's decision to return to scientific adventure and to its questions about nature was so rare in the postwar period that the few other examples of travels like the *Kon-Tiki* were inspired by Heyerdahl. After the *Kon-Tiki* one of the most famous stories of travel in the 1950s was to become Alain Bombard's journey across the Atlantic in a rubber dinghy in 1952, an adventure that ended up as a book entitled *Naufragé Volontaire* (The Voyage of the *Hérétique*) the following year. Bombard, a French physician, had been inspired by the *Kon-Tiki* to explore to what extent a shipwrecked man could survive on what the sea furnished. Bombard's thesis was that it was possible to live a long time at sea by living from what the sea gave, and he chose to prove his thesis by performing the role of the shipwrecked himself.

Bombard had learnt that adventurous science necessitated a lone genius with one idea that braved the clear disapproval of the experts. This dismissal by a faceless and sedentary science provoked the impetuous to prove the theory through a practical experiment. As Bombard put it, it was necessary for his 'hypothesis to stop being only a hypothesis', something that he concluded a 'human experiment', a voyage, could achieve.[17] Bombard's strategy was thus exactly the same as Heyerdahl's; he put a human face to his science and made it physical in that it required a voyage rather than time in the lab or study. Identity and physicality were the two key components of the adventurous science of the lone genius. Bombard also paid tribute to the *Kon-Tiki* in his book and chose the same route over the Atlantic as Columbus had taken on his fourth trip.

He also used both rational and romantic tropes when describing nature, just like Heyerdahl had.

Heyerdahl and Bombard stand out in the 1950s as the figures that invested themselves completely in an attempt to merge science and adventure. Most of the other travellers in the media, their colleagues, answered the question of 'why' with Mallory's retort: adventure was the main reason for adventure. Science was however rarely completely absent from travel literature, especially in the European tradition that Heyerdahl was writing in. In looking more closely at the travel writing of three countries where the *Kon-Tiki* had great success – Sweden, Britain and France – it is possible to start to understand this residue of scientific language and motivation in travel writing, even when science had ceased being the reason for the voyages.

Science in 1950s travel writing, when included, was either described in the rational language of Linnaeus, or in the romantic of Humboldt. It was unusual for these two approaches to be mixed as they had been in Heyerdahl and Bombard. The rational form was the most frequent, completely dominating in Britain and Sweden. French travel writing proved an exception in that it embraced a much more romantic language in its description of both adventure and science. This is instructive as it shows how much romantic language in travel literature is connected to tragic plots. When adversity is encountered in nature it is hard to pretend to be able systematically to make sense out of it; nature hits back. Happy journeys leave more space for the traveller to assert his or her control over nature.

French travel-writers in the 1950s often emphasized the chaotic character of nature in their tortured journeys. Many times this disorderly nature was described in purely sentimental terms without much scientific pretence. This was the case of the young explorer Raymond Maufrais, who was lost in the jungle of French Guyana in 1950 and whose *Aventures au Matto Grosso* (Matto Grosso Adventure; 1951) and *Aventures en Guyana: Carnets* (Journey without Return; 1952) were posthumously published, as well as the less well-known Michel Perrin's *La Tragédie du Haut-Amazone* (The Tragedy of the High Amazon; 1954), and the 1951 international bestseller *Annapurna premier 8.000* (Annapurna, First Conquest of an 8000-meter Peak) by Maurice Herzog.[18] An exception to this rule, where science did play a part, was the popular account of anthropologist Alain Gheerbrant's expedition into the Amazonian jungle, *L'Expédition Orénoque Amazone 1948–1950* (The Impossible Adventure: Journey to the Far Amazon; 1952).

Gheerbrant describes himself and the other men in the expedition who enter the Amazonian jungle as wanting a wild and majestic nature rather than an easily ordered one. This unclassifiable nature is embodied in the dwellers of the jungle who have never before encountered white men and modern society. The French anthropologist's goal is described as 'meeting savage men'. It was important that these savages were indeed the '*vrais sauvages*', the real savages.[19] But this is an overpowering romantic nature that Gheerbrant never develops into a fully fledged science of adventure as he appears constricted in pushing the Humboldtian science into the background and focusing on the story of a tragic adventure of accidents and mishaps. Gheerbrant fails to turn himself into a lone genius fighting a scientific establishment, and as he does not have one theory to 'prove' he cannot construct a story where he can appear to do both adventure and science like Heyerdahl.

In Sweden, where Heyerdahl met with such great success, travel literature was dominated by a young generation of bohemian travellers who embarked on happy exotic voyages around the world. Science still played a background role, but it was a rational science that did not stress the powers of nature. These travellers combined a joy at the ability to explore the foreign after the war with a gentlemanly 'collecting' of artefacts and samples for Swedish scientific institutions. The author, photographer and travel-writer Rolf Blomberg, for example, travelled widely in South America from the mid-1930s to the 1970s and wrote many of his books in the 1950s. In his books nature was simply waiting for the Western traveller to make sense of it. Of Ecuador Blomberg said in his 1949 *Vildar* (The Named Aucas): 'The land of this country is full of archaeological and paleontological remains – it is still virginal soil for the scientist', and shortly afterwards he mentioned *en passant* that he himself is collecting zoological specimens for the Museum of Natural History in Gothenburg.[20] That science is not the 'why' of his journey has however been made clear in the very beginning of his text when he says that his voyage was a consequence of his wish for living adventure and his curiosity, rather than his desire to 'do science'.[21]

Blomberg's way of approaching science in his books was mirrored in the works of figures like Sten Bergman, Arne Hirdman and the Swedish *Kon-Tiki* expedition member Bengt Danielsson, notably in *Den lyckliga ön* (The Happy Island; 1951). Danielsson is an interesting case as he was an anthropologist within the scientific establishment carrying out fieldwork in Polynesia. He does however manage to suggest that he and his wife moved there simply because they wanted to experience another culture (live adventure), but then he goes on to make sense out of the society by describing and labelling it in minute ethnographic detail. Science is not the aim, but rational science is still heavily alluded to throughout this and his other books from the period.

The classifiable nature in the books of the Swedish travel-writer of the 1950s is also present in the few British travel books that make any pretence of having a scientific project as well as in those simply being about adventure. This is the case with a bestselling author Arthur Grimble, a British colonial official who wrote *A Pattern of Islands* in 1952 and *Return to the Islands* in 1957 about his time on the Gilbert (now Kiribati) Islands in Micronesia. Nature is recorded, collected and systematized by the gentleman scientist. Abroad is a land that can be made to make sense. Like most of the Swedish travellers, Grimble did not come from a scientific background, in contrast to figures such as Bombard and Gheerbrant in France.

When discussing the theme of travel and science in postwar Europe it is tempting to include a figure who, although not a popular writer, addressed these questions explicitly. Claude Lévi-Strauss was a French anthropologist who was deeply committed to the project of separating science from adventure while at the same time in 1955 publishing a travel book. The result was the enigmatic classic *Tristes Tropiques*. Lévi-Strauss opened his book with a tirade directed at the likes of Heyerdahl and Gheerbrant, stating that he hated 'travelling and explorers'.[22] He then proceeds to paint a picture of adventure as the enemy of science. If adventure arose when science was 'done', then it was merely an unfortunate side effect.[23] The modern explorers who filled lecture theatres with stupid people and delivered platitudes to them could not lay claim to any vocation outside their own self-fashioned explorer-profession.[24] Lévi-Strauss the scientist lamented having to move, focused on a particular physical spot when in the field and tried to erase himself from his narration. Curiously enough, he wrote a travel book in which he both lends individuality and physicality to his travels, thus achieving the very opposite of what he had set out to do.

*Tristes Tropiques* is interesting as it is, in its motivation, the anti-*Kon-Tiki* of the 1950s. This was no doubt clear for Lévi-Strauss as he took care to reject Heyerdahl and his thesis in the book.[25] Lévi-Strauss's failure in de-romanticizing the displacement of an individual traveller, however, showed how difficult it was to write a purely scientific treatise of travel. If Heyerdahl had included the same level of complexity in terms of self-reflection in his book it would have been inaccessible to the broader popular market. Yet there are some interesting points of convergence between the books, especially when the rational science of Lévi-Strauss in South America is contrasted to a much more romantic description of nature in his sections on India. From two very different starting points, Lévi-Strauss and Heyerdahl reached a consensus that nature was most movingly described as both rational and chaotic.

The polarities of Heyerdahl and Lévi-Strauss illustrate well the stake of science in popular travel writing of the postwar period. Heyerdahl emulated the old masters in his simplified conception of them, merging them in the process, and aligned himself on the side of the lone genius in the popular image of science. Lévi-Strauss in contrast rejected the past of adventurous science, yet *Tristes Tropiques* ended up as something closer to the *Kon-Tiki* than the majority of travel literature in which science was not an issue. Overall it was a safer bet not to engage with science at all; doing so meant having to relate to a field of scholarly literature that was not only challenged by both scientists and adventurers, but that also incorporated differing and complex approaches to nature. And this avoidance of engagement is what the travellers of the 1950s practised for the most part: for them adventure was lived for adventure's sake.

## Adventure and the 'Ulysses Factor'

To write an adventurous science Heyerdahl needed not only to relate to science, but also to adventure. Superficially, adventure can be defined as risk-taking just outside the comfort zones of established norms, though this is not the full explanation. The concept of adventure is as complicated as science and has its own historical trajectory. Whereas science has academies that have defined what can properly be called science, adventure is a more nebulous concept that is constantly being moulded by a myriad actors in popular culture. Understanding the role of adventure in the *Kon-Tiki* is thus a much more complicated process than grasping lone genius science.

Adventure has often been analysed through the prism of psychology; namely in terms of the adventurer's motivation. An interesting attempt to do this was in the little-known 1970 book *The Ulysses Factor* by the British journalist J. R. L. Anderson. This study is not interesting for its rather far-fetched conclusions, but for how these conclusions necessitated the construction of a definition of what adventure is. Anderson himself dismissed the notion of 'adventure', and argued that the secret was to be found in another force, the 'Ulysses Factor', which propels individuals to undertake dangerous feats that might appear purposeless but are 'of value to the survival of the race'.[26]

The Ulysses Factor, according to Anderson, consists in the human qualities of the individuals embarking on adventures. These were things like: courage, selfishness, practical competence, physical strength, powerful imagination, ability to lead, self-discipline, endurance, self-sufficiency, cunning, unscrupulousness and strong sexual appeal.[27] It was important that these qualities were translated into physical action: 'The Ulysses type cannot find fulfilment without personally being *there*: your *own* foot must tread the mountain top, your *own* eyes see the waves, your *own* hand be on the tiller.'[28] Here Anderson invoked the themes of individuality and physical action that were so important for Heyerdahl.

Had Anderson written his book 40 years later he would have spoken of a Ulysses gene instead of type, but what he meant was the same. The Ulysses trait was displayed by, apart from Ulysses himself: Abraham, Pytheas, Leifr Eiríksson, Columbus, Drake, James Cook and, significantly, Thor Heyerdahl. According to Anderson, civilizations too could be influenced by a 'Ulysses Impulse', and here he suggested that this has been the case for the Greeks, Phoenicians, Saxons, Norsemen, Portuguese, Spaniards, English and, possibly, the Polynesians.[29] These individuals and nations had reached beyond 'mere' adventure, giving to the world 'meta-adventure' for the benefit of humanity as a whole.

It is easy to find fault with Anderson's part-psychological and part-biological conclusion but he clearly spelt out a definition of adventure, even though this was not what he claimed to have done. If physical action was there to be performed through traits like courage, selfishness, cunning and so on, then there was adventure. Adventure was thus, in other words, corresponding to an idea that had been in place since the nineteenth century of what masculinity was supposed to entail. That the real man was a strong individual who did not shy away from physical action and risk was a fantasy born out of rapidly industrializing Western societies where life and work became increasingly repetitive and sedentary. The real man came as a dream when the reality of men made this vision of masculinity little more than a nostalgic hope. The return of the real man would be a second coming, like the expected one of Christ. This was also what one can interpret as promised in the word 'adventure': 'to come' from the Latin *ad-venire*.

Anderson claimed that all adventure had to be without practical purpose, but this was an argument that did not take into account what had gone before the split between science and adventure or the stereotype of the lone genius. The truly purposeless physical adventure that Anderson talks about was to be by the 1950s the dominant mode of travel writing. It was the interwar period that saw an increase in the number of completely purposeless adventures that worked as masculine rejections of the perceived effeminate bourgeois values of modern civilization as expressed in the domesticity of postwar culture. It was not only Mallory who risked his life because his life could be risked: there were also figures like Graham Greene, Evelyn Waugh, Robert Byron, André Gide and Michel Leiris. What these figures did was to use Ulyssean traits and direct action as a rebellion. Pure and purposeless adventure was danger, and danger was, as the German right-wing writer Ernst Jünger said in 1931, 'senseless' to the bourgeoisie, a class that saw reason as the power ensuring security.[30]

Jünger accused the bourgeoisie of having become 'intolerably boring', and this was a sentiment with which Heyerdahl surely would have agreed.[31] This was not so strange. Not only had industrialization and urbanization radically changed society, but the possibilities for young men to find controlled and semi-sanctioned adventure in science, commerce, war and colonial service were rapidly decreasing. Science had become stationary; the mechanical revolution in transport meant that drastically fewer people were needed to move commerce around the world; the same mechanical revolution had made wars so dangerous as to become apocalyptic; and the colonial service was becoming both hazardous as well as less glamorous and attractive than in previous eras. Adventure was not becoming senseless just because it was a rebellion against something, but also because the previous avenues to live out the same urge diminished as the century progressed.

Yet the romantic protest of violence and danger that Jünger theorized and advocated was still a fantasy that came from inside the bourgeois class itself. Reading about adventure or following adventurers became a safety valve, a way to daydream one's way out of the boring everyday. Adventure in general, and travel in particular, were important ways of creating a masculine fantasy and delineating the borders of bourgeois norms. The archetypical traveller escaped 'from the constriction of the daily, the job, the boss, the parents' as Paul Fussell said following Freud, to some place where 'a new sense of selfhood can be tried on, like a costume'.[32] The reality and fantasy of escape are about self-development and self-definition.[33] Jünger and the fascists put a misplaced belief in the idea that a more extreme and violent adventure would herald a truer renaissance of the individual, but the Second World War would crush that illusion. The war itself would also raise questions as to whether the postwar world had changed to the extent that adventure and travel no longer held promises to help individuals define who they were.

Adventurous escape suffered a loss of innocence after the Second World War. It was as if that place outside the bourgeois norms, often an exotic abroad, had vanished. There was no longer any place in reality – and nor, increasingly, in fantasy – where the adventurers could find themselves. After the war it also made little sense to dislocate oneself in a world full of 'displaced persons', that constituted a 'great army of men and women without papers, without official existence, [...] refugees and deserters' as Evelyn Waugh stated.[34] On a similar note, many found that civilization had now reached all areas of the globe, penetrated every nook and cranny. There was no wilderness, no exotic, only the disgusting West. As Lévi-Strauss said in 1955, voyages through the modern world showed nothing but our own garbage 'thrown into the face of humanity'.[35]

Waugh famously predicted in 1946 that he did not 'expect to see many travel books in the near future'.[36] He was wrong. Even the old-style masculine adventure survived, as in the conquest of the Everest in 1953. Something, however, did happen. The loss of wilderness that many experienced was countered by a move inwards. Travellers started admitting that abroad was a lot like home. This was to escape from an escape, and the effect was ironic and led to comic narrations of amateurs who played down the classic themes of danger, self-definition and masculinity. An ironic mode of adventure came into being that could be contrasted with an older sincere one.

Two British adventurers, Wilfred Thesiger and Eric Newby, neatly illustrate the difference between the serious, sincere adventure and the comic, ironic one. The ironic traveller Newby recounted a meeting with Thesiger in *A Short Walk in the Hindu Kush* (1958). Thesiger was a stern, romantic and gentlemanly traveller who dressed the part and spoke the local languages, and for whom the abroad represented a possibility for self-definition. He encounters Newby and his friend who have travelled to the mountains of the Hindu Kush in Central Asia on a whim. They know nothing of climbing and their journey is a comic cavalcade of minor disasters and dysentery. They are to some extent awed by the foreign, but most of the time they deflate romanticism with humour, and they also carry conveniences of modern civilization in order to make it more like home. One such luxury appears in the guise of air-mattresses, and the book ends with Thesiger watching them inflate these to make the Hindu Kush more comfortable; he turns away in disgust exclaiming, 'God, you must be a couple of pansies.'[37]

The fact that Newby describes Thesiger is important. Travellers do often meet each other abroad, but such meetings are not often recounted in sincere adventure stories. But Newby does not have to insist on the isolation and uniqueness of the abroad, and Thesiger provides yet another opportunity for the ironic travellers to poke fun at themselves. The same denial of the uniqueness of the abroad in Newby's book is evident in that he does not really think it necessary to prepare too seriously for travelling. He leaves the *haute couture* business in central London for Central Asia with virtually no knowledge of what he is doing. This amateurism leads to mistakes, mishaps, gags, comedy – but it does not lead to self-discovery as the unique abroad does for the professional and prepared traveller Thesiger. For Newby going abroad was only an excuse for eventually being able to go home, home to where subjectivity was *really* created. Abroad was a ludic possibility, not a site of rebellion and redefinition. Ironic adventure was a celebration of the fact that it was, after all, somewhat absurd to justify going to some dangerous and inhospitable place just because it was there.

Heyerdahl wanted to combine adventure and science. He also used two modes that scientific travelling had developed to describe nature: rational or romantic. When it came to how he treated adventure through the *Kon-Tiki* he similarly tried to mediate between the two different forms of adventurous travel in existence in the 1950s. At a first glance the *Kon-Tiki* seems to include mostly the 'initiation to manhood' type of adventure in which Heyerdahl and the crew find themselves in a unique abroad. The scientists in Heyerdahl's narration can stand in for a bourgeois order that he rejects through embarking on a dangerous adventure. This is however not the entire story.

There is an important humorous streak in the *Kon-Tiki*. Heyerdahl constantly stressed that he is a common man embarking on an exceptional adventure. He is not a sailor, and neither are any of the crew, just as Newby was keen to stress that he was not a climber. The narration of the *Kon-Tiki* voyage is full of self-deflating humour and ironic moments like the departure from Callao when Heyerdahl does not manage to explain to the Peruvian tug-boat's crew that the rest of his men are bringing provisions and drinking their last beer on land, partly because he is trying to catch a parrot that has escaped from its cage. His proud voyage starts with a misunderstanding, and he is left alone on the raft with only a sulking Spanish-speaking parrot as company before the crew joins him out at sea.

Heyerdahl and the crew are also surrounded by modern equipment and technology on the raft, which is downplayed yet not denied in the story, and thus travel with a bit of home to the abroad. At the same time there is a meaningful wilderness for Heyerdahl, although it stays in the sea, outside the confines of the raft. Heyerdahl thus creates a situation in which he can use the uniqueness of abroad at the same time as rejecting it. More than anything he proves that one can have both without having to sacrifice one or the other. This was an accomplished piece of mythic mediation that, just like the merger of adventure and science as well as rational and romantic nature, made the *Kon-Tiki* quite unlike any other travel stories in the postwar period.

## Adventure in Postwar Travel

It was the comic and ironic adventure that represented a new departure after the war. Adventure and travel had been mocked and satirized before, but these satiric stories had often been set in contexts of tourism such as Mark Twain's *The Innocents Abroad* (1869) that dealt with his voyage to Europe and the Holy Land. Poking fun at tourists was quite a different thing from travelling alone or with fellow adventurers to some distant place and poking fun at oneself. Tourists rarely travelled in order to define themselves, and when they did it was not through danger that a new definition was achieved. Adventurers had to make fun of adventure, of danger.

The postwar ironic traveller was still only a minority among travel-writers. Most of the profession kept to an older, more sober tradition in which the danger or the enterprise was not questioned or satirized. This would also have been the most natural way for Heyerdahl to write his *Kon-Tiki*. His story of the misunderstood lone genius seemed at first glance to marry itself to a more high-falutin way of narrating. A lone genius that was too comic could run the risk of not being taken seriously. The step between being a Don Quixote fighting windmills and a Galileo standing up to religious dogmatism was not great. It would have been much safer if Heyerdahl had not included so much humour in his adventure, if he had not attempted a difficult merger between the sincere and the ironic.

Taking this risk was in the end a good move as is evident from the attention that Adam Helms gave to the comic elements of the book. Helms also reinforced this side of the *Kon-Tiki* in his much-copied marketing campaign. Heyerdahl was made into a jester and a rogue adventurer at the same time as he was a lone genius. In this way the *Kon-Tiki* could work as a mild challenger of various national traditions of writing adventurous travel stories that focused exclusively on danger and manly bravery. More than anything, this image of Heyerdahl democratized notions of adventure, as well as science. Heyerdahl was neither a hardened super-human adventurer like Thesiger, nor was he a crackpot amateur ending up in extreme situations like Newby. He was a common man, an object of identification.

It was the ironic adventurers of the postwar period who helped Heyerdahl shape his story of adventure into a new and, as would soon be clear, popular fashion. In looking closer at narratives of this type one discovers that they are based on three considerations. First, the book or film or ironic travel does not have to be always ironic or comic, but what is much more important is that it is never tragic. The introduction of a tragic moment like an accident makes it impossible to deny the danger of the adventure. This is why the man-overboard story in the *Kon-Tiki* when Herman Watzinger is saved by Knut Haugland works so well for the narrative. The *Kon-Tiki* is saved from becoming a tragic story about which the question would always be raised whether the 'why' of the adventure merited its sacrifices. The accident also shows that, for all the light-heartedness and humour, the danger is still real.

The second consideration of ironic travel is that the important part is not the end point of the journey, but the passage in the middle. The possibility of reaching a passage in the journey that feels timeless and calm, like the eye of a hurricane, had been discussed for a long time in travel writing, but the postwar ironic travellers made it the aim of their journeys. The passage and the feelings of serenity it could induce were also some of the few things at which they did not poke fun. In *Kon-Tiki* the passage played a very important role, but Heyerdahl still affirmed the importance of the destination. Arriving in Polynesia would, after all, 'prove' his theory. The ironic adventurer without any scientific pretence could reject the destination completely, like the Swedish Arne Hirdman, who stated in his 1954 book: 'I travelled with a rucksack as my only luggage, without itinerary, with chance as my compass and curiosity as a map. Every time the road split I took the path that looked most promising and I never needed to regret my choice; one does not go wrong when one is going nowhere.'[38]

The third element of ironic adventure is that wilderness cannot be radically wild and different from the traveller, which meant that there had to be a bit of home in the foreign. And contrary to Lévi-Strauss, who regretted that it was impossible to travel without encountering the garbage of modernity, the ironic travellers thought that it was something positive that there was no extreme otherness. This was especially clear when interacting with those who lived in the exotic destinations. These people were often described as having a lot in common with those in the home countries of the travellers. This in turn often led ironic travel stories to highlight colonial oppression since if there was a shared humanity it made little sense for some people to claim the right of suppressing others. Heyerdahl's stance on otherness was much more complicated, as the next chapter will make clear, but through his auto-identification with the prehistoric white race he argued that part of the primitive had been white, and that white people therefore had a claim to the primitive.

The absence of tragedy, the unimportance of the destination and the undramatic relationship to the exotic added up to a democratization of the concept of travel. This was travel stripped of all its previous purpose. One needed neither a scientific education nor the ability or preparation to cope with extreme nature. It was, in theory, enough to buy a ticket and go frolicking abroad where the capriciousness of curiosity could be enjoyed. It was, in spirit, a lot like tourism as we know it.

The difference between the amateur travel of the 1950s and tourism lay in certain lingering concepts from the history of travel and adventure. Most importantly, travelling was still an exercise for an individual or small group. There was none of the mass movement that modern tourism entailed. The amateurs were also still seeking out rather extreme places, like Newby's Hindu Kush. Since their project was to debunk the danger of the foreign they often had to endure travail with a happy-go-lucky smile. This discomfort was probably increased by the lack of preparation that their genre stipulated. Maybe it is better to see them as hardy pioneers of a more egalitarian touristic vision that broke new ground for a more thorough democratization of travel that came into force in the 1950s when tourism exploded in the West thanks to the economic upturn and a level of commercial transport by land, sea and air that the world had never seen before.

One of the most extreme examples of the price that the ironic travellers had to pay for their debunking of adventure and of the foreign is the French sailor Eric de Bisschop. He had a long career of sailing fanciful junks and rafts on the Pacific, and was a much less known proto-Heyerdahl – except that Bisschop was convinced that the Polynesians had come from Asia. In the late 1950s Bisschop sailed a bamboo raft from Polynesia to South America, and in his posthumously published book he refused to exaggerate the danger of the journey as it would only 'please the bourgeois'.[39] Bisschop knew the lesson that Ernst Jünger had failed to learn: danger might be abhorrent to the bourgeoisie, but the bourgeoisie still enjoyed feeling that abhorrence as long as the horror came in the mode of a spectacle that they could experience from their armchairs. In the case of Bisschop it was he who paid the price. The French adventurer died on the raft as it sailed back to Polynesia; his desire to debunk adventure was so great that he downplayed all suggestions that sailing a raft made of bamboo was inherently severely risky.

Bisschop's fate illustrates the question of what it was that the postwar readers wanted. Maybe the most extreme amateur travel was too close to tourism to attract the great mass of readers. The escape from the escape that ironic adventure entailed short-circuited the few remaining justifications for adventure after science and adventure had parted ways. At the same time there was something markedly old-fashioned about the serious and sincere adventures of professional travellers as Norman Lewis, André Dupeyrat, Laurens van der Post, Wilfred Thesiger, Maurice Herzog and so on. These figures were popular, but none of them was as popular as Heyerdahl, who took greater care to adapt to the demands of the popular media.

By constructing an adventure that still contained science and a meeting with both a classifiable and a majestic nature and then combining this with a comic amateur touch that also debunked the adventure itself Heyerdahl perfected a story that was exactly right for its time. This might have been the outcome of intuition, conscious crafting or fluke, but what is more interesting is to understand how the narrative itself worked. The *Kon-Tiki* story became a remarkable text that made sense for millions of readers on account of its ability always to appear as in-between. Heyerdahl found just the right ways of combining dissonant tendencies and stories and merging them all into a whole that could give the reader, invariably, what he or she was looking for.

# 8

## White Primitives and the Art of Being Exotic to Oneself

### The Exotic and the Primitive

Besides adventurous science it was the exotic appeal of the *Kon-Tiki* that was most often used as a way of marketing it and to explain its success. Part of this exotic foreign could be found in Heyerdahl's description of nature, for example the sea, as will be discussed in chapter 9. Another great component lay in Heyerdahl's treatment of the foreigner, the native, the primitive. Heyerdahl's theory that an advanced white race coming from the east was the original primitive, the 'true' Polynesian, made it possible for him to overcome two opposite strands when it came to relating to the foreign. These were the desire to become and merge into primitive natives, and the enjoyment of the foreignness of the same primitive without attempting to transgress the boundaries between a Western self and a foreign other. These two conflicting strands can be called primitivism and exoticism, and Heyerdahl was one of the few ever to have proposed a mediation between the two.

The concepts 'exotic' and 'primitive' are often used interchangeably, even in scholarly discourse. There is however a potential gain in trying to see how the terms for the most part indicate different intellectual processes. Both are colonial fantasies of the West; but the desire to become primitive (primitivism) is not, and has not been, the same as the desire to enjoy the foreign (exoticism) by staying in the known self. The starting and end points are, however, always the same: a Western 'civilized' individual. In primitivism this individual wants to shed his or her civilization and regress to a state of nature. In exoticism the individual does not have to shed anything or to regress much in order to enjoy the foreign. Primitivism is thus a more radical way of looking abroad than exoticism, though both terms are deeply problematic as they are Western fantasies of a purportedly uncivilized world.

Heyerdahl's innovative move was in a sense to get rid of the question of the natives altogether. He and his 'fair-skinned' crew of Norsemen emulated that vanished itinerant white race that Heyerdahl claimed had settled Polynesia.[1] This race had sported hair 'reddish to blond', skin 'remarkably pale' and 'blue-grey' eyes.[2] This was the privileged primitive that was at the centre of Heyerdahl's narration. As a background to this white race were the people he and his crew encountered in South America and Polynesia. These were mixed or brown people, irrelevant for the story. In South America the indigenous people were a 'sun-browned wrinkle-faced people' that 'seemed to have grown up out of the earth itself', as plentiful and uninteresting as the pebbles strewn across the gigantic Andean *altiplano*.[3] In Polynesia the white race had been mixed up with others, and the inhabitants were now had 'gold-brown skins, raven hair and flat pulpy noses'.[4]

To understand exoticism and primitivism it is necessary to grasp the fundamentally oppositional concepts 'same' and 'other'. These terms can be translated at the most basic level as a geographical inside and outside, core and periphery. The ancient Greeks had defined what lay inside and outside the bounds of their civilization by calling outsiders 'barbarians'. The idea is here that man defines himself through exclusion. As Jacques Derrida said in *Of Grammatology*, 'Man *calls himself* man only by drawing limits excluding his other […] the purity of nature, of animality, primitivism, childhood, madness, divinity.'[5] This concept of identity creation through exclusion was used by Edward Said in his influential 1978 *Orientalism*, when he discussed French and British construction of an effeminate Oriental other that helped delineate the Western man as strong and masculine. Said influenced an important strand in postcolonial scholarship which looked at how the West had defined itself through processes of constructing others, or 'othering'.

Attempts to break down and redefine the binary of same and other were however made a long time before the invention of the academic discipline of postcolonial studies. Psychological models of how identity and culture were formed had been articulated in the late nineteenth century, chiefly through the new discipline of psychoanalysis developed by Sigmund Freud. Here the focus was on how the split between the inside and outside was reproduced in the human psyche itself. Maybe the most elegant formulation of this came even before Freud in 1871 when the French poet Arthur Rimbaud stated that *Je est un autre* ('I is another' or 'I is someone else').

When discussing the concepts of the Western same and the foreign other it is thus necessary to accept from the outset that these are difficult and problematic constructions. By placing the existence of a foreign other well outside the Western individual, exoticism sustains a fantasy of a primitive animal-like man close to nature and outside history. This is a vision that can be used as a colonial weapon. Partaking of the exotic becomes a form of tourism in which that outside the convention is used as a titillating spice. There is no attempt to understand the foreign above and beyond its existence as an inversion of the values that the West has assigned to itself: rational, masculine, disciplined and rule-bound. But the alternative of placing the foreign within the self, as in primitivism, has often led to an identification of the exotic with a fantasy of a primordial state of childlike lunacy hidden in the Western self.

It was primarily in the arts that primitivism gained momentum in the turn of the last century. In post-impressionistic and later surrealist art the exotic was beginning to be equated with a regressed individuality. The exotic or the primitive was the repressed, the instinctual and the mad for artists such as Pablo Picasso who started celebrating this inner outside as holding the key to a truer artistic expression. Legions of artists started to adopt fantasies of the exotic in order to become other to their societies and cultural norms, a turn that was characterized as a homecoming to a truer self.[6] It was a utopian project that, in the words of Jean-François Staszak, sought to 'grasp a deeper truth beyond deceiving appearances', and to reach, often through regressions, freedom.[7] There were many ways of trying to achieve this; the Dadaists of Zurich, for example, donned improvised African masks and, according to Roger Cardinal, 'turned their noisy cabaret antics into a ritual invoking primeval forces'.[8] This they did to shock and outrage a bourgeois public that might stomach the exotic, but not the transgression into becoming primitive. It did not mean that equating the foreign with regressed instincts led to any greater understanding of the non-Western world. Primitivism was more radical than a tame exoticism that upheld the differences between home and away, but both ways of interpreting the world were based on colonial appropriations of the foreign.

It was a primitivist urge to reject an overly rational and impure West by travelling to a romantic and pure foreign land that had inspired Heyerdahl to leave Norway in late 1936. He was only 22 years old and about to 'return to nature' by going to Polynesia. Heyerdahl was by no means alone in turning to nature for solace in the 1930s, a decade that saw the invention of the term 'Shangri-La'.[9] After the First World War and the Great Depression there was widespread disillusionment with Western civilization. Neither was Heyerdahl's destination a particularly innovative choice when it came to fantasies about noble savagery in pristine nature. The subsequent failure also followed a rehearsed script. To become primitive, either as a regression into a foreign or an internal other, was an impossibility.

Heyerdahl's failure was so stereotypical that it is a good illustration of what can be termed the primitivist's dilemma. Primitivists will never succeed in becoming the foreign other for the simple reason that their vision of this other is only a fantasy. Shedding the impurity and falseness of modern civilization for a true existence in a nurturing and idyllic nature is impossible since the idea of nature being the true home of man is a construct of the very same modern civilization that he is escaping. The same goes for when the primitivist escapes through an internal psychological regression, trying to realize fantasies of more exalted ways of being. It is here the real dilemma comes into play; if the primitivist's fantasy of the foreign would completely correspond to another reality and the primitivist actually become primitive, there would be no way for this other to report back to the former self. Put more directly, as long as the potential of the primitivist's quest is communicated it has not succeeded. If Heyerdahl had become one with nature on his Polynesian island it would have been the end of Heyerdahl as a public figure.

The dilemma of the primitivist traveller has classically been overcome in two interconnected though different ways. In the first scenario the traveller realizes that it is not possible for a Western subject to become primitive 'again', and therefore he or she seeks to leave primitive people alone so that they are not further 'polluted' by the West. The alternative to this solution is for the primitivist to blame the failure on the primitive by claiming that he or she has been pursing a 'false' primitive that under its disguise turned out to be every bit as as postlapsarian as the traveller.

In this case the primitivist's quest for the true primitive can continue elsewhere, only to be thwarted again by another attempt to acculturate to a different false embodiment of the fantastic primitive. Heyerdahl pursued the second option, though adding a peculiar idiosyncrasy.

In the accounts that Heyerdahl wrote about his time on Fatuiva he put the blame squarely on the indigenous people for not living up to his fantasy of the primitive. The fake primitives in Polynesia were feuding, sickly, drunken, unfriendly and obsessed with the entrapments of modernity. The native village on the island is described as a hellish place that constantly threatens to infect Heyerdahl and his wife with the disease elephantiasis that causes terrible swellings of limbs or genitals. True peace comes to Heyerdahl and Liv only when they are alone. In a 1994 documentary about Heyerdahl it is claimed that he and Liv took off all their clothes when they were sure that the natives were not watching in order to enact their fantasy of being Adam and Eve in Eden.[10] It turns out that Heyerdahl and his wife were much better primitives than the Polynesians had ever been.

After returning to Norway Heyerdahl could have started all over again and searched for another place and people less corrupted by modernity. What is fascinating with Heyerdahl is that he instead focused all of his attention on the region whose inhabitants had so disappointed him. In the *Kon-Tiki* book Heyerdahl claimed that he now wanted to 'tackle primitive people'.[11] He was however not questioning the Polynesians for having succumbed to Westernization; instead he made an entire argument out of the fact that he had been a better primitive than they were. In Heyerdahl's universe, the present-day Polynesians were only the mongrel descendants of a white race of bearded men, the true natives of the islands. Heyerdahl would describe this old race in no uncertain words in his pseudoscientific treaty *American Indians in the Pacific* (1952), in which he claimed that its members had 'intelligent features appealing to the European mind and sometimes with a rather European aspect'.[12] They were furthermore 'culture-bearers', or a 'culture-bearing aristocracy' with 'intelligent and determined physiognomies' that were 'European-like'.[13] And to make it really clear that this race differed widely from the other people living in and around the Pacific, he characterized the Melanesians as having 'dark, often black skin, frizzy hair, and negroid appearance', the Malays as 'morose and reserved' with 'flat, broad and pulpy nose; round head' and the indigenous people of South America as primitive and uninventive.[14] How curious, Heyerdahl pointed out, that a people 'more like ourselves than most aboriginal people, was discovered in recent centuries on tiny islands in the midst of the largest of all seas.'[15]

To claim that a white race was the ultimate and preferred primitive added up to a final colonial conquest of the foreign. Heyerdahl's theory reduced the non-white races into being uninventive and unnecessary. His itinerant white race reserved for itself the role not only of being the perfect primitive, but also, paradoxically, the harbinger of civilization. This meant that there was nothing to thank the non-Western and non-white people for, neither civilization nor the primitive. This was, to put it mildly, a problematic argument to put forward during a period when numerous bloody wars raged between Western colonizers and non-Western colonized, from Indonesia where the Dutch were fighting to regain their empire between 1945 and 1949, to Vietnam where the French tried to do the same from 1945 to 1954 and Kenya where the British were battling the Mau Mau guerrillas from 1952 to 1959. Above all it was an ideological argument that had precious little to do with science. This is clear to us today, but even contemporaries of Heyerdahl like Ashley Montagu were at the time saying that to view humanity in terms of races with differing characteristics was a myth and an intellectual fallacy.[16]

## Heyerdahl, Tarzan and the White Core

The theory of the itinerant culture-bearing white race was a diffusionist argument that postulated a physical connection between the world's civilizations. Where Heyerdahl proved innovative was not in the articulation of his theory, which originated in nineteenth-century racist discourse, but in his idea that his theory needed to be performed in order to be proved. The performativity of the *Kon-Tiki* expedition, down to such details as the crew growing beards like the white race, carried the diffusionist idea out of its abstract state and dramatized it as though in a play. This applied diffusionism could have been the result of many sources of inspiration, of which the figure of Tarzan is a fascinating one. Edgar Rice Burroughs's fictional story about an offspring of British aristocrats growing up in the jungle played a part in Heyerdahl's adolescence. This Tarzan can be seen, following Marianna Torgovnick's reading, to embody the main tenets and confusions of diffusionism. Tarzan has been misconceived as being about an escape from Western civilization when Tarzan is in fact a British aristocrat, Lord Greystoke, performing a vigilant battle to civilize the wilderness surrounding and infiltrating him. Tarzan spends 'years learning to read English (before he encounters it as a spoken language), refrains from cannibalism, organises the apes into political factions, and kisses Jane's hand when he first meets her'.[17] Tarzan's whiteness distances him from the primitive even before he has been introduced to the white world he hails from. Whiteness is described as not only a physical trait, but also a mental one.

Just as the Polynesians were not the 'right' primitives for Heyerdahl, neither are the black natives of the jungle for Tarzan. Appropriately enough, Tarzan stumbles over a lost ancient and advanced white civilization, in the middle of primitive nature.[18] This encounter is based, as Torgovnick goes on to point out, on a white-supremacist appropriation of the legacy and material remains of great African pre-colonial civilizations: 'the "best" of Africa is white'.[19] Again, the preferred and original non-West is still the white West. With this knowledge in mind, Tarzan's rejection of what he sees as a corrupt and degenerate modern urban civilization is as minimally radical as Heyerdahl's. Neither Tarzan nor Heyerdahl has any need to become a non-Western primitive; their aim is to stay within their performance of the better Western self.

The diffusionism in the Tarzan narrative was usually framed as a story about a hunt for surviving traces of the great white race that had initiated the world's great civilizations and then vanished. The fantasy was that this race was still out there, somewhere. This made travellers like the British mystic P. H. Fawcett, another Tarzan come to life, venture out into the Amazon jungle in order to locate the lost cities of the master race. Fawcett, syndicated by Jack Wheeler at NANA, disappeared in 1925, and the search for him became worldwide headline material in the 1920s and 1930s.[20] His son, Brian Fawcett, published *Exploration Fawcett* in 1953, a book about his father that would feed the hysteria around the latter, today a well-enshrined New Age myth. Curiously, the most persistent rumour is that Fawcett found his lost city, was adopted by its inhabitants and, appropriately enough, made immortal.

Heyerdahl had as a child read Fawcett, but his approach to diffusionism would be different from that of both Tarzan and his double.[21] Heyerdahl and his crew would perform the very journey of this white race, instead of locating any living remains of it. History was to be restaged and performed. The *Kon-Tiki* book is full of parallels between the crew and the white race:

'The lamp flung huge shadows of bearded men on the sail, and we thought of the white men with beards from Peru.'[22] On that very same sail there were not only the shadows of the bearded crew but also a painting of the leader of the white master race, the god-king *Kon-Tiki* (see front cover). Of course it was Heyerdahl who was Kon-Tiki, suggested Arnold Jacoby in his 1964 biography entitled *Señor Kon-Tiki*. It was therefore natural for Heyerdahl, arriving in Polynesia on his raft, to lecture the 'brown people' there about their once-upon-a-time white history.[23]

The modern white Scandinavians on board the raft had an easy time impersonating the privileged white primitive. Journeys such as Tarzan's and Fawcett's still required exposure to a threatening nature in order to reach a chimerical goal of a lost city. In Heyerdahl's journey through history there was no need to become an unknown and lightly subversive primitive. There was no need to sacrifice rational and conscious control. The primitive hidden in the history of the West was a rational and enlightened one, carrier of great civilizations and ruler of men, and there to be performed rather than hidden away in a jungle. This way of becoming primitive had nothing in common with the libidinal, and fearful, projects of avant-garde art in the interwar period. Maybe their irrational savage still existed in blacks, mentally disturbed people and artists themselves, but it was a mirror of the West too disturbing and too close to home for the majority of the postwar *Kon-Tiki* audience to contemplate. Though after the experience of six years of total war in the West it might have been easy to conceive that man at heart is a bloodthirsty irrational savage, like Joseph Conrad's Kurtz in *Heart of Darkness*, it was more comforting to think of 'true' man as peaceful, judicious, rational – a demi-god that could be re-enacted.

The subservient role that the non-white people play in the *Kon-Tiki* story reinforces Heyerdahl's racist narrative and removes the potential anxiety that the West felt towards the non-West. Heyerdahl does not for a moment contemplate bringing a Polynesian or a South American on board the raft, but a priori dismisses the possibility that any such people would have a better idea of how to build or steer it. Peruvian sailors, 'with Inca blood in the veins', build the raft together with Heyerdahl, but under the close supervision of him and his crew.[24]

One of the most symbolic scenes in the *Kon-Tiki* film operated under the same logic of exclusion of the indigenous people in the book described as brown men in white men's clothes.[25] Heyerdahl's raft lands on an uninhabited island and the crew waits for some time for the scared and superstitious natives to approach from another island. When they do so, the Tarzan he-men of the *Kon-Tiki* wave a huge Norwegian flag to greet their canoe (see plate 14). It is as though the Polynesians are welcomed to a land annexed to Heyerdahl's Norway; the once colonized nation becomes a colonizer. That Heyerdahl and his men have one or two things to teach the natives is soon made clear as they display their radio sets and start curing their sick. Heyerdahl has finally arrived back in Polynesia, and this time it is he who is the undisputed master of the situation.

Even though Heyerdahl displays modern technology for the Polynesians – the same technology that he was careful not to corrupt them with on his previous trip – his main aim is not to modernize the primitives but to primitivize the moderns. Through the *Kon-Tiki* story he supplied a scenario in which the West could embrace its primitive side. This primitive past of the white West was safely put in the past, which helped to make any play-acting of the primitive devoid of risk since it in essence could be nothing else than a reconstruction of a historical event. This is well illustrated in how Heyerdahl and his crew departed from a big mechanized wharf, the Peruvian naval dockyard in Callao, and how they returned to the USA from Polynesia on a modern 4000-tonne freight ship fortuitously named *Thor I*.[26] Heyerdahl entered history on his voyage westwards over the Pacific under his symbolically historic name Kon-Tiki, and returned eastwards to the Americas under his modern name Thor. In between was a reconstruction of the historic event of cultural diffusion by a white race, play-acted by Heyerdahl and his bearded men. The West and its primitive side were thus ideally united, even though factually split by time.

The primitivism of Heyerdahl was a ludic space in which the non-primitive could play at being the primitive that it had once been. This played perfectly into the Californian cultural current of 'Tiki culture', or 'Polynesian Pop', that had begun in the interwar period. In 1937 Ernst Beaumont-Gantt revamped his bar Don the Beachcomber in Hollywood as a 'South-Sea hideaway' with tropic interior, drinks and mock-Polynesian art.[27] Another pioneer, Victor Bergeron, did the same with his Trader Vic's restaurant in Oakland.[28] These were the beginnings of franchising chains of Tiki bars and restaurants that spread across the USA in the 1940s and 1950s, and then also ended up in Europe. There were many more explanations for the popularity of Tiki culture than Heyerdahl's

*Kon-Tiki*. Thousands of returning US soldiers that had had first-hand contact with Pacific cultures returned after the war to the mainland or were stationed in Europe. The collection of short stories *Tales of the South Pacific* by James A. Michener, published in 1946, scored a huge success and was even adapted into a blockbusting musical on Broadway in 1949.[29] Further boosts came when Hawaii was made a state in 1959 and through Elvis Presley's Hawaiian films of the 1960s.

The Tiki culture provided an outlet for having 'fun in an otherwise conservative society', as Sven A. Kirsten put it in *The Book of Tiki* (2000).[30] Polynesian garden parties, often named *luaus* after the Hawaiian model, became a strong presence in US suburbia; complete with Hawaiian shirts, barbecue and garish drinks served from grotesque goblets in fake designs of 'tikis' (Polynesian woodcarvings of deities). This culture 'allowed the man in the grey flannel suit to regress to a rule-free primitive naivety', Kirsten continues.[31] Another major reason why this regression into a fantasy world of exotica was possible was also that Heyerdahl had 'proved' that the original Polynesian was white. There was therefore no reason to fret over the consequences of going native, nor over the possibility that a cultural heritage might be misappropriated. Tiki culture was even imported into Hawaii so as not to confuse tourists or make them anxious were they to find only a real and unfamiliar Polynesian culture.[32]

Tiki culture spread slowly from the USA to Europe, but the concept was not lost on the European audience, as exemplified when a certain chef de cuisine at the Centraal Hotel in Amsterdam named Kraam asked Heyerdahl's permission to name a chicken and fruit dish 'Jambonneau de la Volaille sauté Kon-Tiki' in 1955. Heyerdahl accepted with the proviso that the dish in question was tasty.[33] It was a symbolic answer. The important tenet of Tiki culture was that it was enjoyable, not that it was authentically Polynesian; it was to be an exoticism of pleasure rather than one of anxiety.

Just like the chicken dish at the Centraal Hotel, Heyerdahl's merger of exoticism and primitivism was one that could be bought and sold. Whereas old primitivism and romantic exoticism had stigmatized commercialism as a corrupter of the authentic, the postwar primitive exoticism saw no incompatibility in this regard. The acceptance of commercial exotica as harmless broke down another romantic presupposition; the idea that the true exotic experience was only for an elite avant-garde. Since no experiences or cultures were seen as more authentic than any other they could be exchanged and traded with the help of a 'neutral' monetary system already in place. Popular exotic tourism could conveniently be destigmatized, for example, in a globalizing age when the romantic exoticists bemoaned the disappearance of radical otherness. Tiki culture was a true popular culture, aimed at the mass.

## The Exotic and the Primitive in Postwar Travel Writing

European travel writing after the war was almost entirely focused on describing the exotic not as a foreign that should be joined or emulated, but as something that should be kept separate from the Western self. The primitivism of the interwar period with its experiments in going native had come to a halt. It was as though the travellers and adventurers were tired of the primitivist's dilemma. Regressions or transgressions into the primitive were rarely attempted. The exotic remained as a romantic or aesthetic object to be observed and described, fascinating only for the difference it represented. Heyerdahl's *Kon-Tiki* story was thus rather unusual in comparison to how the postwar journey looked in travel literature. Not only did Heyerdahl retain a measure of primitivism, but he also tried to make a bridge between the exotic and the primitive. Heyerdahl's pseudoscientific and racist diffusionism was not new, but performing it and presenting it as travel literature was.

There were a few isolated individuals who pursued a primitivistic quest to regress to a state of nature in the 1950s, and these would be inconsequential had it not been for the interesting fact that some of these travellers worked as colonial functionaries. This showed the paradoxical nature of racism expressed in primitivism. Going native was as much a colonial fantasy as it was a radical one. This was well illustrated in the French Colonial Exposition in Paris 1931 when the painted primitivist fantasies of the artist Paul Gauguin were featured in the official displays and where primitive artefacts belonging to leading surrealists were showcased in the communist counter-exhibit 'The Truth about the Colonies'.[34] The primitivist drama seemed exhausted, however, in France after the war, whereas it survived in Britain and Sweden.

Arthur Grimble had worked in the British colony of the Gilbert (now Kiribati) Islands, in Micronesia from 1914 to 1920 and published a bestselling account of his experiences as *A Pattern of Islands* in 1952.

Grimble had been on Kiribati during the heyday of primitivism and had also attempted to become the foreign other. Not only had he been adopted by a native family but he had also been tattooed, itself an important marker of transgression into otherness in Western literature from Melville's *Typee* to Norman and Hall's fictional account of the *Bounty* mutiny.[35] Grimble also decided to live in native fashion and had a house built for him into which 'not a fragment of European stuff went [...] except a corrugated-iron kitchen roof for water-catchment'.[36] He did not find any fundamental clash between colonialism and primitivism, as though the function of the colonialist could be to protect the primitive. Missionaries, in this regard, presented a much greater threat as they destroyed 'much that was beautiful and useful in native custom' according to Grimble.[37]

Malcolm MacDonald, Commissioner-General of the United Kingdom in Southeast Asia, published in 1956 a book called *Borneo People* that in many ways echoes Grimble's work. In the book, MacDonald shares the humble life of his Borneo primitives and becomes part of their family structure by adopting a girl. Like Grimble, he is also critical of missionaries who try to change the primitive lives of the jungle-dwellers. MacDonald's desire to become a primitive resonates throughout the book. When pushing ever deeper into the jungle of Borneo he states, 'I felt instantly that I had left the awful, wearying troubles of the modern world and reached a haven where complexity was replaced by simplicity, frustration by contentment and strife by peace'.[38] Speaking about the Dayak people who dwelt in Borneo's interior he puts it more explicitly: 'I wished I were a Dayak and that I need never leave this simple existence with my warm-hearted friends'.[39]

One of the very few primitivist travel accounts from Sweden, where the *Kon-Tiki* achieved such success, was interestingly enough also connected to the European colonial enterprise. Eric Lundqvist wrote *Djungeltagen* (In Eastern Forests) in 1949 about his time in the Dutch logging industry in Indonesia from 1934 to 1939. The very reason for Lundqvist to take the job was because it gave him an opportunity to get away from modern civilization. He emphatically states, 'freedom for the individual is impossible in a civilized society'.[40] He is more acutely self-aware of his own place within the colonial logic than Grimble and MacDonald and watches with horror as he himself erects a miniature version of the civilization he is trying to escape in the jungle in order to satisfy the hunger for profits of the 'Dutch capitalists' that employ him.[41] Although he represents an encroaching white civilization he continues to insist that it is the West that should learn from the 'savages', and not vice versa.

Lundqvist is much more aware of the impossibility of becoming primitive than either Grimble or MacDonald. On a hunting trip he once comes close to the primitive inside himself: 'The conscious ego disappears as fog and smoke. Now it is a savage that stands there with the spear in both hands.'[42] To mark this regression into other he shifts the narrative into third person and describes himself as 'the savage' who dances over his kill and is fulfilled with primeval life. But Lundqvist reads the split between the Western self and the foreign other not as a matter of individual choice or even psychological disposition, but something that is there because of the colonial logic that has brought him to the jungle in the first place. His short entrance into otherness is in the end interrupted by his servant praising his prowess and calling him *tuan* (master in Malay).[43] Lundqvist, a Swede with a proto-postcolonial consciousness in the pay of the Dutch colonial state, ends up blaming the West for the radical impossibility of becoming other. But neither in *Djungeltagen* nor in his other books did Lundqvist give up his primitivist desire in order to become a detached exoticist. Although aware that his desire cannot be fulfilled he cannot stop himself from desiring.

Lundqvist, Grimble and MacDonald thus represent three travel-writers in the postwar period who continue to engage with the vexed theme of going native. When looking more closely at their books it is clear that they have very little to do with the *Kon-Tiki*. There is no trace of diffusionism in these accounts; the primitives are properly foreign and different from the West. They are, in Heyerdahl's universe, 'brown'. These books share much more with Heyerdahl's first one about his time on Fatuiva. They are narrated as classic primitivist going-native stories of a genre that appeared to have its last foothold in the crumbling colonial world.

The absolute majority of postwar travel writing admired the foreign from a distance, and entertained no wish to become a part of it. The interwar desire to regress to the state of some imagined pre-lapsarian primitive had by and large disappeared. What remained was a voyeuristic pleasure derived from romanticizing the foreignness of the non-Western in which the primitive became an *objet d'art*. The amateur travellers like Eric Newby tried to debunk the exotic, but most postwar travellers adopted a romantic stance in which the foreign became something transcendental yet brittle, in danger of being destroyed by exposure.

The romantic exoticist vision led to similar conclusions about modernity and civilization as had the analysis of primitivists. The West was seen as morally corrupt, emotionally inauthentic, set on a course that would lead to its own destruction. The exotic had the possibility of representing the opposite. A traveller in the exotic land should be a harmless observer who let the beatitude of the primitive rub off, without in turn leaving any traces. As Wilfred Thesiger said when speaking of his time with the Bedouin of Arabia, 'I wished only to live as they lived and, now that I have left them, I would gladly think that nothing in their lives was altered by my coming.'[44] Polluting the exotic was, however, almost unavoidable. Even walking slowly by the side of the primitives was dangerous. Thesiger himself came to understand that his wish not to affect 'his' Bedouin by his stay in the desert was in vain: 'I realize that the maps I made helped others, with more material aims, to visit and corrupt a people whose spirit once lit the desert like a flame.'[45]

The French excelled in this romantic and defeatist notion of the exotic that characterized the other as weak and easily crushed. The books of Alain Gerbault, Françoise Balsan, Raymond Maufrais, Michel Perrin and Jean Raspail all contain it. Their travels were tortured spiritual searches for a pure exotic other that they could not join and were condemned to pollute almost by observation alone. Since the exotic is an aesthetic object, very clear parameters were set up as to what made it beautiful or not. Most authors considered it very important that the exotic was pure, and miscegenation was often openly abhorred; some, like Gerbault, carried this so far that, in the posthumously published *Un paradis se meurt* (A Paradise Dies; 1949), he suggests that a South African-type system of racial segregation be put in place in Polynesia to protect the Polynesians from the Europeans.[46] Gerbault and Jean Raspail are good examples of romantic exoticism going hand-in-glove with racist and reactionary politics. Gerbault was a Vichy supporter stuck in a Polynesia controlled by the Free French forces during the war, and Raspail who wrote *Terre de Feu – Alaska* in 1952 would later write one of the most canonical white-supremacy novels, *Le Camp des saints* (The Camp of the Saints), in 1972.

For the romantic exoticists it is not the content of the exotic that is important at the end of the day, but its radical difference from the known. As long as the exotic and primitive are pure and untainted nothing beyond their status as being non-Western matters. An uncontaminated instance of the exotic promised the possibility of the survival of West–non-West difference. The science of the non-West, anthropology, had been obsessed with this problem from its very inception. Malinowski, the modern father of the discipline, had proclaimed in 1922 in *Argonauts of the Western Pacific*, 'Alas! the time is short for Ethnology, and will the truth of its real meaning and importance dawn before it is too late?'[47] This was what George E. Marcus has called the 'Salvage Mode' within ethnography, defined as when 'the ethnographer portrays himself as "before the deluge," [...] fundamental change [in the society] are apparent, but the ethnographer is able to salvage a cultural state on the verge of transformation', a mode that was still very much the orthodoxy during the postwar period.[48] It was not only anthropologists and ethnographers that were working in salvage mode; the majority of travel-writers through the twentieth century were too.

In an essay on exoticism written over the period 1904 to 1918 and published posthumously in 1955 the French poet Victor Segalen argued that the exotic was 'eternally incomprehensible'.[49] The true exotic was impossible to understand, the very inverse of the known and comprehensible that was an entropic world conceived, by Segalen, as a 'terrible monster of emptiness'.[50] Although Segalen's impact came later, it was as though his spirit hovered over postwar French travel writing. Claude Lévi-Strauss wrote about meeting a tribe previously not studied by saying that it was, fittingly, like seeing a reflection in the mirror that he could not understand.[51]

Alain Gheerbrant in his 1952 book about an anthropological expedition in the Amazon described probably the most extremely romantic meeting with the incomprehensible exotic. His expedition, like Lévi-Strauss's, intended to discover previously 'unstudied' Indians who were still unpolluted by the West. Gheerbrant was very happy when he eventually encountered the perfectly exotic Guaharibo tribe. It was impossible for the young French anthropologists to communicate with the Guaharibo and vice versa. Gheerbrant saved the day by a Schopenhauerian trick. He took his tape recorder and played Mozart to establish communication. The capitalism and colonialism of the West might destroy the exotic, but its romantic art will not. Art speaks on a level of abstraction and does not commit Gheerbrant to share anything that could pollute the natives.

The brief glimpse that the impure West gets of the disappearing pure non-West, as in Gheerbrant and Lévi-Strauss, was as close as the romantic exoticist got to the foreign. Throughout the West writers lamented the 'suburbanization' of the exotic as Gavin Maxwell, travel companion to Wilfred Thesiger, put it in his 1957 *A Reed Shaken by the Wind*. According to Maxwell, the monster of sameness was attacking from all directions: 'The margins of the atlas were closing in: the journeys I had dreamed in years before were blocked by the spreading stains of new political empires and impenetrable frontiers behind which, if propaganda is to be believed, the suburbanising process progressed but the faster.'[52] Whether it was Western colonialism or political regimes based on a Western model in the Third World, change meant a 'wiping out of local culture', words the *Kon-Tiki* crew member Bengt Danielsson used when describing the Polynesian situation.[53] The true exotic was rapidly disappearing, and there was nothing to be done about it.

## The Exotic is Dead, Long Live the Primitive

The romantic exotic that was so celebrated in postwar travel literature was of little or no significance for Heyerdahl in the *Kon-Tiki*. He was more interested in a primitive removed in time, a primitive that had been white, than in the difference between the West and the existing exotic peoples or locations. By not paying any attention to the brown endangered exotic he could celebrate the white primitive who was safely removed to some distant historical domain. This was a unique way of approaching the problem of the exotic that seemed to have been on the verge of disappearing for such a long time that the disappearing had become part of its essence. There was however some travel writing that tried to counter this trend during the period, though not through Heyerdahl's argument. The exotic was debunked either by saying that it would not hurt it to modernize or through a tongue-in-cheek questioning of how exotic the exotic really was.

The exotic had been demystified before the postwar period, but this mode did receive something of a boost from the ironic amateur travellers and adventurers. These travellers often questioned the difference between them and their destination by imagining their behaviour though the eyes of the other, a trope pioneered in the *Persian Letters* by Montesquieu in 1721. Everyone was not the same, but differences existed on an equal level and were the picturesque quirks of humanity. Therefore we could all be exotic to each other and trade our differences. Capitalism and consumerism were no threats. The traveller was a tourist in a bewildering marketplace, much like a member of the white urban middle class strolling through a multicultural district of a Western city today.

Unromantic exoticism was not straightforwardly racist, but failed to account for the very real power relationships that existed between people of the West and the non-West. The Western traveller-tourist experimented with the difference between himself and the exotic at a cost no higher than a humorous embarrassment, a privilege that was not shared by the colonial subject even though this possibility was often implied in the narratives. At a time when the initial steps towards colonial liberation were being taken, this was tantamount to trying both to deny the momentous aspects of what was happening and to smooth over the problems. In the mock equality of the colonial with the colonized, the Western same with the primitive other, unromantic exoticism constructed a subterfuge through which exoticism could be saved for the future postcolonial world. Since this future of exoticism equalled the commodification of the exotic, it was paramount to curing the neurosis in romantic exoticism that everything had to be authentic.

To rob the exotic of its exclusive, romantic and slightly pompous veneer also laid the ground for a democratization of the exotic throughout the 1950s; Tiki culture was very much a part of this trend. Travellers like Elspeth Huxley wrote about previous exotic locales like Africa telling the reader not to expect any 'lonely deserts, empty forests, hunted game and primitive tribes'.[54] The reader would join Huxley on 'the beaten track'.[55] This was how readers teamed up with Christopher Isherwood, Eric Newby, Jean Chegaray, Rolf Blomberg and many others through the period. The conclusion was even in some cases that the difference of the exotic was not even that interesting in the first place. Isherwood's description of the 'madly ungay' Inca empire in the 1948 *The Condor and the Cow* is a good example: 'It was a culture of mass, of authority, order. A culture based upon natural law; materialistic, reasonable, and, within its graded social limits, strictly just. A mountain culture, solid, magnificent and sombre. Much ritual, little spirituality. Much gold, little elegance. Much feasting, little fun.'[56] His Incas sounded like the Nazis Isherwood had escaped in 1939 when he left Berlin.

Debunking the exotic would eventually lead to a mode in travel writing that Paul Fussell has characterized as post-tourism: travel in a globalized world where real difference is no longer possible.[57] These are the grumpy and satirical travels through a landscape in which the exotic has been converted into tacky souvenirs, like the journeys of the US travel-writer Paul Theroux. Post-tourism shares a lot with another 'post,' post-modernity, as Casey Blayton has argued, being characterized by 'in-your-face playfulness, reflexivity, and dark humor'.[58] This is important to note for one reason alone: it shows us how this type of debunking the exotic led to a radically different result from Heyerdahl's. In the *Kon-Tiki* story Heyerdahl did question the attraction that the exotic natives represented, but he did not do away with the desire for difference. The survival of this desire also meant that Heyerdahl used legend as a narrative mode rather than playful reflexivity.

The exotic might be dead, or dying, in a rapidly globalizing world, but Heyerdahl's message was that as long as the West had been the white primitive this did not matter. Heyerdahl had developed a most timely compromise. He could have had aligned himself with an old tradition of primitivism, but he had experimented unsuccessfully with that in his first book; moreover, it was also an elitist mode of writing that would limit his readership. The second alternative would have been to adopt some kind of exotic vision, be it romantic or inspired by amateurism and tourism. But then Heyerdahl would have had to relate to themes such as globalization and colonialism, themes that would anchor his story in the present and make it hard to communicate as a legend. The solution was as simple as it was brilliant: the authentic primitives had been white, and therefore there was no need to grant the same status to the real people in the exotic locales that he visited.

Heyerdahl's compromise preserved some of the most compelling aspects of primitivism and the two kinds of exoticism. He regressed to the primitive who was but a version of himself removed in time and he therefore remained free to debunk the exoticism of the real natives of South America and Peru. The end result was a story that did not sacrifice its claim to legend but instead used it, and through its workings managed to become both romantic and unromantic, mythic and ironic, elitist and egalitarian. Heyerdahl saved the legendary potential of travel, maybe for the last time, with his compromise. No one would later do it as successfully as he did, even though there was no dearth of those who tried. Adventurers like Maurice Herzog and Alain Bombard became hugely successful in the 1950s, but they never managed to overcome the important question of elite versus popular adventure. Heyerdahl had succeeded in becoming 'universal' by introducing a radically non-elitist and democratic concept of the foreign that at the same time did not degenerate into crass tourism. Look at your history, Heyerdahl told his Western audiences, and realize that you were once the primitive.

# 9

## The New Postwar Sea and the Pacific Frontier

### The Aquatic Frontier of the American Lake

Heyerdahl's most innovative and successful legendary mediation in the *Kon-Tiki* took place in his writing of the sea. He had previous resuscitated old genres, adventurous science and primitivism, and dressed them in new garbs tailored to suit the times. When evoking the sea Heyerdahl did not suggest a compromise between two known positions, but juxtaposed an old established image of the oceans with a new one that that he helped to pioneer. Heyerdahl described the sea as being both fathomless and sublime nature as well as a controllable and peaceable realm. We are today used to the image of a threatened sea that suffers pollution and depletion of its species. The aquatic world is weak and delicate, in need of our protection. This idea of the fragile seascape owes a lot to Heyerdahl's writing about the sea, a writing that began with the *Kon-Tiki*.

The sea was the true protagonist of the *Kon-Tiki* story, and was almost unanimously identified as such by the reviewers of Heyerdahl's book and film. More than 40 years of environmentalism separate us from the 1950s, a decade in which the ocean played centre-stage in popular culture as the new wilderness and frontier.[1] That the sea has progressively been reduced to irrelevance in twenty-first-century culture makes it more difficult to understand its role in the postwar world. Never before in modern history have so many people in the West been so removed from the world's bodies of water. Ocean liners are a thing of the past, and the few cruise ships that remain are introverted floating hotels that have substituted indoor shopping arcades for their promenade decks. Freight traffic is carried out by a handful of professionals on computerized container ships. The moment in flight-safety demonstrations where stewards show how to fit the ubiquitous life jacket before the aircraft takes off often represents the largest presence of the sea in many people's lives today.

Being removed from the sea and thinking of it as threatened by pollution makes it almost difficult to imagine the seascape as a daunting and dangerous environment. Only a few films like James Cameron's *Titanic* (1997), Wolfgang Petersen's *The Perfect Storm* (2000) and Roland Emmerich's *The Day after Tomorrow* (2004) depict a sea that is powerful, unpredictable and able to devour. To think of the sea as a threatening, rather than threatened, environment, was the norm before the Second World War. This started to change in the 1950s, largely thanks to Heyerdahl writing a new, delicate sea into existence. This new sea was a benign one that gave life rather than an evil one that took it. After the *Kon-Tiki*, a number of immensely popular works would explore this tension between the old and new sea: Rachel Carson's *The Sea Around Us* (1951, filmed in 1952); Ernest Hemingway's *The Old Man and the Sea* (1952); Alain Bombard's *Naufragé volontaire* (The Voyage of the *Hérétique*; 1953); and Jacques-Yves Cousteau's *Le Monde du silence* (The Silent World; 1953, filmed in 1956). The books were all international bestsellers and one of them, Hemingway's, led to the author's becoming a Nobel laureate. Heyerdahl, Carson and Cousteau also won Oscars for the documentary films that resulted from their voyages and books.[2] With the advent of the 1960s the scene was set for the wholesale inversion of the dangerous into the endangered sea through the worldwide environmentalist movement in which Heyerdahl would also play a major role.

That the sea was Heyerdahl's preferred setting is clear in the *Kon-Tiki*; he is very careful to describe his raft as being in total isolation, drifting on the Pacific. The crew appropriate the 'whole sea' as theirs.[3] They live 'in close converse' with this sea and find it to be home to 'real peace and freedom'. It was a place where life was 'fuller and richer' than in the modern world.[4] Heyerdahl and his men drifted outside time on the vast and welcoming sea belonging to them. But it is essential to understand what this meant and how Heyerdahl's audience read it. The Pacific Ocean was not an innocent space outside time and place. It was the postwar sea *par excellence*, a perfect environment in which to engage with the role of the sea in the culture of the times.

The conception of the ocean in the twentieth century was characterized, as Gary Kroll has discussed in his *America's Ocean Wilderness* (2008), by a movement in which the sea was first thought of as a frontier, but then later also as an entity that takes up most of the world's surface. This vision of the planet as a water world, pioneered by figures such as William Beebe, Rachel Carson and Thor Heyerdahl, Kroll fittingly called 'oceanocentric'.[5] These two ways of viewing the sea as a vast wilderness to discover and maybe even inhabit and as a frontier converged in the postwar period in the world's largest ocean, the Pacific, which was the scene of a US imperial advance and the reopening of the Western frontier. Heyerdahl's *Kon-Tiki* cannot be read outside this context. Not only was Heyerdahl sponsored by the most important player in the expansion, the US Navy, but he was also arguing an appropriately allegorical theory of a culture-carrying white race fanning out into the Pacific.

It was in the Pacific that the imperial ambitions of the USSR and USA met, but the Pacific rose to importance even before becoming the quintessential sea of the Cold War. Improved communications, first with steam traffic in the mid-nineteenth century and then with commercial airline traffic, the Pan-Am China clipper flights, opened the west coast of the USA to Asia. This development could be seen as both positive and negative. The 1941 Japanese attack on Pearl Harbor clearly illustrated that the USA needed, once and for all, to stop thinking of the Pacific as a large and impenetrable wilderness offering protection. The Frank Capra film, *Prelude to War* (1942), which was the first in the *Why We Fight* series (obligatory viewing for all US servicemen), featured a world map with the Americas in focus; in the film an arrow is drawn to Japan, measuring a distance of 8000 miles, and then a similar arrow drawn to continental Europe, measuring 3500 miles. There are threats out there and distances are no protection, the speaker tells us: 'we were [pre-Pearl Harbor] still hypnotized by the fact that two broad oceans stood between us and the rest of the world', but now all that had changed as the ocean could be bridged in days or hours. The world was becoming a water world, which also meant that the oceans were paradoxically becoming finite as they could no longer be viewed as abstract obstacles. The very same logic lay behind the more positive image of Allied convoys that with the help of the vast, though penetrable, oceans made it possible for the war to be waged by Allied countries so geographically dispersed as the USA, the USSR and Britain.

The war led the USA to take over Japan's domination of a large part of the Pacific Ocean, an annexation that was institutionalized as the war ended.[6] That the USA would so readily take on the Japanese colonial project, which included territorial acquisitions in Micronesia, was not surprising. Incorporating the Pacific into the messianic frontier story of US westward expansion was the most obvious and easiest way to bring the Pacific wilderness under control, even though it again involved the USA in the colonial practices that it had vowed to discontinue. As early as 1850, Melville had satirized the notion that the West was the timeless solution when he let Taji, the protagonist of *Mardi*, exclaim: 'West, West! Whitherward mankind and empires – flocks, caravans, armies, navies; worlds, suns, and stars all wend! – West, West! – Oh boundless boundary! Eternal goal!'[7]

That Heyerdahl was part of the continuation of the frontier was evident to a latter-day Taji, Georges Carousso, who in 1950 stated in the *Brooklyn Eagle Sun* that, when he reached California, Heyerdahl had solved the problem of there being no 'Westering' left to do by opening the Pacific as a new frontier.[8] But it was not Heyerdahl who did this all by himself. In 1945, when the US Navy ruled or controlled almost all of the area, General MacArthur appropriated the term 'the American Lake' for the Pacific. In 1870 this had been what US Navy Commodore Robert Shufeldt called the Mexican Gulf, designating the Pacific as 'the ocean bride of America'.[9] If the Spanish-American War of 1898 confirmed the Mexican Gulf as the pivotal sea for the USA, the Second World War firmly shifted the attention to the Pacific. In 1946 the US Navy tested nuclear weapons on Bikini as if to announce the consummation of the marriage between the USA and the Pacific. This time the message was directed to Moscow. The USSR and global Communism were the new enemy, and since no 'broad oceans' could save the USA it shifted its frontier right to the doorstep of the communist foe. The era of the 'new atomic imperialism', as Moscow would call it, had begun.[10]

Controlling some Micronesian islands and ruling the surface of the sea were not enough to sustain a frontier; it was the sea itself that needed to be controlled. In September 1945 the USA took the unprecedented step of unilaterally claiming ownership of all the territory of the continental shelves, stretching roughly 200 nautical miles out into the ocean, as well as extending national control over fishing. The seventeenth-century concept of 'freedom of the seas' was radically questioned, and soon many other countries followed suit. The US declaration unleashed frantic international activity to regulate the new postwar sea, a work that would lead to three major UN Conferences on the Law of the Sea (UNCLOS) during the latter half of the twentieth century.[11] There were economic interests at stake, especially fishing and oil extraction. The USA had repeatedly declared that it did not wish to enlarge its territory in the Atlantic Charter, the Cairo Declaration, Truman's Potsdam statement and the United Nations Charter.[12] Soon after the war had ended the USA took a significant step towards doing this on its Pacific frontier.

The postwar focus on the sea in the West cannot be separated from the final opening of the identifiable Pacific frontier by the USA. Becoming frontier entailed trying to rein in the wilderness. There had to be some way to control and domesticate the oceanic expanses. That the war should lead to this new Pacific that was not as radically wild as the preceding one was in some ways counter-intuitive. After all, the sea had been the scene of so much terror and destruction during the war, with huge parts of it transformed into blood-drenched oceanic battlefields. This was not easily erased. In 1942 the journalist Roger Trumbull wrote *The Raft*, which recounted the ordeal of three navy airmen who survived for 34 days in a small rubber dinghy in the shark-infested Pacific. Other stories could soon be added, real stories with less fortunate outcomes like that of the sinking of the *USS Indianapolis* in 1945. The cruiser's crew had been five days in the water before they were found, but by this time most of them had been consumed in a horrific shark banquet. The *Indianapolis* would go on to become an integral part of a postwar trauma centred on the sea's capacity to devour man. The story has been retold in countless books, plays and films, and was even mentioned in Steven Spielberg's film *Jaws* of 1975 that was, and is, perhaps one of the most evocative portrayals of the fear-instilling sea in modern times.

Many postwar accounts of the sea thus continued to stress its status as a man-engulfing radical wilderness, among them Gore Vidal's *Williwaw* (1946), Nicholas Monsarrat's *The Cruel Sea* (1951), Herman Wouk's *The Caine Mutiny* (1951) and William Golding's *Pincher Martin* (1956). The British sailor and author Jonathan Raban has even claimed that the postwar sea was mostly 'cruel' as 'its coldness and turbulence reflects the universal derangement of a world at war'.[13] The British writer Monsarrat's book *The Cruel Sea* is a good example of this, not only on account of its title. Monsarrat even found it easier to forgive the German enemy than the sea, as he stated in the foreword to his novel: 'the men are the stars of this story. The only heroines are the ships: and the only villain the cruel sea itself.'[14] The friends of the protagonist get taken by the ocean one by one, all 'robbed' by the 'same enemy'.[15] Mercilessly, the sea devoured man.

What Raban missed out was that the interesting thing about the postwar sea was not the survival of the old paradigm, but the introduction of a new. The benign, nurturing, penetrable, relaxing, domestic and beautiful sea started to make its first appearance. The old sea had a competitor. Heyerdahl was at the very forefront of this challenge that would spawn more practical crazes for scuba- and skin-diving and surfing. The making of this new sea was thus not only a US creation, but also one in which the West as a whole took part. Recreational scuba-diving was pioneered in France, for example.[16] The father of the scuba, Jacques-Yves Cousteau, was also the man who in 1953 bombastically announced that the era of the sea was approaching.[17] This new era would come and go in record time, for when it was found out that the world's oceans were under threat they needed to be preserved and protected. The frontier closed before it had even opened, but its brief existence provides us a with a good understanding of how the sea became what it is today.

## The Sublime and the Beautiful

The difference between the two ways of describing the seascape in the *Kon-Tiki* can be explained by the concepts of the sublime and the beautiful. These terms come from eighteenth-century aesthetic theory and were developed by thinkers such as Edmund Burke in *Philosophical Enquiry into the Origin of our Ideas of the Sublime and Beautiful*, published in 1757, and Immanuel Kant in *Observations on the Feeling of the Beautiful and Sublime* (1764). They argued that the sublime and the beautiful were the antithesis of each other: the sublime was large, rough, robust and infinite, while the beautiful was small, smooth, delicate and finite. A flower was beautiful, a mountain range sublime. The beautiful tempted us with love, the sublime with violent passion. The arguments of Burke and Kant were more complex than this, especially those of Kant who developed his position in *Critique of the Power of Judgement* (1790), but the dichotomy that was created through their separate writings put into words two ways of viewing nature.

It was the rebellion of the Romantics with their love of nature against the straight lines of Neoclassicism that had introduced the idea that untamed wilderness could be attractive; a pull to the dangerous, to the fear that intensified life. This wilderness was often the mountains or the sea, as in the work of the German Romantic painter Caspar David Friedrich (1774–1840). Writers such as Anthony Ashley Cooper, John Dennis and Joseph Addison had in the late seventeenth and early eighteenth centuries started to divide up nature between the beautiful and sublime, putting the sea in the latter category. Addison wrote in 1712 about the 'agreeable horrour [sic]' arising from the prospect of a tempestuous sea.[18] Burke also discussed the sea in his 1757 text, comparing the feeling it inspired to what he identified as the most pivotal in the sublime: terror. The beautiful was harmonious and pleasing, the sublime was captivatingly terrifying.[19]

In fact, the sublime sea was already an outworn cliché by 1817, when Jane Austen satirized Byron in her unfinished novel *Sanditon*, as Jonathan Raban has noted.[20] The predominantly English poets like Byron, Coleridge and Shelley had already waxed so lyrical about the sublime sea that this image was becoming institutionalized. Not even the epically foolish last voyage of Shelley in the Tyrrhenian Sea in 1822 could put an end to it, although, arguably, it moved across the Atlantic. US writers like Edgar Allen Poe in 'A Descent into the Maelstrom' (1841) and Herman Melville in *Moby Dick* (1851) wrote of the terror of the sublime sea with a poetic genius and force that seemed to suggest that they had invented the expression all over again.

Poe endowed the sublime sea with its ultimate symbol: the whirlpool. This was the terrific gaping mouth of a sea that took life. It almost swallowed the narrator in Poe's short story 'A Descent into the Maelstrom', who is sucked down into the sea off the Norwegian coast. A year after Poe's story the mature Turner tried to sink a steamboat in his canvas *Snowstorm* (1842) by turning sea and sky around it into a dazzling maelstrom. A decade after Poe, Melville had Ahab and the *Pequod* disappear down a vortex in the sea in *Moby Dick*. In 1870 Jules Verne, the French science-fiction writer, in his *Vingt mille lieues sous les mers* (Twenty Thousand Leagues Under the Sea) revisited the maelstrom of Poe, located off Lofoten, and there introduced Captain Nemo of the *Nautilus* to his destiny. The whirlpool was a grand, terrifying spectacle; it was thrilling and untamed, a mindless devouring orifice of nature.

The tropes of a sublime sea that consumed man and a beautiful one that nourished him were both used for full effect in the *Kon-Tiki*. The sea does indeed threaten to eat the crew. The episode when Watzinger falls overboard and is saved in the last moment is a good illustration of the sea as a terrifying consumer. Sharks, featuring extensively in the book and film, are also taken as symbols of this menacing sea (see plate 8). In the *Kon-Tiki* film considerable amount of time is spent on the dented, devouring holes of the sharks' mouths as if to show that the sea still contains terror. But the sea is at the same time that which nourishes Heyerdahl and his crew. He claims that it would not have been possible to go hungry with such a plentiful supply of fish.[21] The crew even eat plankton, something that had been mentioned as a possible food source for humans by the US oceanographer William Beebe as early as in 1926.[22] Nature also gave the *Kon-Tiki* crew water in the form of rain, as well as the liquid from the lymphatic glands of fish and sea water itself that the crew mixed with their sweet water.[23]

Heyerdahl's introduction of a nourishing sea rather than a sublime one was new, but not entirely without precedent. A similar depiction is to be found in Verne's *Twenty Thousand Leagues Under the Sea*, which Heyerdahl might very well have read as a child. Verne's hero Nemo who sails around the world in a submarine can, as Heyerdahl would, live off the sea. He hunts in the depths and he harvests it. All his food is from the watery expanse, as are his cigars and his clothes; the sea provides for all his needs, as he informs his prisoner Arronax.[24] The sea is furthermore a space of freedom, a refuge for Nemo's radical politics. It is beyond the reach of despots, something that a man with portraits of liberal heroes like Thaddeus Kosciusko, Daniel O'Connell, George Washington, Daniele Manin, Abraham Lincoln and John Brown on the walls of his study knows how to appreciate.[25] In the sea Nemo is free; he does not have to obey superiors; he is independent.[26] Verne's sea does however still contain devouring monsters, like the giant squid that attacks the submarine *Nautilus*; and it still claims life just as much as it gives, as exemplified by one of the crew being taken by this terrific creature.[27] The sea is both a utopia and dystopia. In contrast to Heyerdahl's sea, the sublime sea of Verne finally wins out when it sucks the submarine into the archetypical manifestation of the eighteenth-century sublime, a whirlpool.

In writing the sea as potentially beautiful Verne was, as so often, ahead of his time. Up until the *Kon-Tiki* the sea was described almost exclusively as a threatening space. Classic sea fiction abounded with sublime images of the sea. In Herman Melville's *Moby Dick* the sea attracts the protagonist Ishmael from the very first paragraphs, luring him to sign up for a whaling ship. The same pull will eventually show its destructive side when the sea opens up and swallows the *Pequod* in the end. There is titillation in the sea, it attracts, but in the end the agreeable *horreur* just becomes horrific. This ambiguous pull is evident in the most famous writer of the sea there has ever been, Joseph Conrad, who in stories like *Youth* (1902) and *The Mirror of the Sea* four years later accused the sea of coldly giving nothing back for all the passion that was poured into it.[28]

Conrad and Melville often invoked Job-like sea heroes from whom mindless sacrifice is demanded. The figure of Job can also be argued to make an appearance in Jack London's novel *Sea-Wolf* (1904). The story that unfolds is simple: God, Lucifer, or some inexorable mix of the two puts a man in a situation in which he is challenged. The Job figure is very nearly destroyed and then admonished by a God that, significantly enough in the real biblical book of Job (38:1), speaks from a 'whirlwind', leading the thoughts to the whirlpools and maelstroms of Melville, Poe, Verne and Turner. In these accounts the sea swallows everything in its path. This was also the sea of Hemingway in his *To Have or Have Not* (1937). The sea takes Mr Sing, killed by the protagonist Captain Henry Morgan, and it swallows the bootleg liquor he has to throw overboard; it also takes his arm that is shot to pieces by the Cuban coastguards. After this mutilation the sea marks Morgan, as his stump becomes nothing but a limp 'flipper'.[29] Morgan accepts maiming and death in a paradoxical life-affirming celebration in the face of the 'genuine meanness' of it all, in the words of Henry David Thoreau, as the scholar of sea literature Bert Bender has argued.[30] But Morgan can as little bring himself to accept the sea as Job can a despotic God.

Compared with the seas of the past, the *Kon-Tiki* crew enjoyed a pleasure cruise. Heyerdahl accepted the sea, and the sea accepted him. The sharks were menacing, but they did not bite the crew, and the man who falls overboard is saved. Heyerdahl was not writing another aquatic Job story, but a text of the frontier. Even though this story was religious as well, it was so in a simple, messianic way rather than the much more ambiguous book of Job. The frontier myth held land, and now sea, as penetrable territories that could be annexed and controlled. It was exactly this idea that Melville had criticized in his *Moby Dick*, which was in part an allegorical response to the US annexation of new territories after the Mexican-American War that ended in 1848.

The sea-as-frontier position made it to appear as something that was in between the sublime and the beautiful. The frontier challenged the hardy frontiersmen, as well as nourished them. It was also finite; the future closing of the frontier was part of its very conception since new territories were to be settled and claimed. At the same time the frontier had to be wild enough to provide suction and attract its frontiersmen. It still had to be a place where masculinity could be proved in the face of a stagnant and effeminate urban population. If the frontier became too tame it had became another nature to protect and conserve, rather than one to assert mastery over and exploit.

Although Heyerdahl showed the necessity of the sea-as-frontier to be both sublime and beautiful, he neglected to mention that the sublime terror had in fact transmuted and inverted itself in the postwar period. Heyerdahl sailed in an atomic age on an atomic sea. The Pacific and Bikini were home to the new Romantic whirlpool in the shape of the bomb. The atomic sublime was so radical that it threatened the Pacific as a frontier, which was probably part of the reason why Heyerdahl with his journey into a pre-atomic past was so welcomed. Heyerdahl made an ideal frontier of the Pacific where he censored out the reappearance of the horrific sublime. He was not alone in trying to neutralize the impact of the bomb; the naming of the harmless two-piece bathing costumes for women after Bikini was another example.

That the bomb challenged the frontier by reintroducing the sublime is evident in a number of other sea accounts of the time. The 'stupendous and terrifying' mushroom cloud, as one contemporary observer described it, made its appearance in two important films in the 1950s.[31] In Richard Fleischer's film of Verne's *Twenty Thousand Leagues Under the Sea* from 1954, starring James Mason and Kirk Douglas, the director significantly did not allow the *Nautilus* to disappear down the whirlpool imagined by Poe. Instead he had as his finale Nemo blowing up an industrial complex on the island Volcania where his 'secret', too dangerous for man to handle, was hidden. The viewers understand the veiled reference to the bomb when Volcania explodes and a terrific mushroom cloud rises to the skies. Two years afterwards, in the 1956 film *Moby Dick* by John Huston, the finger of Ahab (Gregory Peck) points to a location on the map with the name 'Bikini' when he shows Starbuck where the showdown with the whale will take place. Melville made no mention of Bikini, and Huston's reading of it is completely post-atomic. Heyerdahl might have been interested in toying around with the sublime, but he was consciously avoiding its terror as that would directly have challenged his frontier story.

## The Image of the Raft

Heyerdahl worked carefully to establish a sea that was balanced, in equilibrium: part wilderness and part domesticated nature. The terror was taken out of the sublime, but the attraction and public appeal of danger still contributed to the working of the story. It is in this light that Heyerdahl's decision to travel on a raft can be understood. Part of the reason why he had chosen a raft was to be able to enact a primitive fantasy of communion with nature. His way of approaching the surface of the sea was thus, as he described it, less intrusive than that which an engine-propelled vessel would have provided. Modern man travelled in ways that scared away the inhabitants of the sea and made it appear an empty and desolate place.[32] Besides bringing Heyerdahl physically closer to the sea, the raft was in itself also an extraordinarily powerful image of the terror that travelling on the oceans had promised since the Romantics.

It is for us today hard to understand just how negative the image of the raft was in the postwar period. At the mention of the word, an association would directly be made with shipwrecked sailors or downed airmen during the war, like the unfortunates in Trumbull's *The Raft* or the men of the *USS Indianapolis* that were devoured by sharks. Heyerdahl skilfully played on this connection between raft and disaster. The sailors he spoke to before his voyage told him that a raft was just something to use for flotation if disaster struck.[33] One of them had been torpedoed during the war and drifted on a raft for three weeks. Even though this had made him respect the sea-worthiness of rafts he still warned that a raft could not be steered and was thus completely at the mercy of the wind.[34] Travelling on a raft was tantamount to signing away control. When Heyerdahl came to the point of building the raft in Peru he reports the scepticism of onlookers. The crew would be washed overboard, and if that did not happen the proximity to salt water would tear the skin off their feet.[35] There was no doubt that the sea would suck them into its depths and devour them if they braved it on a raft.

The raft as an image of disaster had been well enshrined before the war. It was the lowest-standing sea craft, literally and metaphorically. Nothing protected its inhabitants from the sea. Like on Théodore Géricault's great Romantic canvas *Le Radeau de la Méduse* (The Raft of the *Medusa*) painted between 1818 and 1819 it is the lack of freeboard that makes the sea appear to be nibbling on the twisted, tortured and prostrate bodies of the shipwrecked. Two framing naked figures to the lower left and right appear to be in the act of sliding off the slippery raft into the menacing sea. The water is agitated and the sky dark; nature is not benign. Géricault depicted an actual event: the frigate *Medusa* had sunk off the coast of West Africa in 1816 leaving the crew enough time to construct a raft, but not enough time to make it large enough for all of them. What followed was a horrifying history of murder and cannibalism. Géricault's painting would firmly link the image of the raft to the terrible devouring sea, also helped by the sublime connotations of the female mythological monster Medusa, attractive as a virgin but terrifying after having been raped by Poseidon, the Lord of the Sea.

If there was anything in which people braving the open seas in small vessels had put their faith it was the existence of a freeboard. This was the case in the real-life open-boat journey of Commander William Bligh, a follower of Captain Cook, whose exploit stunned Europe in 1789. Bligh had been put in a small open launch by the mutinous crew of the *Bounty* in Polynesia and he sailed across the Pacific to safety in Timor without losing a single man at sea. The journey itself was a torturous and spectacular feat of man against nature. The sea was a constant enemy that had to be kept away by bailing the overloaded launch. Bligh's journey became a popular sensational story at the time, and has since been described in countless books and films. Heyerdahl might have even seen Clark Gable in the 1935 film *The Mutiny on the Bounty* in Norway before he left for his first voyage to Polynesia.

Another famous representation of a freeboard saving men from the ocean can be found in Stephen Crane's short story *The Open Boat* from 1898. Crane, a friend of Joseph Conrad, wrote an account based on his experiences as a journalist in the Spanish-American War. He had been shipwrecked in the Caribbean and ended up sharing a lifeboat with three other men. On the vessel the freeboard was the only barrier between them and a sea described as grim, terrible and indifferent. They bail constantly as the seas break into the boat wishing to devour the men, who frenetically try to keep out of its reach. Only when they are close enough to land to swim ashore, does the boat sink. The sea has been cheated of its catch.

Heyerdahl shunned the protection of the freeboard which Bligh and Crane thanked for their lives, a decision he describes as a wager. When the journey starts the crew do not know if the sea with which they have willingly sought close communion will prove to be a 'friend or enemy'.[36] One day at sea is, however, enough to show to them that the sea has accepted them. It did not matter that there was a high sea because the raft gently rolled over the waves. If a wave broke over the raft the lack of freeboard was only a positive, as the water could pour off though the logs. The raft had no hull that had to be bailed.[37] This effectively inverted the image of the raft by claiming that this absence made it more secure than a boat. If a vessel did not displace water it could not sink through leaking. The absence of intrusive action in the sea, displacing it or whipping it with a propeller, also made the sea accept Heyerdahl as though it repaid his trust. Remora and pilot fish attach themselves to the raft as it becomes part of the sea and a 'Center of Fishy Social Life' as one of Heyerdahl's articles has it.[38]

The sea that Heyerdahl braved with his raft was for the most part docile, domestic and benign. The crew soon lose their remaining respect for waves and sharks. Heyerdahl describes both fishing for sharks and riding out storms as almost harmless forms of 'sport'.[39] If Heyerdahl departed on the sea of Géricault and Crane, he was soon sailing on something completely different. First the terror is taken out of the sublime, and then the sublime is almost removed. In the end the sea is beautiful, not only because it is benign and nourishing, but also because it is finite.

Heyerdahl concedes that the sea is virtually 'bottomless', but he nonetheless does all that he can to impose finitude on this environment.[40] When the men of the *Kon-Tiki* peep under the surface of the sea even the 'eternal black night' seemed to carry a 'pleasant light blue' on account of the sun's rays being reflected back to them.[41] The images that Heyerdahl uses to describe the world below the surface contain the sea and lend it a delineated appearance. The raft is a 'moving roof' for the fish enjoying the shade, and the space below the raft becomes its aquatic 'basement', a 'floating aquarium' to be studied and entertained by.[42] This is also exactly how the *Kon-Tiki* rests today in its Oslo mausoleum-like museum; taking the staircase down to the basement from the raft leads the visitor to a mock aquarium that shows the raft from below.

The delineation of the sea made it possible for the men of the *Kon-Tiki* to seek mastery and control over the nature they drifted through. They carry out a wholesale slaughter of sharks, and the remora fish that had lived on the vanquished beasts attach themselves to the logs of the raft, which now becomes their 'new lord and master'.[43] Heyerdahl puts himself highest in the pecking order when he realizes that he can rule over the sea. At one point he even describes how the crew bring 'order' to a chaotic sea full of fighting fish by themselves fishing.[44] The non-intrusive primitive coexistence with nature is soon abandoned as Heyerdahl dons the crown of Poseidon. In 1966, referring to Heyerdahl's fish sections, Edward de Roo advised high-school English teachers that 'this is a splendid time for you and the class to discuss the origin of the species and the survival of the fittest'.[45]

Heyerdahl let the images of the sublime sea and the shipwreck meet in the shape of the raft in order to accentuate what a momentous shift it was to write the sea as benign nature, especially in popular culture. The 1950s saw an explosion of improvised raft journeys around the world in the wake of the *Kon-Tiki*. What had previously been seen as a suicidal way to meet a dangerous ocean was now transformed into a safe method to approach an unthreatening seascape. The flimsy raft in the open seas also became a symbolic representation of humanity under threat, just like Planet Earth on the 'Earthrise' photo taken by astronaut William Anders some twenty years later, in 1968. Heyerdahl himself was fully conscious of this symbolism and wrote an article in the *New York Times* saying that his crew's experience of peaceful cohabitation on a small raft was a 'tale for statesmen' to be inspired by.[46]

Not all of the journeys in the footsteps of Heyerdahl shared his rhetorical verve. In 1952 four youngsters sailed down the Mississippi on a raft as a social-psychological experiment to see if living close to each other made men apter for peaceful coexistence. One of the crew bluntly announced their failure at the end of the journey: 'We find each other repulsive'.[47] The same year other young adventurers sailed a raft made of 75,000 ping-pong balls from Paris to the Mediterranean in order to prove that one did not have to prove anything, thus combining the popular image of the *Kon-Tiki* with the fad of existentialism.[48] There were also more straightforward copycat expeditions, including more than a dozen that performed the same feat in the Pacific as Heyerdahl's.[49]

A serious dent had been put in the image both of the terrifying sea and of the raft as only the last recourse of man in an emergency. But this did not mean that the paradigm shift was complete. The devouring sea still played an important role in postwar novels like those of Vidal, Monsarrat, Wouk and Golding. It also persisted in sensationalist non-fiction stories, like that of the Finnish deserter from the French Foreign Legion, Ensio

Tiika, who jumped ship with a comrade in the Straits of Malacca in order to avoid having to fight in Indochina. The story became an international media event and in 1954 a book with the appropriate title *The Raft of Despair*. In the harrowing story Tiika's comrade dies on their raft, and he gives him to the sharks in order to save himself. The sublime sea had not been completely dispelled, it had only found a strong challenger.

## The Sea in Focus: Carson, Hemingway and Bombard

The works that would help the *Kon-Tiki* in creating a new postwar sea, like Rachel Carson's *The Sea Around Us* (1951), Ernest Hemingway's *The Old Man and the Sea* (1952) and Alain Bombard's *Naufragé volontaire* (1953), all focused on the sea. This might appear self-evident, but the fact is that sea literature of the past was singularly devoted to man's activity in the sea rather than to the sea itself. The most famous writer of the sea, Joseph Conrad, attested as much towards the end of his life when he admitted that 'I have written of the sea very little [...] It has been the scene, but very seldom the aim.'[50] It was 'the unappeasable ocean of human life' that had been Conrad's subject, not the real physical sea.[51] The constricted life on a ship at sea was in most cases only an allegorical reading of humanity, something that should be borne in mind when contemplating Melville's line from *Moby Dick* describing 'the rivers and oceans' as a place in which 'we ourselves see', like Narcissus in his pond.[52] This allegorical function of sea literature did not disappear with Heyerdahl or his followers; what changed was that the sea also became a protagonist in its own right.

This elevated position of the postwar sea was most forcefully depicted in 1951 when Rachel Carson, a 44-year-old marine biologist in the US Fish and Wildlife Service, published her non-fictional *The Sea Around Us*. Carson's book was extraordinary as it depicted a seascape in which almost no land, no ship or boat nor any human being was visible. It was an 'oceanocentric' book in which the planet was described as being made up of vast seas from which islands of land rose only at some point to be swallowed again.[53] The only chapter that is truly about mankind in the book, 'The Encircling Sea', appears last as a discordant and unnecessary appendix. In the bulk of the book the shores recede and the landmasses shrink as the sea rises.[54] There is the *Beagle* of Darwin to be spotted sometimes on the horizon, or the ships of some other naturalist. In the 'eerie, forbidding regions' of the ocean's netherworld the famed oceanographers William Beebe and Otis Barton appear for a brief spell as vulnerable aliens in their bathysphere.[55] For the most part, there is just 'that great mother of life, the sea.'[56] It was not the first time the sea had been called a mother, but *The Sea Around Us* was one of the first coherent narrations in which this was argued both figuratively and materially.

Carson's sea was both the scene and aim, a subject that demanded attention in its own right. Land was a thin crust upon the seas that could easily dissolve again.[57] For man to turn his back on the sea in the urban environment was to live artificially and to deny the importance of the sea from which he came and to which he would return.[58] For Melville and Conrad the sea was a mirror of man, but for Carson the sea was something vastly greater than man himself. Her sea was endowed with a dimension more than the classic surface descriptions of sea literature. And in the mysterious and eternally dark depths of the ocean man could definitely not live, nor find his mirror.[59] Here was only a cold Darwinian primal dusk that moved on mercilessly in violent cycles of eating and being eaten.[60]

That the sea was both omnipresent and Darwinian for Carson meant that it was in some ways unforgiving and sublime. At the same time it was both a mother and a home to man. An organic tie existed between mankind and the sea. This stipulated that the sea should be treated with reverence as it provided solace and redemption to those who ventured out on it.[61] Carson had been thrilled with the *Kon-Tiki* expedition and even asked Heyerdahl to write a small section of *The Sea Around Us*, which he did.[62] For her, Heyerdahl had found a way to live in close proximity to the encircling sea that was endless and sublime, at the same time as it was a finite home and beautiful mother. Even though there are many similarities between Heyerdahl and Carson, it is however important to remember that Heyerdahl wrote of the sea as beautiful, fragile and finite in order to install himself as a classic patriarch over it, which was not the case with Carson. Heyerdahl never called the sea his mother in the *Kon-Tiki*; it was, if anything, his bride.

In 1952, one year after Carson's book, Ernest Hemingway published his novella *The Old Man and the Sea* that was to become another important text of the new sea. The story of the Cuban fisherman Santiago's fight with a marlin was in some ways an inversion of the author's *To Have and Have Not* of 1937. The nominal geography was the same, the Straits of Florida between Havana and the Florida Keys, but the sea was radically different. Santiago celebrates the sublime terror of the Darwinian universe, for he, a poor fisherman, lives in it more completely than Captain Morgan. Furthermore, Santiago also questions the mean biological order with a distinct dose of sentimentality. The terror of the sublime is not empty and hollow for Santiago as it was for Morgan. Santiago is an undoubting Job. And he is helped in this by the fact that the sea he is sailing on is the one of Heyerdahl and Carson. For Santiago the sea is everything; it is that which gives and takes life, and he celebrates it for its omnipotence. Captain Morgan in 1937 loved his 38-foot motorboat; Santiago in 1952 loves the sea. This is spelt out lucidly when Santiago says that those who love the sea know that she is a woman. The young fishermen with their motorboats and advanced equipment have distanced themselves so far from the sea that they have lost this knowledge.[63] The sound of engines makes man remote from the female space of the sea.

Santiago finds it much easier to say the *Hail Marys* than the *Our Fathers*.[64] Both Santiago and the fish come from the womb of the sea. He has to kill the marlin he is pursuing in order to survive, but it saddens him as it amounts to slaying his brother.[65] Captain Morgan would not have mourned a fish as a brother if he had ever managed to catch one, just as little as he mourns Mr Sing whom he does kill and dump into the sea. In comparison with Santiago there is precious little transcendentalism in Hemingway's pre-war *To Have and Have Not*. For Morgan the sea is a *place*: a place to be traversed with cargo, to fish in, to make money out of, to survive in and to stay out of reach of the petty rules and decadence of the *Waste Land*. Santiago, in contrast, is one with the sea. And the blows he receives he can accept not as those given by a mean place, but as those emanating from the force that takes and gives life. This is the mature, and surprisingly transcendental, manifestation of Hemingway's Eucharist, complete with heavy symbolism at the end when Santiago carries his mast like a cross. We may dislike it; 'the imagery of Christ's suffering is melodramatically tacked on to a story where there has been no credible belief in redemption', as David Castronovo put it in *Beyond the Grey Flannel Suit* (2004), but it is still important to note the differences that separate Morgan from Santiago.[66]

It is possible to consider *The Old Man and the Sea* as an important proponent of the new postwar sea. The ocean still retains its sublime qualities, though these are now balanced by a move towards a more beautiful and maternal seascape. Hemingway, like Heyerdahl, was eager to underline that physical rapprochement with the surface is important, and the small skiff of Santiago replaces the powerful motorboat of Morgan for this reason. There was scope for a primordial union with the sea, if it was approached without engines and the trappings of modern civilization. The sea could redeem a technological society gone awry. It is difficult to assess how much of this sea was directly influenced by Heyerdahl and Carson. Hemingway had been working on his novella for quite some time, but it is easy to find the sea of Heyerdahl and Carson in his book of Santiago that in many ways breathed new life into the influential writer's career and won him both a Pulitzer Prize in 1953 and the Nobel Prize for Literature in 1954.[67]

A third important and popular account of the postwar sea was Alain Bombard's bestseller *Naufragé volontaire* from 1953. Bombard was more directly indebted to Heyerdahl than Carson or Hemingway as he sought to use the experiences of the *Kon-Tiki* crew in order to show how shipwrecked men could survive at sea. Bombard, a French medical doctor working at the Oceanographic Museum of Monaco, had the idea that the sea was not an evil, devouring monster, but a space that man could inhabit. For this end Bombard sailed the fifteen-foot rubber dinghy *Hérétique* across first the Mediterranean and then the Atlantic in 1952. He did not have to travel far from shore before he rejoiced over the fullness of life on the sea as opposed to the artificiality of land-life.[68] Then he proceeded to live off the sea, drinking seawater and eating raw fish, events that he somewhat disingenuously celebrated as breaking of taboos even though both Heyerdahl and Hemingway had been writing about the same.

Bombard puts forward a thesis that one can live on and off the sea if one accepts it. If one rejects the sea, the sea will become a devouring monster. Again the prerequisite for accepting the sea, and reaching a communion with it, is to be in physical proximity to it. Bombard has only the tiniest of freeboards on his little dinghy. At the same time Bombard is careful not completely to erase the sublime from this nurturing sea that dominates his world as he drifts across the Atlantic. As in the *Kon-Tiki* and *The Old Man and the Sea* it is the trusty sharks that again have to take the responsibility of embodying the terror of the sea. Fighting with sharks also establishes Bombard as the patriarchal master of his patch of the ocean as it did for Heyerdahl. The moment he starts fighting the sharks Bombard's dinghy is surrounded by small fish seeking protection.[69]

That the sea is the protagonist of Bombard's story is clear when he arrives back in Paris and is greeted by a stormy but welcoming sea of people.[70] A sea both sublime and beautiful is now an allegory of humanity. Bombard approached this sea by trying to establish himself as its master just as Heyerdahl had done, thus creating a sea that was both omnipresent as well as finite. For Carson and Hemingway it was more a question of finding a mystical union with the nurturing sea, but physical proximity was still key to this. The surface world of the sea was where it was benign. Under the surface were the sharks or the endless depths that still contained the terror. The postwar sea would not be freed from this terror until the depths of the seas were approached as nurturing and beautiful places for man.

## Cousteau's Penetration of a Closing Aquatic Frontier

Jacques-Yves Cousteau's book *The Silent World*, published in 1953 and released as a film in 1956, represents one of the most extreme attempts to write a radical new postwar sea. It was Cousteau who finally penetrated the surface to show not a cold and forbidding netherworld but an extension of the domestic sea that Heyerdahl had pioneered. Cousteau did not lack precursors. William Beebe had explored the depths of the ocean in the interwar period in his bathysphere, and Carson had through her prose freed this inhospitable realm from the portholes, tubes and other nuts and bolts of the cumbersome technology that made Beebe's explorations possible. Heyerdahl had also worked towards creating the image of a safe sea by likening it to an aquarium. What Cousteau did was finally to free man from the firmament of land by constructing the technology that made it possible for him to exist underwater.

In 1943, at the height of the war, Cousteau had developed his aqua-lung in the French Vichy Navy. His invention consisted of a harness attached to a cylinder containing a compressed mix of oxygen and different gases. A regulator equalized the pressure of the air supply, and a hose from the regulator led to a mouthpiece, which allowed the diver to breathe. With this equipment man could move completely freely under water without either being trapped in a submersible vessel or bell or having to rely on air being pumped to a clumsy diving suit as before. Cousteau's technology was not the only one of its sort during a war that saw the introduction of manned underwater sabotage activity on a large scale, but what Cousteau did with his new sets of lungs was revolutionary.

Before the war Cousteau sailed the seas as a gunnery officer in the French Navy and was an avid swimmer. But he did not discover what lay under the surface, according to his story, before he first put on a pair of goggles, an event that was nothing short of a revelation.[71] His life changed, and Cousteau began skin-diving in the late 1930s, mostly to hunt fish in the Mediterranean.[72] When the war came the French Navy asked him to develop oxygen diving equipment and in a matter of a few years the first fully functioning prototypes were ready. It was now that Cousteau could start to explore fully what the forbidden and mysterious depths had hidden.[73]

At first Cousteau did not dare enter the depths of the sea without the harpoon he had used closer to the surface when fishing. Soon, however, he is able to leave it behind as the depths prove to be a peaceable realm. The dangers from sharks is vastly overrated, Cousteau states; the terror of the sea is no more.[74] That this is important for Cousteau is evident when an attacking shark does not even make him change his mind. He does grudgingly accept that sharks might be dangerous, but only close to the surface.[75] Significantly, depth gives security; it is the surface that is the dangerous place, as well as the sea closest to land. Full immersion in the benign sea away from both surface and land is the best protection. Jules Verne had developed this theme already, but Cousteau forcefully restated it to illustrate the harmlessness of the postwar sea.[76]

Cousteau and his men became human fish intermingling with the real fish that in the film were anthropomorphized as cuddly and child-like rather than cold-blooded. This domestication of the depths reached such an extent that a portrait of the whole Cousteau family underwater featured in his book. The sea had truly become a safe home, lacking in any terror. Cousteau is constantly stressing this harmlessness in his story of the sea. It does not much matter that one of his men, Maurice Fargues, died as he tried to break the record for the deepest descent with the aqua-lung.[77] In his narration Cousteau does not for a moment stop and reflect on the fact that the sea has devoured one of his men. In the next breath he tells us of when he taught his children how to dive. The sea is not for a moment allowed to be a forbidding place as he stakes everything on becoming the first truly aquatic man since the mythological half-fish half-man Glancus.

Suspended in water the aquatic men surveyed a new world of submerged plains and valleys. The world above the surface does not interest Cousteau at all. In the hugely popular film that Cousteau made together with director Louis Malle, the spectator is invited to replace his eye with that of the camera, and allow him- or herself to be guided mutely by one of Cousteau's aquatic men. The ground unfurls under us as though we were flying above it, but the constant reminders of the buoyancy of water through seeing other divers and fish saves the spectator from vertigo. The muteness and infantile friendliness of the indigenous population, the fish, almost make the depths into a potential colonial mindscape that invites paternal care. The sea is finite and harmonious, a beautiful damsel awaiting its knight. The remaining sublime that had led to mystic unions with nature in Carson and Hemingway, and Darwinian fights against it in Heyerdahl and Bombard, had now dissolved. The sea home of Cousteau was almost a bourgeois creation.

Cousteau predicted in 1953 that man was facing the era of the sea.[78] He had torn down the last obstacles with his technology and his final domestication of the sea. Now it could be the real home of humanity; it was only for the settlers to move in. The writings of Heyerdahl, Carson, Hemingway, Bombard, Cousteau and others had constructed a sea previously unknown. Popular interest in the planet's aquatic expanses was at a peak. The Earth had finally become a water planet. But postwar man did not find his new abode in the sea. The fascination with the new sea fizzled out, and the hopes of Cousteau came to nothing.

By the end of the 1950s the aquatic frontier had closed almost as soon as it had opened. The frontier as such did not, however, disappear; rather, it was moved. Now it was located in outer space.[79] Sea and space as frontier environments shared many properties. Space needed hardy frontiersmen to probe the sublime terror of the apparently inhospitable emptiness and gradually to dismiss its dangers with infantile frolics in weightlessness. It also promised redemption for man as the postwar sea had; man would live in it, feed off it and so on in increasingly fantastic scenarios. This time the USSR was to participate and compete in creating the new global space frontier. Indeed the USSR shocked the world by initially beating the USA in the space race. In 1957 Sputnik, the first satellite, was communist, as was the first manned space journey in 1961 by Yuri Gagarin on the Vostok.

As if to underline that a simple replacement of space for sea had taken place, the galactic frontier inherited the nautical terms of its predecessor. Space travellers became 'astronauts' in the USA, and 'cosmonauts' in the USSR. The inspiration was Jason's sailors on the *Argo*, the Argonauts. The suffix '-naut' came from the Greek word for 'sailor'. And the vessels of the space sailors were appropriately enough named 'space-*ships*'.[80] This inheriting of vocabulary did not bode well. The space frontier did not close as quickly as the sea of the postwar period, but it did not take much more time for it to fail to live up to its promises, despite NASA consuming up to four percent of the national budget of the USA in the mid-1960s.[81] Visions of human beings making their home in outer space, or in the oceans, returned to the fictional surroundings that had spurred them in the first place; they regressed into books and films and other media that could encourage the fantasy without having it punctured by reality.

The demise of both the sea and the space frontier can be attributed to the fact that living in these environments was neither practical nor especially rewarding scientifically or in other terms. They were imaginary frontiers, fantasies that could not survive being realized. There were also other reasons for the closing of the sea frontier in the mid-1950s. The postwar sea was such an attractive idea because it promised to be romantic and sublime at the same time as finite and beautiful. Cousteau's final penetration into a postwar sea had the effect of removing the last danger and thus rendering it harmless and domestic. The frontier was supposed to be a possible space, but it was not to be without perils. If it was, then there was no incitement for a celebration of masculinity in wilderness. When Cousteau suburbanized the sea it was clear that the frontier was doomed.

The real-life frontier of the USA in the Pacific had in any case never been much more than a fantasy. The small Micronesian islands now under US rule would never lend themselves to exploitation; if anything they needed conservation. That other sublime, the atomic bomb, did in any case cast its vast shadow over the entire colonial enterprise. On top of this it was becoming apparent that not only were the seas finite, they were also fragile and already suffering heavily from man's activities connected with them. If the seas were in need of man's help they could no longer hold any promise of being redemptive or providing a transcendental experience. The sea reverted to being a clear mirror for humankind when it became clear that its health depended directly on human actions.

Not surprisingly, it was the writers who had started to take the sublime out of the sea who moved on in the 1960s, except Hemingway who committed suicide in 1961, to construct a new and entirely beautiful ecological sea. This was to become the same sea by the shores of which we live today. This time round it was not Heyerdahl who was the first, but Rachel Carson. In 1962 her book *Silent Spring* was published, a book that in many ways was the first text of the modern environmentalist movement in the West.[82] Rather than focusing on the unfathomable wonders of nature, Carson described the negative effect of man on the environment. Nature was no longer a transcendental nurturing mother that dwarfed man; now nature needed protection from man. The sea was once and for all secularized. It has been argued that science emptied the sea,[83] but it was pollution that was responsible for this. From being imbued with a terrific sublime, nature now became a delicate and finite resource that man was destroying. The only redemption possible for humanity was to conserve the precious nature of the planet.

Heyerdahl underwent a similar development to Carson in the late 1960s when he embarked on new expeditions of experimental archaeology on reed boats across the Atlantic. In the 1969 and 1970 *Ra I* and *Ra II* voyages from the north of Africa to the Caribbean, Heyerdahl and his crew became aware of how heavily polluted the seas were. The proximity to the surface that had in the *Kon-Tiki* voyage ensured such a strong communion with aquatic nature here enabled Heyerdahl to become privy to the threat that human activity posed to the water world. Heyerdahl's old ocean bride was ailing and in desperate need of protection. Through the efforts of Heyerdahl and many others international co-operation started to come into place to deal with the man-made contamination of land and sea. The United Nations Conference on the Human Environment in Stockholm in 1972 brought environmentalism into global politics for the first time. The Earth's nature seemed never again to be able to provide a frontier for man.

Like Heyerdahl, Alain Bombard and Jacques-Yves Cousteau also became internationally famous environmentalists from the 1970s to their deaths. Bombard and Cousteau even joined in the same environmental pressure group in 1974, Groupe Paul-Emile Victor pour la Défense de l'Homme et de son environnement. Bombard served briefly as minister of environment in 1981 under Mitterrand. That year Bombard also became a deputy in the parliament of the European Community, in which he argued for environmental issues until 1994. Cousteau similarly tried to champion environmentalism, work which as early as 1977 had secured him a UN medal. Just as with Heyerdahl and Bombard, Cousteau's interest in environmentalism grew stronger over time. As late as the 1990s the latter was advising the UN and the World Bank on environmental issues. Her premature death from breast cancer in 1964 meant that Carson herself could not participate in the movement she had been so instrumental in creating.

The postwar sea thus represented a brief window in time when the planet's last possible frontier was explored. Heyerdahl's importance in contributing to writing a sea that was both sublime and beautiful cannot be exaggerated. This is also why this mythic mediation was the most accomplished and influential of all the ones in the *Kon-Tiki* event. If the role of Heyerdahl and the *Kon-Tiki* in creating a bridge between the sublime sea of the past and the beautiful one of the present is so important, it is largely because the image of the threatened ecological sea has now so completely coloured the way the seas are viewed. In a period where the oceans seem so small and vulnerable as today and when the world is once again a land planet, Heyerdahl's mediation between the sublime and the beautiful sea is a historic relic, but a more interesting and important one than the mere physical *Kon-Tiki* raft lying in state in an Oslo museum. Global warming and rising sea levels might change this in the future, which could lead to a return of the aquatic frontier.

# Conclusion

The first chapter of this book about the maker of legends Thor Heyerdahl began with an interrupted evening prayer in his Norwegian childhood home. This was the scene that Heyerdahl and his biographers so often used to illustrate how he had from an early age been torn between religion and science. What the scene explains is, however, something more complicated: it is a symbolic representation of how Heyerdahl created a world divided into almost irreconcilable parts that he would have to bring together in his own story. This is how heroes are created, or create themselves, in the Atomic Age as well as in any other era. Heyerdahl became through the *Kon-Tiki* a figure that embodied the mediating function of myth by bridging science and adventure, the exotic and the primitive, and the sublime sea of the past with the beautiful one of the present. That story of evening prayer showed the task ahead, for which the *Kon-Tiki* was the solution.

Thor Heyerdahl lived a long and eventful life after his success with the Pacific raft expedition that enthralled the world after the Second World War. This story of the Norwegian adventurer ends when his public life in many ways began. It does not claim to explain his later career, but through understanding how Heyerdahl propelled himself onto the world's media stage it is possible to grasp how he could remain there for over half a century. The full analysis of all of Heyerdahl's adventures still awaits its author. This book will have to leave Heyerdahl in the early 1950s.

It is a dark November night in Oslo in 1952. Heyerdahl is fussing over his luggage together with his wife Yvonne. He is used to the procedure, having more or less lived out of a suitcase since 1939 when he left for Canada. The destination is familiar as well, the USA. He has been back at least once a year ever since he left to organize his raft expedition in 1946. That time he had travelled with a wild idea; now he has published his scholarly tome *American Indians in the Pacific*, and has been travelling to academic conferences with his controversial thesis – followed by journalists, of course. This time it is not yet another conference that leads him to cross the Atlantic. He is about to depart for his first major expedition since the *Kon-Tiki;* he has done enough stationary science for the moment.

Heyerdahl's final destination was the Galapagos islands of Darwin and Melville, where he stayed for some months trying to gather evidence for people from the American mainland having travelled there in pre-Columbian times, something he claimed would further prove his thesis. Heyerdahl had begun his search for a new great sensation. In 1955 he would leave again, this time to the Rapa Nui he had dreamt of since he was a child. Heyerdahl had hired a ship that departed from Oslo full of scientists whom he had invited to carry out excavations and whose work he had promised not to interfere with. In addition to the scientific reports the expedition gave rise to, Heyerdahl published *Aku-Aku, the Secret of Easter Island* in 1957 in which he furthered his theory of the South American connection through a language infused with romantic and spiritual images. *Aku-Aku* was to become an enormously successful international bestseller, but it did not surpass the *Kon-Tiki*. Heyerdahl would never be able to repeat the first sensation.

When Heyerdahl died in 2002 he had sailed reed boats across the Atlantic (*Ra I* and *Ra II* in 1969 and 1970) and from Iraq to Djibouti (the *Tigris* in 1977–8). He had carried out excavations all over the world, from Peru to the Maldives. His initial fascination with the lost white culture-bearing race had not disappeared, and he made references to it throughout his life, but later he elaborated the theme of the historical interconnectedness of man and tried to shine a more general light on the maritime prowess of ancient people. He continued to argue for literal interpretations of these people's legends and tales, even to the extent of carrying out excavations in Azerbaijan towards the end of his life to link a mysterious people – white-skinned of course – to the Vikings. Heyerdahl claimed that the god Odin of the Norse legends had been a real chieftain from southeast Caucasus. This time Heyerdahl brought upon himself more heated accusations of being a pseudoscientist than ever before. The old battle between the lone genius and academic dogma flared up yet again as Heyerdahl's life approached its end.

Why the academic establishments were so unable to handle Heyerdahl deserves a book on its own. At times he was courted and praised for his work, though rarely for his conclusions. That Heyerdahl used, from the beginning of the 1950s, a large part of his considerable income from book sales to finance independent research was something that earned him a certain goodwill as it showed that he was at least not in it for base private gain. That so many of the archaeologists and anthropologists in the field had themselves been inspired in their choice of career and area of expertise by the charismatic Heyerdahl did not make the situation less complex. The scientists that did criticize Heyerdahl in the media, his own preferred battle ground, often used such heated language that their writings ended up looking like a child's rebellion against the father. Heyerdahl's calm, demure and expert handling of the role of being the lone scientist frequently gave him the upper hand.

With the greater non-academic audience Heyerdahl managed to build a less complicated relationship that moved and developed with the times. He was a citizen of the world who argued that human beings have always been interconnected and that there was a shared responsibility for the planet at the time of the prolonged and divisive Cold War and the environmental awakening. He was both the last great explorer as well as a non-affiliated personality who represented a conscientious engagement with the world. He also wore the badges to prove it; he was an ardent supporter of the United Nations and of the idea of world federalism, as well as being engaged in both the World Wildlife Fund and the Green Cross International. It was as though he came to represent the hope that the wise advocate of international understanding and environmentalism could be combined in the same body as that of the hardy and manly adventurer.

The *Kon-Tiki* was the original story and the foundation myth behind the remarkable human destiny that was Thor Heyerdahl. The *Kon-Tiki* was also his most perfect legend as it truly took root after the initial success that has been described and explained in this book. Not only is Heyerdahl's story of the raft read all over the world to this day, but he and his publishers were so successful in creating a brand that *Kon-Tiki* is now more known as a symbol than as an historic event, especially for younger generations. Almost anything that can be sold has at some point been marketed with the name Kon-Tiki, from chocolate bars to motor homes. In the worldwide tourist industry there are hotels, restaurants, resorts, travel agents and operators, diving clubs, camping sites and cruise ships named with variations on 'Kon-Tiki'. Heyerdahl would have been an astronomically rich man if he had managed to protect his trademark.

The omnipresence of a distilled *Kon-Tiki* working as a byword for the exciting and exotic carries the risk of imposing itself on the historical event of Heyerdahl's media sensation that Bjørn Rørholt, Adam Helms, Olle Nordemar and all the others involved helped to create. This book has hopefully shown just how complicated and particular that origin was. The beginning of the *Kon-Tiki* phenomenon was in many ways much more interesting than the voyage itself. In unpacking *Kon-Tiki* it is also inevitable to reflect on the fact that Heyerdahl made his Kon-Tiki white, and, moreover, the leader of a white culture-bearing race. It is inevitable because it is all there, expressed in no uncertain terms by Heyerdahl himself. One might exonerate Heyerdahl the person for this mistake because of his other contributions. Or one could dismiss the racist discourse by that convenient excuse that he was a child of his time. My choice has been to do neither, and that is because this is a book about the *Kon-Tiki* and its time rather than a verdict on Heyerdahl. The mysterious white race is interesting because it is so inextricably linked through allegory to the voyage itself and to a denigrating way of viewing indigenous achievements that has been widespread, but not monolithic. To take this into account is important, especially when we try to understand the trajectory of a Polynesia largely colonized by foreign powers that have many times tried to destroy the local culture as well as nature. Truly interesting reconstructions of ancient voyages has been taking place under the auspices of the Polynesian Voyaging Society in Hawaii since the 1970s, and one would wish that these attempts to show the greatness of prehistoric Polynesian sailing techniques, and not only those of a great white race, could have received some of the media coverage that the *Kon-Tiki* gained.

Are heroes dictated by some law of our culture? Maybe. But this is no excuse for shying away from understanding what heroes do; how their stories are created; with which political and cultural background they resonate; all the people and structures needed to make one person famous. Thor Heyerdahl did not like the God proclaimed by haughty priests, or the Law declared by scholars in ivory towers. The iconoclast Heyerdahl deserves better than having his *Kon-Tiki* adventure ossify into a stale chapter in a hagiography.

# Notes

Material in the Kon-Tiki Archive at the Kon-Tiki Museum, Oslo, is designated under the abbreviation KTA Oslo. The archive had not been catalogued at the time it was consulted, which is why no more detailed reference is given.

## 1   The Man and the Myth

1   Thor Heyerdahl, *Grønn var jorden på den syvende dag* (Oslo: Gyldendal, 1991), 32. Thor Heyerdahl, *I Adams fotspor, en erindringsreise* (Oslo: J. M. Stenersens Førlag AS, 1998), 32. Arnold Jacoby, *Señor Kon-Tiki: boken om Thor Heyerdahl* (Oslo: J. W. Cappelen, 1965), 18–19. Ragnar Kvam Jr, *Thor Heyerdahl: Mannen og havet* (Oslo: Gyldendal, 2005), 42–3. Christopher Ralling, *The Kon-Tiki Man: An Illustrated Biography of Thor Heyerdahl* (London: BBC Books, 1990), 12–13.
2   Kvam, *Mannen og havet*, 53.
3   Heyerdahl, *I Adams fotspor*, 35.
4   Heyerdahl, *Grønn var jorden*, 32.
5   Claude Lévi-Strauss, 'The Structural Study of Myth', *Journal of American Folklore*, 68/270 (1955), 440–3.
6   Alan Dundes, 'Binary Opposition in Myth: The Propp/Lévi-Strauss Debate in Retrospect', *Western Folklore*, 56/1 (1997), 46–7. William Bascom, 'The Forms of Folklore: Prose Narratives', *Journal of American Folklore*, 78/307 (1965), 4.

7   On Lévi-Strauss see John Oliver Robertson, *American Myth, American Reality* (New York: Hill and Wang, 1980), 21. That Heyerdahl used legend in this way is suggested by Michael Carroll, 'Of Atlantis and Ancient Astronauts: A Structural Study of Two Modern Myths', *Journal of Popular Culture*, 11/3 (1977), 541–50.

8   Jacoby, *Señor Kon-Tiki*, 12. Kvam, *Mannen og havet*, 48–54, 58.

9   Kvam, *Mannen og havet*, 41.

10  Ibid., 41–2.

11  Jacoby, *Señor Kon-Tiki*, 28.

12  Heyerdahl, *I Adams fotspor*, 40. Jacoby, *Señor Kon-Tiki*, 29–31. Ralling, *The Kon-Tiki Man*, 15–16.

13  Renato Rosaldo, 'Imperial Nostalgia', *Representations*, 26 (1989), 117. David Leverenz, 'The Last Real Men in America: From Natty Bumppo to Batman', in Peter F. Murphy (ed.), *Fictions of Masculinity: Crossing Cultures, Crossing Sexualities* (New York and London: University of New York Press, 1994), 33.

14  Theodore Roosevelt, *An Autobiography* (1913; New York: Charles Scribner's Sons, 1946), 14, 19–20.

15  Jacoby, *Señor Kon-Tiki*, 16, 32–3.

16  Ibid., 43.

17  Ibid., 33.

18  Ibid., 35–6.

19  Ibid., 37. Arnold Jacoby, 'Kimen og røttene', in Jacoby (ed.), *Thor Heyerdahl: festskrift til 75-årsdagen* (Larvik: Sjøfartsmuseum, 1989), 19.

20  Jack London, 'Call of the Wild', in London, *The Call of the Wild, White Fang, and Other Stories* (New York and London: Penguin Books, 1981), 110.

21  Jacoby, *Señor Kon-Tiki*, 37.

22  Ibid., 38.

23  Ibid., 42.

24  Heyerdahl, *Grønn var jorden*, 37. Heyerdahl, *I Adams fotspor*, 70–1. Jacoby, *Señor Kon-Tiki*, 42–3. Kvam, *Mannen og havet*, 18–19. Ralling, *The Kon-Tiki Man*, 26–8. Roar Skolmen, *I skyggen av Kon-Tiki* (Gjøvik: N. W. Damm & Søn, 2000), 44.

25  Ralling, *The Kon-Tiki Man*, 26.

26  Kvam, *Mannen og havet*, 146–7.

27  Jacoby, *Señor Kon-Tiki*, 50.

28  Roosevelt, *Autobiography*, 24.

29  Jacoby, *Señor Kon-Tiki*, 49–50.

30  John F. Kasson, *Houdini, Tarzan, and the Perfect Man: The White Body and the Challenge of Modernity in America* (New York: Hill and Wang, 2001), 196.

31  Skolmen, *I skyggen*, 30–41.

32  The spelling of Polynesian names is a difficult question. For spelling of Fatuiva see Nicholas Thomas, *Marquesan Society: Inequality and Political Transformation in Eastern Polynesia* (Oxford: Clarendon Press, 1990), ix. Rather than referring to the Marquesas islands I have, following Greg Dening, used the term Fenua Enata; see Dening's *Beach Crossings: Voyaging Across Times, Cultures and Self* (Philadelphia: University of Pennsylvania Press, 2004). The name 'Polynesia' itself was coined by the Frenchman Charles de Brosse (meaning 'many islands' in Greek), and it has been accepted in the various versions of the indigenous language (in Hawaiian *Polenekia* and in Tahitian *Porinetia*), which is why it is also used in this text; see Ben Finney, *Voyages of Rediscovery* (Berkeley: University of California Press, 1994), 10.

33  Jacoby, *Señor Kon-Tiki*, 33.

34  Kvam, *Mannen og havet*, 33, 131–2.

35  Jacoby, *Señor Kon-Tiki*, 57–60. Heyerdahl, *I Adams fotspor*, 77–8. Kvam, *Mannen og havet*, 36–9.

36  Jacoby, *Señor Kon-Tiki*, 53. Kvam, *Mannen og havet*, 26.

37  Heather Pringle, *The Master Plan – Himmler's Scholars and the Holocaust* (New York: Hyperion, 2006), 146–7. Christopher Hale, *Himmler's Crusade* (London: Bantam, 2003), 103–5.

38  Torgeir Skorgen, *Rasenes oppfinnelse: Rasetenkningens historie* (Oslo: Spartacus, 2002), 223–4.

39  Heyerdahl, *Grønn var jorden*, 87. Thor Heyerdahl, *Fatu-Hiva: Back to Nature* (London: Allen & Unwin, 1974), 78. Kvam, *Mannen og havet*, 137, 194. This had been argued in works like Edward Treager's *The Aryan Maori* of 1885.

40  Jacoby, *Señor Kon-Tiki*, 66.

41  Heyerdahl, *Fatu-Hiva*, 56.

42  Skolmen, *I skyggen*, 53.

43  Thor Heyerdahl, 'Turning Back Time in the South Seas', *National Geographic Magazine*, 79/1 (1941), 135.

44  Skolmen, *I skyggen*, 55.

45  Jacoby, *Señor Kon-Tiki*, 61–84. Skolmen, *I skyggen*, 56–7.

46  Thor Heyerdahl, *På jakt etter paradiset: et år på en sydhavsø* (Oslo: Gyldendal, 1938), 64–5. Heyerdahl, *Fatu-Hiva*, 120.

47 Jacoby, *Señor Kon-Tiki*, 79.

48 Kvam, *Mannen og havet*, 199.

49 Ibid., 188.

50 Jacoby, *Señor Kon-Tiki*, 86.

51 Thor Heyerdahl, *The Kon-Tiki Expedition: By Raft Across the South Seas*, tr. F. H. Lyon (London: George Allen & Unwin, 1950), 15. All subsequent citations from the *Kon-Tiki* book will be from this edition unless otherwise stated.

52 Letters cited in Kvam, *Mannen og havet*, 194, 196–7. This translation is my own, as are all translations in this book unless otherwise stated.

53 Ibid., 194–6.

54 Kjetil Korslund, 'Heyerdahl og Nazi-Tyskland', *Dagbladet*, 28 Nov. 2005. Jon Røyne Kyllingstad, 'Heyerdahl og Günther', *Dagbladet*, 5 Dec. 2005. Torgeir Skorgen, 'Thor Heyerdahl og norsk raseforskning', *Dagbladet*, 26 Nov. 2005.

55 Jon Alfred Mjøen, 'Der Mensch des Nordens', in *Nordland Fibel. Gerausgegeben von der Nordischen Gesellschaft* (Berlin: Wilhelm Limpert Verlag, 1938), 24.

56 Heyerdahl, *Kon-Tiki*, 15.

57 NOK 3000. Thor Heyerdahl, letter to the director of Norsk Telegrambyrå, 29 Dec. 1947, KTA Oslo.

58 This book has been referred to as 'In Search of Paradise' in English, though it was never translated (see for example footnote 1 on page 45 of the 1968 English version of Jacoby's *Señor Kon-Tiki*). *Jakt* literally means 'hunt' in Norwegian, and has a much more aggressive connotation than 'search'; 'pursuit' conveys this linguistic nuance better.

59 Skolmen, *I skyggen*, 60.

60 Kvam, *Mannen og havet*, 205.

61 Ibid., 206.

62 As argued in Skolmen, *I skyggen*, 80.

63 Thelma Silkens, 'Thor Heyerdahl Revisits the Northwest Coast' [online journal] <http://northislandlinks.com/campbell_river/archives/Thelma/9810thelma/thelma.htm> accessed 8 May 2003.

64 Though he does discuss Cook and Voss in his 1952 *American Indians in the Pacific*.

65 Snorre Evensberget, *Thor Heyerdahl: Oppdagaren* (Oslo: J. M. Stenersens Forlag, 1994), 8–9. Jacoby, *Señor Kon-Tiki*, 89–90. Ralling, *The Kon-Tiki Man*, 81–2.

66   Heyerdahl, *I Adams fotspor*, 100. Kvam, *Mannen og havet*, 246.

67   Eva Henderson (vice-consul at the Swedish Consulate in Vancouver), email to the author, 18 May 2004 and 16 Dec. 2009. A Charles B. Stahlschmidt is listed as having been born 1865 in BC in the 1901 Victoria Census hosted at RootsWeb [online resource] <http://www.rootsweb.ancestry.com/~canbc/1901vic_cen/div05/d05p01.htm>. The same document also states that he died in Vancouver in November 1940, which corresponds to date of the death of the C. B. Stahlschmidt listed as Norwegian consul.

68   Heyerdahl, *I Adams fotspor*, 104–5. Kvam, *Mannen og havet*, 262.

69   Kvam, *Mannen og havet*, 267.

70   Jacoby, *Señor Kon-Tiki*, 126.

71   Heyerdahl, *I Adams fotspor*, 111.

72   Kvam, *Mannen og havet*, 269, 276.

73   Ibid., 277.

74   Cited in ibid., 276–8.

75   Anders Johansson, *Den glömda armén. Norge–Sverige 1939–1945* (Rimbo: Fischer & Co., 2005), 39.

76   Ivar Kraglund of the Norwegian Resistance Museum, letter to the author, 4 May 2004. See also T. K. Derry, *A History of Modern Norway 1814–1972* (Oxford: Clarendon Press, 1973), 387.

77   Harshe-Rotman Inc., 'A Brief Biography of Thor Heyerdahl', Newberry Library, Chicago, Rand McNally Archive, Series 3, Box 16, Folder 227.

78   Thor Heyerdahl, 'Epilogue', in *The Kon-Tiki Expedition* (1950; London: Flamingo, 1996), 242.

79   Heyerdahl, *Kon-Tiki*, 21.

80   Kvam, *Mannen og havet*, 334, 336. Harald Sandvik, *Frigjøringen av Finnmark 1944–1945* (Oslo: Gyldendal, 1975), 94–6.

81   Johansson, *Den glömda armén*, 298.

82   Sandvik, *Frigjøringen*, 201.

83   Jacoby, *Señor Kon-Tiki*, 161.

84   Heyerdahl, *I Adams fotspor*, 155.

85   Thor Heyerdahl, letter to Herbert Spinden, 16 Dec. 1945, Brooklyn Museum Archives, Records of the Department of the Arts of Africa, the Pacific & the Americas: Research & Writing. General Corresp [01], 1935–1947.

86   Heyerdahl, *I Adams fotspor*, 155. Jacoby, *Señor Kon-Tiki*, 200.

87   Kvam, *Mannen og havet*, 356.

88  'Et symbol og et forbilde', *NRK* [online journal], (18 April 2002), <http://
    www.nrk.no/nyheter/innenriks/1795525.html> accessed 14 May 2002.
    Heyerdahl, *I Adams fotspor*, 129. Kvam, *Mannen og havet*, 320.
89  Thor Heyerdahl, letter to Thomas Olsen, 27 Nov. 1946, KTA Oslo.
90  Tony Judt, *Postwar: A History of Europe Since 1945* (London: William
    Heinemann, 2005), 85.
91  Yngvar Ustvedt, *Det skjedde i Norge, i: 1945–52: Den varme freden, den
    kalde krigen* (1978; Oslo: Gyldendal, 1981), 125.

## 2   Making the *Kon-Tiki*

1   Rob Kroes, *If You've Seen One, You've Seen the Mall: Europeans and
    American Mass Culture* (Urbana and Chicago: University of Illinois
    Press, 1996), 13. John Coles, *Experimental Archaeology* (London:
    Academic Press, 1974), 25–6, 77–8.
2   Ivar Kraglund, letter to the author, 7 Feb. 2007.
3   Tor Bomann-Larsen, *Roald Amundsen: En Biografi* (Oslo: J. W.
    Cappellens Forlag, 1995), 409.
4   Heyerdahl, *Kon-Tiki*, 22.
5   Jacoby, *Señor Kon-Tiki*, 204.
6   Thor Heyerdahl, letter to Herbert Spinden, 16 Dec. 1945, Brooklyn
    Museum Archives, Records of the Department of the Arts of Africa,
    the Pacific & the Americas: Research & Writing. General Corresp [01],
    1935–1947.
7   Heyerdahl, *I Adams fotspor*, 211.
8   Herbert J. Spinden, letter to the membership committee of the
    Explorers Club, 16 May 1942, Explorers Club New York Archives,
    Membership Files, Heyerdahl.
9   Thor Heyerdahl, letter to Thomas Olsen, 27 Nov. 1946, KTA Oslo.
10  Bjørn Rørholt, letter to Knut Haugland and Torstein Raaby, 23 Jan.
    1947, KTA Oslo.
11  Kvam, *Mannen og havet*, 395.
12  Thor Heyerdahl, letter to Dr Gilbert Grosvenor, 18 Nov. 1946, KTA
    Oslo.
13  J. R. Hildebrand, letter to Thor Heyerdahl, 21 Nov 1946, KTA Oslo.

14  Claim repeated in Jacoby, *Señor Kon-Tiki*, 193. Ragnar Kvam Jr, *Thor Heyerdahl: Mannen og verden* (Oslo: Glydendal, 2008), 17.

15  Heyerdahl, *Kon-Tiki*, 28–30. Heyerdahl does not give a date for this event, but it is possible that it was 26 Nov. 1946; see Thor Heyerdahl, letter to Thomas Olsen, 27 Nov. 1946, KTA Oslo. Haskin was probably Lieutenant Colonel Millard L. Haskin, 22nd Bombardment Group, USAF.

16  Bjørn Rørholt, letter to Thor Heyerdahl, 6 Dec. 1946, KTA Oslo.

17  Oberst Munthe Kaas, letter to Den Kgl. Norske Ambassade, 17 Dec. 1946, KTA Oslo.

18  Memorandum, 'Principal Items to be discussed with the War and Naval Departments', 12 Dec. 1946, KTA Oslo. Thor Heyerdahl, letter to Torstein Raaby, 15 Dec. 1946, KTA Oslo.

19  Colonel Lumsden (Chief of Combined Operations Representative in Washington), letter to the Chief of Combined Operations in London, Dec. 1946, KTA Oslo.

20  'Prospectus of the Kon-Tiki Expedition', 16 Jan. 1947, KTA Oslo. Thor Heyerdahl, letter to Bengt Danielsson, 28 Nov. 1947, KTA Oslo. The latter figure is excluding a debt that was later not claimed.

21  Heyerdahl, *Kon-Tiki*, 37.

22  Colonel Lumsden (Chief of Combined Operations Representative in Washington), letter to the Chief of Combined Operations in London, Dec. 1946, KTA Oslo.

23  Captain T. Harland for Chief of Combined Operations, letter to Chief of Combined Operations Representative in Washington, 7 Jan. 1947, KTA Oslo.

24  Peter Collins, 'The Floating Island', *Cabinet Magazine*, 7 (2002).

25  Heyerdahl, *Kon-Tiki*, 39.

26  Hans Houteman and Jeroen Koppes, 'World War II: Unit Histories & Officers', [website] <http://www.unithistories.com/officers/RM_officersL.html> accessed 17 Sept. 2008.

27  Bjørn Rørholt, letter to Thor Heyerdahl, 6 Dec. 1946, KTA Oslo.

28  Lloyd J. Graybar, 'The 1946 Atomic Bomb Tests: Atomic Diplomacy or Bureaucratic Infighting?', *Journal of American History*, 72/4 (1986), chiefly 905. Lloyd J. Graybar, 'Bikini Revisited', *Military Affairs*, 44/3 (1980), 118–23. David Alan Rosenberg, 'American Atomic Strategy and the Hydrogen Bomb Decision', *Journal of American History*, 66/1 (1979), 62–87.

29 Hadley Cantril and Mildred Strunk, *Public Opinion, 1935–1946* (Princeton, NJ: Princeton University Press, 1951), 24, cited in Lloyd J. Graybar and Ruth Flint Graybar, 'America Faces the Atomic Age: 1946', *Air University Review*, 2 (Jan.–Feb. 1984), [website] <http://www.airpower.maxwell.af.mil/airchronicles/aureview/1984/jan-feb/graybar.html> accessed 28 Sept. 2009.

30 Paul Fussell, *Wartime: Understanding and Behavior in the Second World War* (New York and Oxford: Oxford University Press, 1989), 155.

31 Ibid.

32 Jacoby, *Señor Kon-Tiki*, 209.

33 'War Dept Public Relations Div. Release For A.M. Papers Friday December 27, 1946', 26 Dec. 1946, KTA Oslo.

34 Bjørn Rørholt, letter to Colonel Palmstrøm, 14 Jan. 1947, KTA Oslo.

35 Bjørn Rørholt, letter to Torstein Raaby and Knut Haugland, 14 Jan. 1947, KTA Oslo. For Heyerdahl and Watzinger urging them to arrive in uniform see Herman Watzinger, letter to Knut Haugland, 12 Jan. 1947, KTA Oslo.

36 Gary Kroll, 'Federal Science and the Exploration of the Pacific Ocean: Preparation and Preservations of a New Last Frontier' in 'Exploration in the Mare Incognita: Natural History and Conservation in Early-Twentieth Century America', PhD dissertation, University of Oklahoma, 2000. Gary Kroll, 'The Pacific Science Board in Micronesia: Science, Government, and Conservation of the Postwar Pacific Frontier', *Minerva*, 41 (2003), 25–46. Gary Kroll, *America's Ocean Wilderness* (Lawrence: Kansas University Press, 2008), 154–5. Arrell Morgan Gibson, *Yankees in Paradise: the Pacific Basin Frontier* (Albuquerque: University of New Mexico Press, 1993). Jean Heffer, *Les États-Unis et le Pacifique; Histoire d'une frontière* (Paris: Albin Michel, 1995). Philip E. Steinberg, *The Social Construction of the Sea* (Cambridge: Cambridge University Press, 2001), 121. Charles Olson, *Call Me Ishmael* (New York: Reynal & Hitchcock, 1947), 114, 117.

37 Hal M. Friedman, *Creating an American Lake: United States Imperialism and Strategic Security in the Pacific Basin, 1945–1947* (Westport, CT: Greenwood Press, 2001), 147.

38 Ibid., 5.

39 Press release, 'War Dept Public Relations Div. Release for A.M. Papers Friday December 27, 1946', 26 Dec. 1947, KTA Oslo.

40 Cited in Reinhold Wagnleitner, *Coca-Colonization and the Cold War: the Cultural Mission of the United States in Austria after the Second World War* (Chapel Hill: University of North Carolina Press, 1994), 83.

Stephen Vincent Benét, *America* (New York: Overseas Editions, 1944), 1, see also 80.

41 Bjørn Rørholt and Bjarne W. Thorsen, *Usynlige soldater: Nordmenn i Secret Service forteller* (Oslo: Aschehoug, 1990), 405–7.

42 Minutes, 'Meeting December 5. 1946. between: Eigil Tresselt, Bob Durham, John Whitmore, Thor Heyerdahl, H. Watzinger. Comments to discussion', 14 Dec. 1946, KTA Oslo.

43 Heyerdahl, *Kon-Tiki*, 42.

44 Tom Gjesdal, letter to Thor Heyerdahl, 23 Oct. 1950, KTA Oslo.

45 Mark D. Alleyne, *Global Lies? Propaganda, the UN and World Order* (Houndmills: Palgrave, 2003), 1–2, 12.

46 Thor Heyerdahl, letter to Torstein Raaby, 15 Dec. 1946, KTA Oslo. See also Bjørn Rørholt, letter to Trygve Lie, 22 Jan. 1947, KTA Oslo.

47 Vicecónsul Cristobal Montero, letter to Señor Administrador de Aduanas Guayaquil, 20 Dec. 1946, KTA Oslo.

48 As mentioned in Thor Heyerdahl, letter to Thomas Olsen, 27 Nov. 1946, KTA Oslo.

49 Graham E. L. Holton, 'Heyerdahl's Kon-Tiki Theory and the Denial of the Indigenous Past', *Anthropological Forum*, 14/2 (2004), 177–8.

50 Thor Heyerdahl, letter to Rear Admiral Frederico Diaz Dulanto, 7 Jan. 1947, KTA Oslo.

51 Steinberg, *The Social Construction of the Sea*, 139–40.

52 Written Agreement, 'Expedition Kon-Tiki Kontorordning', 2 Jan. 1947, KTA Oslo. This document is a proposal by Rørholt, but all other documents confirm that everything he requested was granted.

53 Bjørn Rørholt, letter to Colonel Palmstrøm (of the Norwegian Army), 14 Jan. 1947, KTA Oslo. 'Constitution' (of the *Kon-Tiki* Expedition), 7 Jan. 1957, KTA Oslo.

54 Opposition hinted at in Gerd Vold, letter to Generalkonsulent Bahr, 4 Jun. 1947, KTA Oslo.

55 Bomann-Larsen, *Amundsen*, 348–9.

56 Report, 'Rapport for desember 1946' by Oberst Munthe-Kaas, 2 Jan. 1947, KTA Oslo.

57 Gerd Vold, letter to Peter Celliers, 10 May 1947, KTA Oslo. The underlining is Vold's.

58 Oberst Munthe Kaas, letter to Den Kgl. Norske Ambassade, 17 Dec. 1946, KTA Oslo.

59 Thor Heyerdahl, letter to Torstein Raaby, 15 Dec. 1946, KTA Oslo.

60 Invitation list for cocktail party for the *Kon-Tiki* Expedition at the Norwegian Embassy, 4 Oct. 1947, KTA Oslo.

61 Memorandum, telephone conversations between Department of State and Norwegian Embassy on 26 Sept 1947 and 29 Sept. 1947, KTA Oslo.

62 'The President's Calling List', *Washington Post*, 4 Oct. 1947. 'Truman Gets Ensign Flown on Kon-Tiki', *New York Times*, 4 Oct. 1947.

63 Harry S. Truman, letter to Thor Heyerdahl, 16 May 1951, KTA Oslo.

64 Miss Royce Moch, US Department of State, letter to Thor Heyerdahl, 20 Oct. 1947, KTA Oslo. Major Henry E. Jackson, letter to Hans Olav, 10 Nov. 1947, KTA Oslo.

65 Thor Heyerdahl, letter to Thomas Olsen, 27 Nov. 1946, KTA Oslo.

66 Evensberget, *Oppdagaren*, 96. Evensberget, 'Bøker over alle grenser: Begynnelsen på et bok-eventyr', in Arnold Jacoby (ed.), *Thor Heyerdahl*, 52–3.

67 Shawn J. Parry-Giles, *The Rhetorical Presidency, Propaganda, and the Cold War, 1945–1955* (Westport and London: Praeger, 2002), 32.

68 Thor Heyerdahl, letter to Thomas [Olsen], 10 Jan. 1947, KTA Oslo. Kvam, *Mannen og havet*, 385.

69 'Copy of letter containing contract between N.A.N.A. and Th. Heyerdahl', John N. Wheeler, letter to Thor Heyerdahl, 15 Jan. 1957 [accepted 4 Feb. 1947], KTA Oslo.

70 As mentioned in Thor Heyerdahl, letter to the director of Norsk Telegrambyrå, 29 Dec. 1947, KTA Oslo.

71 Heyerdahl, *Kon-Tiki*, 33.

72 Appendix H – Kon-Tiki Prospectus, 'Communications', by Bjørn Rørholt, 19 Feb. 1947, KTA Oslo.

73 Knut Haugland, letter to Brigadier F. W. Nicholls, 21 Feb. 1947, KTA Oslo.

74 Knut Haugland and Torstein Raaby, letter to Bjørn Rørholt, 22 Jan. 1947, KTA Oslo.

75 Torstein Raaby, letter to Herman Watzinger, 21 Feb. 1947, KTA Oslo.

76 Report, 'Rapport for mars 1947' by Oberst Munthe-Kaas, 1 April 1947, KTA Oslo.

77 'The History of K3CR … The Penn State Amateur Club', [website] <http://www.clubs.psu.edu/up/k3cr/history.html> accessed 5 March 2005.

78 Written agreement between Thor Heyerdahl and Bjørn Rørholt, 'Sambandsarrangementet for Ekspedisjonen Kon-Tiki', 7 March 1947, KTA Oslo. Gerd Vold Hurum, *En kvinne ved navn 'Truls': Fra motstandskamp til Kon-Tiki*, ed. Cato Guhnfeldt (Oslo: Wings, 2006), 224.

79 As described in report, 'Rapport for mars 1947' by Oberst Munthe-Kaas, 1 April 1947, KTA Oslo.

80 Knut Haugland, letter to Mr. William Ready (National Company), 18 Nov. 1947, KTA Oslo.

81 Peter Celliers, letter to Gerd Vold, 25 June 1947, KTA Oslo.

82 Susan J. Douglas, *Listening In: Radio and the American Imagination, from Amos 'n' Andy and Edward R. Murrow to Wolfman Jack and Howard Stern* (New York: Random House, 1999), 340.

83 John N. Wheeler, letter to Bjørn Rørholt, 23 Jan. 1947, KTA Oslo.

84 Peter Celliers, telegram to Thor Heyerdahl, 20 June 1947, KTA Oslo.

85 Gerd Vold, letter to Peter Celliers, 24 June 1947, KTA Oslo.

86 Peter Celliers, letter to Gerd Vold, 25 June 1947, KTA Oslo.

87 Ibid.

88 Peter Celliers, letter to Gerd Vold, 17 June 1947, KTA Oslo.

89 Thor Heyerdahl, letter to John N. Wheeler, 24 Oct. 1947, KTA Oslo.

90 John N. Wheeler, letter to Thor Heyerdahl, 7 Oct. 1947, KTA Oslo.

91 Thor Heyerdahl, telegram to Hans Olav, 31 June 1947, KTA Oslo.

### 3   From Raft to Brand

1 'Overenskomst Mellom Deltagerne Paa Kon-Tiki Ekspedisjonen', signed by Heyerdahl and Herman Watzinger, Jan. 1947, KTA Oslo.

2 As evident in Thor Heyerdahl, letter to Ingeborg Barth, 21 May 1949, KTA Oslo.

3 'Prospectus of the Kon-Tiki Expedition', 16 Jan. 1947, KTA Oslo.

4 John N. Wheeler, letter to Thor Heyerdahl, 7 Oct. 1947, KTA Oslo.

5 Report, 'Kon-Tiki Usage check MAY 1, 1947 to JUNE 7, 1947', 19 Jun. 1947, KTA Oslo. Thor Heyerdahl, 'Raft in High Seas Rides Easy and Dry', *New York Times*, 20 May 1947.

6 'Six Men on A Raft', *New York Times*, 12 Aug. 1947.

7 DeWitt Wallace, letter to Thor Heyerdahl, 11 Feb. 1948, KTA Oslo.

8 Thor Heyerdahl, letter to the other five Kon-Tiki expedition members, 25 March 1948, KTA Oslo.

9 Thor Heyerdahl, letter to Knut Haugland, 9 Aug. 1948, KTA Oslo.

10 Evensberget, 'Bøker over alle grenser', in Jacoby (ed.), *Thor Heyerdahl*, 52–3. Thor Heyerdahl, letter to Harald Grieg, 13 Dec. 1946, KTA Oslo.

11  Thor Heyerdahl, letter to Bengt Danielsson, 17 Jun. 1948, KTA Oslo.
12  Harald Grieg, letter to Thor Heyerdahl, 19 Jun. 1948, KTA Oslo. Thor Heyerdahl, letter to Ingrid Moshus, 10 July 1948, KTA Oslo.
13  Sir Stanley Unwin, 'Publishing The "Kon-Tiki"', *W.H. Smith Trade Circular*, 16 Dec. 1950.
14  H. M. Brenner, letter to Thor Heyerdahl, 22 March 1948, KTA Oslo. The article, "Sechs Mann auf einem Floss" appeared in the 15 Jan. 1948 number of the magazine.
15  F. A. Brockhaus, letter to Thor Heyerdahl, 11 Dec. 1947, KTA Oslo.
16  Thor Heyerdahl, letter to F. A. Brockhaus, 22 Aug. 1948, KTA Oslo.
17  Ibid.
18  Thor Heyerdahl, letter to H. M. Brenner, 1 Oct. 1948, KTA Oslo.
19  Hans F. K. Günther, *Mon témoignage sur Adolf Hitler* (Puiseaux: Pardès, 1990), 8.
20  Herbert R. Lottman, 'Norway's Gyldendal: A Question of Patriotism', *Publishers' Weekly*, 12 Aug. 1968.
21  Thor Heyerdahl, letter to Knut Haugland, 18 Nov. 1948, KTA Oslo.
22  Bomann-Larsen, *Amundsen*, 434.
23  Thor Heyerdahl, letter to Knut Haugland, 18 Nov. 1948, KTA Oslo.
24  Peter Quennell, 'Kon-Tiki Book Review', *Daily Mail*, 8 April 1950.
25  Thor Heyerdahl, letter to the other five Kon-Tiki expedition members, 26 April 1949, KTA Oslo.
26  Finn Carling, 'En Varmhjetet Klovn?', in Nils Kare Jacobsen (ed.), *Erindringer om en forlegger: forfattare om Harald Grieg* (Oslo: Gyldendal, 1994), 38–9.
27  Thor Heyerdahl, letter to Oscar Bahr, 18 Nov. 1948, KTA Oslo.
28  Erling Christie, '"Kon-Tiki" som tiasdokument', *Verdens Gang*, 27 Oct. 1951.
29  'What is a bestseller?' *John O'London's Weekly*, 29 Feb. 1952.
30  Adam Helms, letter to Harald Grieg, 22 Jan. 1949, KTA Oslo.
31  Adam Helms, *En förläggare fattar pennan* (Stockholm: Forum, 1969), 57–8.
32  Adam Helms, letter to Harald Grieg, 22 Jan. 1949, KTA Oslo.
33  Harald Grieg, letter to Thor Heyerdahl, 26 Jan. 1949, KTA Oslo.
34  Thor Heyerdahl, letter to Knut Haugland, 9 Aug. 1948, KTA Oslo. Thor Heyerdahl, letter to Harald Grieg, 28 Jan. 1949, KTA Oslo.
35  Thor Heyerdahl, letter to Knut Haugland, 18 Nov. 1948, KTA Oslo.
36  Helms, *En förläggare*, 57–8.

37  Per I. Gedin, 'Adam Helms – ett liv för boken', in Märta Bergstrand et al. (eds), *Stockholms universitetsbibliotek 25 år* (Stockholm: Universitetsbiblioteket, 2002), 54–5. Gunder Andersson, 'Unik boksamling tillgänglig', *Kulturrådet*, 6 (1995), 16–18.

38  Eduoard Théodore-Aubanel, *Comment on lance un nouveau Livre* (Paris: L'Intercontinentale d'édition, 1937), 9–13, 17–18. See also Donald Sassoon, *The Culture of the Europeans: From 1800 to the Present* (London: HarperCollins, 2006), 1025.

39  The collection was opened in 1993. Gedin, 'Adam Helms', 56. Andersson, 'Unik boksamling', 20.

40  Adams Helms, *Kollektiv reklam: föredrag vid 'Vadstenamötet' Svenska Bokhandlarföreningens studiedagar den 22–25 maj 1952* (Stockholm: Forum, 1952), 17.

41  Al and Laura Ries, *The 22 Immutable Laws of Branding* (1998; London: HarperCollins, 2000), 25–37.

42  Adam Helms, letter to Messrs Allen & Unwin, 28 Sept. 1949, KTA Oslo.

43  Adam Helms, postcard to the Swedish booksellers, 10 Aug. 1950, KTA Oslo.

44  Helms, *En förläggare*, 75.

45  'Kon-Tiki-Utställning', *Svenska Dagbaldet*, 12 Aug. 1949. 'Kon-Tikiflotte på PUB-expo', *Morgon-Tidningen*, 12 Aug. 1949.

46  'Kon-Tiki at PUB – a marvellous adventure in modern time', *Svenska Dagbladet*, 12 Aug. 1949.

47  Adam Helms, letter to Thor Heyerdahl, 8 Aug. 1949, KTA Oslo.

48  John M. Murphy, 'What is Branding?', in Murphy (ed.), *Branding: A Key Marketing Tool* (1987; Houndmills: Macmillan, 1992), 3.

49  Jacoby, *Señor Kon-Tiki*, 238.

50  'Mason Interviews Rand McNally Editor-In-Chief', Jane Mason (WGN Chicago, 24 August 1951) [radio interview].

51  Jane McGuigan, letter to Thor Heyerdahl, 10 Mar. 1948, KTA Oslo.

52  Thor Heyerdahl, letter to Marion Dittman, 10 Sept. 1948, KTA Oslo.

53  Marion Dittman, letter to Thor Heyerdahl, 16 Sept. 1948, KTA Oslo.

54  Thor Heyerdahl, letter to the other five Kon-Tiki expedition members, 26 April 1949, KTA Oslo.

55  Cited in Arthur T. Vanderbilt II, *The Making of a Bestseller: From Author to Reader* (Jefferson, NC: McFarland, 1999), 57.

56  Thor Heyerdahl, letter to Ingeborg Barth, 21 May 1949, KTA Oslo.

57  Thor Heyerdahl, letter to the other five *Kon-Tiki* expedition members, 26 April 1949, KTA Oslo.

58  Ibid.

59  'Mason Interviews Rand McNally Editor-In-Chief', Jane Mason
    (WGN Chicago, 24 August 1951) [radio interview].

60  B. B. Harvey, letter to Sir Stanley Unwin, 21 Sept. 1951, Reading
    University Library Archive, Allen and Unwin Collection, AUC 511–13.

61  Heyerdahl, *I Adams fotspor*, 174.

62  Kvam, *Mannen og verden*, 42.

63  Philip Unwin, letter to Thor Heyerdahl, 26 April 1949, Reading
    University Library Archive, Allen and Unwin Collection, AUC 405–14.

64  F. H. Lyon, reader's report on 'The Kon-Tiki Expedition by Thor
    Heyerdahl', Reading University Library Archive, Allen and Unwin
    Collection, AURR 16/3/43. Geoffrey Malcolm Gathorne-Hardy, 'Report
    on KON-TIKI EKSPEDISJONEN by Thor Heyerdahl From G. M.
    Gathorne-Hardy', Reading University Library Archive, Allen and
    Unwin Collection, AURR 16/1/08.

65  Philip Unwin, '*Kon-Tiki* in Colour', *The Bookseller*, 31 July 1965.

66  Sir Stanley Unwin, 'Publishing The "Kon-Tiki"', *W. H. Smith Trade
    Circular*, 16 Dec. 1950.

67  Adam Helms, *En förläggare*, 72.

68  Cited in Adrian Room, 'History of Branding', in Murphy (ed.),
    *Branding*, 16–17.

69  Ibid., and Adrian Room, *Dictionary of Trade Name Origins* (London:
    Routledge, 1984), 195–6.

70  Kevin Lane Keller, 'Branding and Brand Equity', in Barton Weitz and
    Robin Wensley (eds), *Handbook of Marketing* (London: Sage, 2002), 157.

71  Philip Unwin, letter to Thor Heyerdahl, 20 June 1949, Reading
    University Library Archive, Allen and Unwin Collection, AUC 405–14.

72  Thor Heyerdahl, letter to Philip Unwin, 28 May 1949, Reading
    University Library Archive, Allen and Unwin Collection, AUC 405–14.

73  Philip Unwin, letter to Thor Heyerdahl, 20 June 1949, Reading
    University Library Archive, Allen and Unwin Collection, AUC
    405–14. Thor Heyerdahl, letter to Philip Unwin, 28 June 1949, Reading
    University Library Archive, Allen and Unwin Collection, AUC 405–14.

74  Adam Helms, letter to Messrs Allen & Unwin, 28 Sept. 1949, KTA Oslo.

75  Adam Helms, letter to Thor Heyerdahl, 16 Aug. 1950, KTA Oslo.

76  Adam Helms, letter to Messrs Allen & Unwin, 28 Sept. 1949, KTA Oslo.

77  Allen & Unwin, letter to Adam Helms, 4 Oct. 1949, KTA Oslo.

78  Sir Stanley Unwin, 'Publishing The "Kon-Tiki"', *W. H. Smith Trade
    Circular*, 16 Dec. 1950. 'How *Kon Tiki* became a best seller', *The*

*Bookseller*, 3 June 1950. Philip Unwin, 'Kon-Tiki in Colour', *The Bookseller*, 31 July 1965.

79   Sir Stanley Unwin, 'Publishing The "Kon-Tiki"', *W. H. Smith Trade Circular*, 16 Dec. 1950.

80   'Heyerdahl's Kon-Tiki Expedition: 200,000 sold in 9 Months', *The Publishers' Circular and Booksellers' Record*, 16 Dec. 1950.

81   'Rekord men "Kon-Tiki"', *Ringsaker Blad*, 24 Feb 1951.

82   'Reassembly Of Parliament Anxious Weeks For Government, Finance Bill Hazards', *The Times*, 12 June 1950.

83   Carl Werner (Imperial War Museum), email to the author, 10 Oct. 2005.

84   Thor Heyerdahl, letter to Marion Dittman, 26 Oct. 1949, KTA Oslo.

85   Thor Heyerdahl, letter to Bennet B. Harvey, 23 Oct. 1950, KTA Oslo.

86   Thor Heyerdahl, letter to Marion Dittman, 26 Oct. 1949, KTA Oslo.

87   In the budget over $10,000 class, see 'Best Ad Campaigns of 1950 receive Pw-Adclub Awards', *Publishers' Weekly*, 19 May 1951.

88   Bennet B. Harvey, letter to Thor Heyerdahl, 1 May 1950, KTA Oslo. See also Frederic Babcock, 'Among the Authors', *Chicago Daily Tribune*, 30 July 1950.

89   Bennet B. Harvey, letter to Thor Heyerdahl, 1 May 1950, KTA Oslo.

90   'A Secret Longing', *Time Magazine*, 26 March 1951.

91   Bennet B. Harvey, letter to Thor Heyerdahl, 11 Oct. 1950, KTA Oslo.

92   A figure to be found in Gorham Munson, 'Adventure Writing in Our Time', *College English*, 16/3 (1954), 153.

93   Vanderbilt, *The Making of a Bestseller*, 57.

94   Alice Payne Hackett, *80 Years of Best Sellers: 1895–1975* (New York and London: R. R. Bowker Company, 1976), 153.

95   Hemingway's book was released on 7 Sept., two days after the *Kon-Tiki*, by Charles Scribner and sold around 140,000 copies in 1949 during the same time it took for Heyerdahl to sell almost 130,000 copies. Hackett, *80 Years*, 153.

96   Evon Z. Vogt, 'Anthropology in the Public Consciousness', in *Yearbook of Anthropology* (Chicago: University of Chicago Press, 1955), 361.

97   Vanderbilt, *The Making of a Bestseller*, 139–40.

98   Thor Heyerdahl, letter to Marion Dittman, 5 Sept. 1950, KTA Oslo.

99   Ries, *Immutable Laws of Branding*, 39.

100  Thor Heyerdahl, letter to Håkan Nörholm, 24 Oct. 1950, KTA Oslo.

101  Evensberget, *Oppdagaren*, p. 97.

102  Thor Heyerdahl, letter to Esther M. Dimchevsky, 1 June 1955, KTA Oslo.

## 4 The Seamless Craft of Writing Legend

1 'Guilty as Charged', *Time Magazine*, 4 June 1951.
2 Mary B. Campbell, *The Witness and the Other World: Exotic European Travel Writing, 400–1600* (Ithaca, NY: Cornell University Press, 1998), 1–2.
3 Tzvetan Todorov, 'Structural Analysis of Narrative', *Novel*, 3/1 (1969), 75. Tzvetan Todorov, 'Les voyages et son récit', in Todorov, *The Morals of History* (Paris: Grasset et Fasquelle, 1991), 95–108.
4 Michael Kowalewski (ed.), *Temperamental Journeys: Essays on the Modern Literature of Travel* (Athens: University of Georgia Press, 1992), 7. Jean-Xavier Ridon, *Le voyage en son miroir: essai sur quelques tentatives de réinvention du voyage au 20e siècle* (Paris: Éditions Kimé, 2002), 19.
5 Germaine Brée, 'The Ambiguous Voyage: Mode or Genre', *Genre*, 1 (1968), 88.
6 For various interpretations of 'passage' see Michael Harbsmeier, 'Spontaneous Ethnographies: Towards A Social History of Traveller's Tales', *Studies in Travel Writing*, 1 (1997), 216–38; Eric Leed, *The Mind of the Traveler: From Gilgamesh to Global Tourism* (New York: Basic Books, 1991), 25–101; Anthony Pagden, *European Encounters with the New World: From Renaissance to Romanticism* (New Haven, CT: Yale University Press, 1993), 3.
7 Casey Blanton, *Travel Writing: The Self and the World* (New York: Routledge, 2002), 2.
8 Leed, *The Mind of the Traveler*, 54–6.
9 Heyerdahl, *Kon-Tiki*, 80.
10 Ibid., 186.
11 Ibid., 97.
12 Ibid., 133.
13 Ibid., 91.
14 Ibid., 101.
15 Thor Heyerdahl, letter to Marion Dittman, 26 Oct. 1949, KTA Oslo.
16 Heyerdahl, *Kon-Tiki*, 229.
17 Claude Lévi-Strauss, 'The Structural Study of Myth', 430. See also: Claude Lévi-Strauss, *The Naked Man: Introduction to a Science of Mythology IV* (1971; London: Jonathan Cape, 1981), 644.
18 Erich Auerbach, *Mimesis: The Representation of Reality in Western Literature* (1946; Princeton, NJ: Princeton University Press, 2003), 19.

19  Ibid., 17. G. Robert Carlsen, 'To Sail Beyond the Sunset', *The English Journal*, 42/6 (1953), 300.

20  Tzvetan Todorov, *Genres in Discourse* (Cambridge: Cambridge University Press, 1990), 31.

21  Heyerdahl, *Kon-Tiki*, 69. Heyerdahl does not mention what film they saw, but it was most probably *Rainbow Island* (directed by Ralph Murphy) from 1944 in which Lamour played the role of a white girl raised as a native on a tropical island.

22  Heyerdahl, *Kon-Tiki*, 11.

23  John Emerson and Anita Loos, *How to Write Photoplays* (Philadelphia: George W. Jacobs & Co., 1920), 95. Cited in David Bordwell, 'Chapter 3. Classic Narration', in Bordwell et al. (eds), *The Classical Hollywood Cinema: Film Style & Mode of Production to 1960* (1985; London: Routledge, 1988), 28, 37.

24  Ibid., 28.

25  Heyerdahl, *Kon-Tiki*, 12.

26  Bordwell, 'Chapter 3. Classic narration', in Bordwell, *op. cit.*, 28, 32–3, 37.

27  Bordwell, 'Chapter 1. An excessively obvious cinema', in Bordwell, *op. cit.*, 3.

28  Bordwell, 'Chapter 2. Story causality and motivation', in Bordwell, *op. cit.*, 16.

29  Frances Marion, 'Scenario writing', in Stephen Watts (ed.), *Behind the Screen: How Films Are Made* (New York: Dodge, 1938), 33. Cited in ibid., 19. This process is evident in the beginning of the *Kon-Tiki* book when the encounters, trials, and success of Heyerdahl simply befall him, being a consequence of purely his actions alone.

30  Heyerdahl, *Kon-Tiki*, 152.

31  Ibid., 133–4.

32  Ibid., 15.

33  Ibid., 20, 134. Heyerdahl claims that the battle with Cari took place on an island in Lake Titicaca, but refers to Tiwanaku as 'Kon-Tiki's ruined city'. Tiwanaku is situated close to Titicaca. Heyerdahl's inspiration here is Pedro Cieza de León's *La Crónica del Perú* (1550).

34  Ibid., 17–21.

35  Ibid., 18.

36  Skolmen, *I skyggen*, 20.

37  Heyerdahl, *I Adams fotspor*, 192. Bennett simply refers to the statue, which he himself excavated, as the 'Small bearded statue'; see Wendell

Clark Bennett, 'Excavations at Tiahuanaco', *Anthropological Papers of the American Museum of Natural History*, 34 (1934), 441.

38 Pringle, *The Master Plan*, 180–3, 195. Hale, *Himmler's Crusade*, 120. Michael H. Kater, *Das 'Ahnenerbe' der SS 1935–1945* (Stuttgart: Deutsche Verlags-Anstalt, 1974), 97. Kiss, in contrast to Heyerdahl, was an adherent of Hans Hörbriger's Welteislehre, and argued that the blond race had lived in Tiahuanaco/Tiwanaku much earlier than Heyerdahl would.

39 Heyerdahl, *Kon-Tiki*, 19.

40 Ibid.

41 Adolph F. Bandelier, 'Traditions of Precolumbian Landings on the Western Coast of South America', *American Anthropologist*, 7/2 (1905), 251–2.

42 See book 6, ch. 7. Arthur de Gobineau, *Essai sur l'inégalité des races humaines*, ii (Paris: Firmin Didiot, 1855), 492–525.

43 Heyerdahl, *Kon-Tiki*, 56.

44 Ibid., 19, 133–4.

45 Ibid., 20–1.

46 Ibid., 45.

47 Ibid., 49–50.

48 Ibid., 18.

49 Ibid., 64.

50 Ibid., 214.

51 Ibid., 221–2.

52 Ibid., 12, 98.

53 Although the English translator, F. H. Lyon, refers to the parrot as 'he' or 'it', its gender and name are made plain in the *Kon-Tiki* film.

54 Heyerdahl, *Kon-Tiki*, 147.

55 Ibid., 15.

56 Ibid., 63.

57 Ibid., 216.

58 Ibid., 182.

59 Marianna Torgovnick, *Gone Primitive: Savage Intellects, Modern Lives* (Chicago and London: University of Chicago Press, 1990), 17.

60 Ibid.

61 J. M. Blaut, *The Colonizer's Model of the World: Geographical Diffusionism and Eurocentric History* (New York: The Guilford Press, 1993), 17.

62 Ibid.

63  K. R. Howe, 'Maori/Polynesian Origins and the "New Learning"', *Journal of Polynesian Society* 108/3 (1999), 308–9. See also Holton, 'Heyerdahl's Kon-Tiki Theory', 164.

64  W. J. Perry, *The Children of the Sun: A Study in the Early History of Civilization* (London: Methuen & Co., 1923), 141. G. Elliot Smith, *In The Beginning: The Origin of Civilization* (1932; London: Watts & Co., 1937), 96.

65  See for example Hans Günther, *Rassenkunde Europas* (Munich: J. S. Lehmans Verlag, 1929), 76.

66  Howe, 'Maori/Polynesian Origins', 310.

67  Arturo Escobar, *Encountering Development. The Making and Unmaking of the Third World* (Princeton, NJ: Princeton University Press, 1995), 23–4.

68  Ibid., 8, 26, 39.

69  Holton, 'Heyerdahl's Kon-Tiki Theory', 163.

70  Ibid., 175.

71  Edward Norbeck, 'Book Review: American Indians in the Pacific: The Theory Behind the Kon-Tiki Expedition', *American Antiquity*, 19/1 (1953), 93. For discussions of this review see Robert Wauchope, *Lost Tribes & Sunken Continents: Myth and Method in the Study of American Indians* (Chicago & London: University of Chicago Press, 1962), 120. The existence of a trace of racism in Heyerdahl's thesis was also pointed out in 1958; see Marian W. Smith, 'Book Review: Aku-Aku: The Secret of the Easter Island', *Geographical Journal*, 124/3 (1958), 385–6.

72  Sir Stanley Unwin, 'Publishing The "Kon-Tiki"', *W. H. Smith Trade Circular*, 16 Dec. 1950, 35–6.

73  David Thomson, '"The Kon Tiki Expedition" A Dramatisation of the Book by Thor Heyerdahl', Reading University Library Archive, Allen and Unwin Collection, AUC 403–15.

## 5    To Review a Classic

1  'Three Years to Make a Legend', *The Times*, 9 April 1953.

2  Judt, *Postwar*, 89.

3  Bernt Bernholm, 'Forskning per flotte', *Expressen*, 19 Aug. 1949.

4  Bk., 'Kon-Tiki-äventyret', *Arbetet*, 5 Oct. 1949.

5    Bernt Bernholm, 'Forskning per flotte', *Expressen*, 19 Aug. 1949. Gunnar Frösell, 'KON TIKI – det livslevande äventyret', *Aftonbladet*, 21 Aug. 1949.

6    S. Barrington Gates, 'Six Men on a Raft', *The Times Literary Supplement*, 7 April 1950.

7    H. M. Tomlinson, 'Down Among the Flying Fish', *John O'London's Weekly*, 20 April 1950. Sir John Squire, 'Escape From the Twentieth Century – By raft', *Illustrated London News*, 29 April 1950. Howard Spring, 'New Books: By Raft Across the Pacific', *Country Life*, 14 April 1950.

8    S. Barrington Gates, 'Six Men on a Raft', *The Times Literary Supplement*, 7 April 1950. Peter Quennell, 'The Kon-Tiki Expedition: Daily Mail Book of the Month of April', *Daily Mail*, 8 April 1950.

9    Arthur Ransome, 'Reviews of the Week: Stone-Age Voyage', *Spectator*, 31 March 1950.

10   Van Allen Bradley '"Kon-Tiki" Sea Exploit Outdoes "Moby Dick" In Sheer Excitement', *Chicago Daily News*, 6 Sept. 1950.

11   Joseph Henry Jackson, 'A Perilous Trip on a Balsa Raft in Support of a Theory', *San Francisco Chronicle*, 3 Sept. 1950.

12   'Stone Age Voyage', *The Atlantic*, 186/4 (1950).

13   Carl Skottsberg, 'Polynesisk historia', *Göteborgs Handels- och Sjöfartstidning*, 26 Nov. 1949.

14   Stig Rydén, 'Kon-Tiki, Tihuanacukulturen och Heyerdahl', *Göteborgs Handels- och Sjöfartstidning*, 24 Dec. 1949.

15   Thor Heyerdahl, letter to Adam Helms, 17 July 1951, KTA Oslo.

16   Carl Skottsberg, 'Polynesisk historia', *Göteborgs Handels- och Sjöfartstidning*, 26 Nov. 1949.

17   '"That Kon Tiki Raft Business" Makes Sir Peter Buck Laugh', *The Auckland Star*, 7 Feb. 1949.

18   Richard Hughes, 'The Kon-Tiki Expedition', *Observer*, 2 April 1950.

19   Harry Gilroy, 'Six Who Dared To Live a Legend: An Incredible Saga of Men and Sharks, Big Seas and Life on a Primitive Raft', *New York Times*, 3 Sept. 1950.

20   Peter Quennell, 'The Kon-Tiki Expedition', *Daily Mail*, 8 April 1950.

21   Sir John Squire, 'Escape From the Twentieth Century – By raft', *Illustrated London News*, 29 April 1950.

22   'Etnologiskt sjöäventyr', *Morgon-Tidningen*, 24 Aug. 1949.

23   B+C, 'Litteratur: Expedition Kon-Tiki "alla tiders bok"', *Sundsvalls Tidning*, 23 Oct. 1949.

24  Frederick Laws, 'Thor Had a Theory', *News Chronicle*, 3 April 1950.

25  Bk., 'Kon-Tiki-äventyret', *Arbetet,* 5 Oct. 1949.

26  Sterling North, 'Book News and Reviews', *Buffalo Courier-Express*, 17 Sept. 1950.

27  Lunkan, 'Sex man på en flotte', *Totem*, 8 Nov. 1949.

28  Robert H. Prall, 'Hero of Pacific Crossing By Raft Is New "Columbus"', *Herald Post*, 10 May 1951.

29  'Cruise of the Kon-Tiki: Modern Vikings Sail 101 Days Across the Open Pacific', *Life Magazine*, 22 Oct. 1947.

30  Joel Fine, 'Raft Odyssey "Proves" Peru to Pacific Theory of Migration', *Oakland Tribune*, 24 Sept. 1950.

31  'By Raft Across the Pacific', *The Times*, 25 Feb. 1950.

32  Van Allen Bradley, '"Kon-Tiki" Sea Exploit Outdoes "Moby Dick" in Sheer Excitement', *Chicago Daily News*, 6 Sept. 1950.

33  Alice Dixon Bond, 'The Case for Books: "Kon Tiki" Story of Dream Turned Into Thrilling, Modern Odyssey', *Boston Sunday Herald*, 17 Sept. 1950.

34  Lewis Gannett, 'Books and Things', *Herald Tribune*, 5 Sept. 1950.

35  Harry Gilroy, 'Six Who Dared To Live a Legend', *New York Times*, 3 Sept. 1950.

36  'En fantastisk sjöfararbragd', *Helsingborgsposten*, 21 Sept. 1949.

37  Raymond Mortimer, 'A Glorious Feat', *Sunday Times*, 2 April 1950.

38  Peter Quennell, 'The Kon-Tiki Expedition', *Daily Mail*, 8 April 1950.

39  James A. Michener, '4,100 Miles on a Raft', *Saturday Review of Literature*, 23 Sept. 1950.

40  'Kon-Tiki', *Newsweek*, 9 Oct. 1950.

41  Harry Gilroy, 'Six Who Dared To Live a Legend', *New York Times*, 3 Sept. 1950.

42  'Stone Age Voyage', *The Atlantic*, 186/4 (1950).

43  Alfred Stanford, 'They Floated Across the Pacific on a Vine-Tied Raft', *New York Herald Tribune*, 3 Sept. 1950.

44  Harry Gilroy, 'Six Who Dared To Live a Legend', *New York Times*, 3 Sept. 1950. Julian Symons, 'Life, People and Books … By raft across the Pacific', *Manchester Evening News*, 6 April 1950.

45  Alfred Stanford, 'They Floated Across the Pacific on a Vine-Tied Raft', *New York Herald Tribune*, 3 Sept. 1950.

46  Bill Robinson, 'Amazing Adventure', *Newark News*, 17 Sept. 1950.

47  Edward Shanks, 'They Went to Sea on a Raft', *Daily Graphic*, 5 April 1950.

48 Sean Fielding, 'Hope for Humans', *Tatler*, 12 April 1950. 'Blam' means 'sound of a shot, explosion, etc.' (Webster's *New World College Dictionary*).

49 'Rekord men "Kon-Tiki"', *Ringsaker Blad*, 24 Feb. 1951.

50 Raymond Mortimer, 'A Glorious Feat', *Sunday Times*, 2 April 1950.

51 Michael Korda, *Making the List: A Cultural History of the American Bestseller 1900–1999* (New York: Barnes & Noble Books, 2001), 86–7.

52 Harrison Smith, 'A Great Narrative of the Sea: Six on a Raft Against Pacific', *Washington Post*, 8 Sept. 1950.

53 Peter Quennell, 'The Kon-Tiki Expedition', *Daily Mail*, 8 April 1950.

54 H. M. Tomlinson, 'Down Among the Flying Fish', *John O'London's Weekly*, 20 April 1950.

55 Heyerdahl, *Kon-Tiki*, 78.

56 Georges Carousso, '101 Days on a Raft: Kon-Tiki by Thor Heyerdahl', *Brooklyn Eagle Sun*, 19 Nov. 1950.

57 Original emphasis. Arthur de Gobineau, *The Moral and Intellectual Diversity of Races*, trans. H. Hotz (Philadelphia, J. B. Lippincott & Co, 1856), translator's note 1, 457–8.

58 Frederick Laws, 'Thor Had a Theory', *News Chronicle*, 3 April 1950. Sir John Squire, 'Escape From the Twentieth Century – By raft', *Illustrated London News*, 29 April 1950.

## 6   The *Kon-Tiki* Film and the Return to Realism

1 Memorandum, 'Principal Items to be discussed with the War and Naval Departments', 12 Dec. 1946, KTA Oslo.

2 Thor Heyerdahl, letter to Philip Unwin, 4 Jan. 1950, KTA Oslo.

3 Knut Haugland and Svein Sæter, *Operatøren* (Oslo: Cappelen, 2008), 228.

4 Thor Heyerdahl, letter to Bengt Danielsson, 15 Oct. 1947, KTA Oslo. Thor Heyerdahl, letter to Olle Nordemar, 8 Nov. 1950, KTA Oslo.

5 Ibid., and Olle Nordemar, letter to Thor Heyerdahl, 4 Nov. 1950, KTA Oslo. It is unclear whether it was Paramount or RKO that made this offer.

6    Gunnar Iversen, 'Chapter 5. Norway', in Iversen, Tytti Soila and Astrid Söderbergh Widding (eds), *Nordic National Cinemas* (London: Routledge, 1998), 122–3.

7    Iversen, 123. Richard M. Barsam, *Nonfictional Film: A Critical History* (1973; Bloomington and Indianapolis: Indiana University Press, 1992), 213–14.

8    Thor Heyerdahl, letter to the other five Kon-Tiki expedition members, 25 March 1948, KTA Oslo.

9    Salve Staubo, letter to Thor Heyerdahl, 1 April 1948, KTA Oslo.

10   Herman Watzinger, letter to Thor Heyerdahl, 9 April 1948, KTA Oslo.

11   Bengt Danielsson, letter to Thor Heyerdahl, 4 July 1948, KTA Oslo.

12   As hinted in Salve Staubo, letter to Titus Vibe Müller, 4 May 1948, KTA Oslo. Salve Staubo, letter to Thor Heyerdahl, 24 May 1948, KTA Oslo.

13   Per Lönndahl and Olle Nordemar, 'Olle Nordemar Berättar Filmhistoria' (sound recording), recorded 5 July 1988, Svenska Filminstitutets Bibliotek, Stockholm.

14   Olle Nordemar, letter to Thor Heyerdahl, 2 Nov. 1949, KTA Oslo.

15   'Kon Tiki-männens färd blir dokumentär Svensk långfilm', *Stockholms-Tidningen*, 25 Nov. 1949.

16   Thor Heyerdahl, letter to Philip Unwin, 13 Dec. 1949, KTA Oslo.

17   Per Lönndahl and Olle Nordemar, 'Olle Nordemar Berättar Filmhistoria' (sound recording), recorded 5 July 1988, Svenska Filminstitutets Bibliotek, Stockholm. For more on OWI see Barsam, *Nonfictional Film*, 219.

18   'Filmfotograf på studieresa till Hollywood', *Dagens Nyheter*, 20 Feb. 1945.

19   Leonard Clairmont, 'Svensk Tornado tog Andan ur Hollywood', *Film Journalen*, 27/29 (1945), 14.

20   'Sverige producerar färgfilm redan nästa år!', *Stockholms-Tidningen*, 30 July 1945.

21   Per Persson, 'Kultur-Sverige på film lockar USA:s filmmän', *Svenska Dagbladet*, 26 July 1945.

22   Thomas Doherty, 'Documenting the 1940s', in Thomas Schaltz (ed.), *History of the American Cinema, vi: Boom and Bust: American cinema in the 1940s* (1997; reprint, Berkeley: University of California Press, 1999), 402.

23  Jack C. Ellis, 'American Documentary in the 1950s', in Peter Lev (ed.), *History of the American Cinema, vii: Transforming the Screen 1950–1959* (New York: Charles Scribner & Sons, 2003), 257–9.

24  Doherty, 'Documenting the 1940s', 406–7.

25  Ibid., 408–10.

26  Ibid., 408.

27  See review after first screening: 'Films at Edinburgh: Record of the Kon-Tiki Expedition', *The Times*, 31 Aug. 1950.

28  Olle Nordemar, letter to Thor Heyerdahl, 21 Aug. 1950, KTA Oslo. Olle Nordemar, letter to Philip Unwin, 22 March 1950, Reading University Library Archive, Allen and Unwin Collection, AUC 434–11. Olle Nordemar, letter to Philip Unwin, 30 Oct. 1950, Reading University Library Archive, Allen and Unwin Collection, AUC 434–11.

29  Olle Nordemar, letter to Philip Unwin, 30 Oct. 1950, Reading University Library Archive, Allen and Unwin Collection, AUC 434–11.

30  Thor Heyerdahl, letter to Philip Uniwn, 20 Nov. 1951, Reading University Library Archive, Allen and Unwin Collection, AUC 504–9.

31  Per Lönndahl and Olle Nordemar, 'Olle Nordemar Berättar Filmhistoria' (sound recording), recorded 5 July 1988, Svenska Filminstitutets Bibliotek, Stockholm.

32  Olle Nordemar, letter to Thor Heyerdahl, 5 Oct. 1950, KTA Oslo.

33  Edwin Schalert, 'Goldwyn Slates Barbara Worth', *Los Angeles Times*, 16 Oct. 1950.

34  Olle Nordemar, letter to Thor Heyerdahl, 4 Nov. 1950, KTA Oslo.

35  Paul F. Ellis, 'Dr. Heyerdahl Unable to See Movie Preview', *New Register*, 30 Nov. 1950.

36  Thor Heyerdahl, letter to H. M. Brenner, 8 Jan. 1951, KTA Oslo.

37  Kate Cameron, 'Kon-Tiki Author Here to See Film Launched', *Sunday News*, 15 April 1951.

38  'Swank "Kon-Tiki" Premiere at Sutton Theater', *RKO Ned Depinet Drive*, 7 April 1951.

39  'Kon-Tiki Points Way to More Travel Type Documentaries', *Washington Post*, 27 July 1952.

40  Frank Capra, *The Name Above the Title: An Autobiography* (1971; New York: Vintage, 1985), 400–1. Schaltz, *History of the American Cinema: Boom and Bust*, 350.

41  Sassoon, *The Culture of the Europeans*, 1012.

42  'Kontikifilmen verdens mest dekorerte film', *Aftenbladet*, 4 July 1952.

43  Dilys Powell, 'Home Made Epic', *Sunday Times*, 12 Oct. 1952.

44  Nils Beyer, 'Grand: Kon-Tiki', *Morgon-Tidningen*, 14 Jan. 1950.

45  Carl Björkman, 'Grand: "Kon-Tiki"', *Dagens Nyheter*, 14 Jan. 1950.

46  'New Film in London: From Our London Film Critic', *Manchester Guardian*, 11 Oct. 1952.

47  'Kon-Tiki: The Film of the Voyage', *The Times*, 8 Oct. 1952.

48  C. A. Lejeune, 'At the Films: Top of the Bills', *Observer*, 12 Oct. 1952.

49  Jean Péray, 'SUR LES ÉCRANS: Groenland et l'expédition du "Kon-Tiki"', *Croix du Dimanche*, 4 May 1952.

50  Eleanor Wintour, 'Films', *Time & Tide*, 33/42, 18 Oct. 1952.

51  André Bazin, 'Kon-Tiki et Groenland: Poèsie et Aventure', *Parisien-Libèrè*, 28 April 1952.

52  Pem., 'Två Glänsande Dokumentärfilmer', *Göteborgs-Posten*, 17 Jan. 1950.

53  Dilys Powell, 'Home Made Epic', *Sunday Times*, 12 Oct. 1952.

54  Jean Nary, 'L'Expédition du Kon Tiki', *Franc-Tireur*, 26–7 April 1952. André Bazin, 'Kon-Tiki et Groenland: Poèsie et Aventure', *Parisien-Libèrè*, 28 April 1952.

55  C. A. Lejeune, 'At the Films: Top of the Bills', *Observer*, 12 Oct. 1952.

56  'Kon-Tiki: The Film of the Voyage', *The Times*, 8 Oct. 1952.

57  'Kon-Tiki', *Image et Son*, 55 (July 1952).

58  Jean-Jacques Gautier, 'Les Films Noveaux: "L'Expédition du Kon-Tiki" et "Groenland"', *Le Figaro*, 26–7 April 1952.

59  Jim O'Conner, 'Kon-Tiki: Fine Drama on Raft', *New York Journal*, 4 April 1951.

60  Though of course there are examples of this being spelt out: 'The picture, unlike most Hollywood productions, was strictly unglamorous but highly realistic' ('Kon-Tiki Shown Here; Is Fine Adventure Film', *Honolulu Advertiser*, 16 Oct. 1951).

61  'Kon-Tiki is the documentary record of a true adventure that even Hollywood might hesitate to offer as fiction' ('New Picture: Kon-Tiki', *Time*, 16 April 1951).

62  Arthur Knight, 'SRL Goes to the Movies: Authentic and Otherwise', *Saturday Review of Literature*, 14 April 1951.

63  André Bazin, *Qu'est-ce que le cinéma?* (1958; Paris; Les Éditions du Cerf, 1994), 26–7.

64  Ibid.

65  Ibid., 31.

66  Ibid., 29.

67  Robert Sklar, *Movie-Made America: A Cultural History of American Movies* (1975; New York: Vintage, 1994), 280.

68  Nancy and Robert Katz, 'Documentary in Transition, Part II: The International Scene and the American Documentary', *Hollywood Quarterly*, 4/1 (1949), 55.

69  Capra, *The Name Above the Title*, 127–8, 197.

70  Barsam, *Nonfictional Film*, 225.

71  Doherty, 'Documenting the 1940s', in Schaltz, *History of American Cinema: Boom and Bust*, 408. Lewis Jacob, 'World War II and the American Film', *Cinema Journal*, 7 (1967–8), 1–5, 18.

72  Doherty, 'Documenting the 1940s', in Schaltz, *History of American Cinema: Boom and Bust*, 410.

73  Nancy and Robert Katz, 'Documentary in Transition, Part I: The United States', *Hollywood Quarterly*, 3/4 (1948), 429–30.

74  Cited in Slavoj Zizek, *Jacques Lacan in Hollywood and Out: Enjoy Your Symptom!* (1992; London: Routledge, 2001), 42.

## 7  A Lone Hero of Adventurous Science

1  Davida Charney, 'Lone Geniuses In Popular Science: The Devaluation of Scientific Consensus', *Written Communications*, 20/3 (2003), 217–18.

2  Ibid., 218, 237.

3  Victoria O'Donnell, 'Science Fiction Films and Cold War Anxiety', in Lev, *History of the American Cinema: Transforming the Screen*, 169–85.

4  Susan Sontag, 'The Imagination of Disaster', in Sontag, *Against Interpretation* (1966; London: André Deutsch, 1987), 211.

5  Kroll, 'Exploration in *Mare Incognita*', 51.

6  Apsley Cherry-Garrard, *The Worst Journey in the World: Antarctic 1910–1913* (London: Constable and Company, 1922), xvii, 545–6.

7  Kroll, 'Exploration in *Mare Incognita*', 51.

8  The quotation has been ascribed to Mallory. He is supposed to have said it in a lecture in New York in 1923. Dudley Green, *Mallory of Everest* (Burnley: Faust, 1991), 123. David Robertson, *George Mallory* (1969; London: Faber & Faber, 1999), 215–17.

9  Cited in Whit Burnett, 'Adventure is a Human Need', in Burnett (ed.), *The Spirit of Adventure* (New York: Henry Holt & Company, 1955), xiii.

10  Campbell, *The Witness*, 18.

11  Cited in Leed, *The Mind*, 179.

12 Ibid., 181–3.
13 Mary Louise Pratt, *Imperial Eyes: Travel Writing and Transculturation* (London: Routledge, 1992), 23.
14 Ibid., 31.
15 Ibid., 120.
16 Ibid., 124.
17 Alain Bombard, *Naufragé volontaire* (Paris: Éditions de Paris, 1953), 38.
18 Perrin's book has not been translated into English, so the translation of the title used here is mine.
19 Alain Gheerbrant, *L'Expédition Orénoque Amazone 1948–1950* (Paris: Gallimard, 1952), 189.
20 Rolf Blomberg, *Vildar: En berättelse om aucaindiarnerna i Ecuador* (1949; Stockholm: Tiden, 1954), 116, 124.
21 Ibid., 11.
22 Claude Lévi-Strauss, *Tristes tropiques* (1955; Paris: Plon, 1984), 9.
23 Ibid.
24 Ibid., 10.
25 Ibid., 295.
26 J. R. L. Anderson, *The Ulysses Factor: The Exploring Instinct in Man* (London: Hodder & Stoughton, 1970), 16–17.
27 Ibid., 31.
28 Ibid., 34. Original emphases.
29 Ibid., 42.
30 Ernst Jünger, 'On Danger', in Jay Kaes and Edward Dimensberg (eds), *The Weimar Sourcebook* (Berkeley: University of California Press, 1994), 370.
31 Ibid.
32 Paul Fussell, *The Norton Book of Travel* (New York: Norton, 1985), 13.
33 Eric Leed, *Shores of Discovery* (New York: Basic Books, 1995), ix–x. Leed, *The Mind*, 50.
34 Evelyn Waugh, *When the Going was Good* (London: Duckworth, 1946), 11.
35 Lévi-Strauss, *Tristes tropiques*, 36.
36 Waugh, *When the Going was Good*, 11.
37 Eric Newby, *A Short Walk in the Hindu Kush* (London: Secker & Warburg, 1958), 247.
38 Arne Hirdman, *Med äventyret i ryggsäcken* (Stockholm: Folket i Bilds Förlag, 1954), 9.
39 Eric de Bisschop, *Cap a l'est: première expédition du Tahiti-Nui: Tahiti–Santiago du Chili* (Paris: Plon, 1958), 94.

## 8 White Primitives and the Art of Being Exotic to Oneself

1 Heyerdahl, *Kon-Tiki*, 64.

2 Ibid., 19.

3 Ibid., 49–50.

4 Ibid., 19.

5 Jacques Derrida, *Of Grammatology* (Baltimore: Johns Hopkins University Press, 1974), 244. Original emphasis.

6 Torgovnick, *Gone Primitive*, 185. Heyerdahl, *Kon-Tiki*, 123. Norbert Lynton, *The Story of Modern Art* (1980; London: Phaidon, 1999), 16–17.

7 Jean-François Staszak, 'Primitivism and the other: History of art and cultural geography', *GeoJournal*, 60/4 (2004), 353–4.

8 Roger Cardinal, 'Primitivism', in Jane Turner (ed.), *The Dictionary of Art, xxxv: Pittoni to Raphael* (London & New York: Grove, 1996), 585.

9 From James Hilton's 1933 novel *Lost Horizons*, filmed by Frank Capra in 1937.

10 *Thor Heyerdahl, explorer & scientist*, directed by Christopher Ralling (Sebra Film AB; 1994) [television series].

11 Heyerdahl, *Kon-Tiki*, 15.

12 Thor Heyerdahl, *American Indians in the Pacific: The Theory Behind the Kon-Tiki Expedition* (Stockholm: Forum, 1952), 13.

13 Ibid., 229, plates XXVI, XXVII.

14 Ibid., 15, 17, 91, 229.

15 Ibid., 3.

16 M. F. Ashley Montagu, *Man's Most Dangerous Myth: The Fallacy of Race* (1942; New York: Columbia University Press, 1945), 1–8.

17 Torgovnick, *Gone Primitive*, 44.

18 Ibid., 60. See also Holton, *Heyerdahl's Kon-Tiki Theory*, 177.

19 Torgovnick, *Gone Primitive*, 10.

20 P. H. Fawcett, *Exploration Fawcett: Arranged from his manuscripts, letters, log-book, and records by Brian Fawcett* (London: Hutchinson, 1953), 278.

21 Heyerdahl, *Fatu-Hiva*, 12–14.

22 Heyerdahl, *Kon-Tiki*, 133.

23 Ibid., 214.

24 Ibid., 64.

25 Ibid., 206.

26 Ibid., 228.

27  Sven A. Kirsten, *The Book of Tiki* (Cologne: Taschen, 2000), 69–70.

28  Kroll, *America's Ocean Wilderness*, 165.

29  John Bush Jones, *Our Musicals, Ourselves: A Social History of the American Musical Theatre* (Lebanon, NH: Brandeis University Press, 2003), 149–63.

30  Kirsten, *The Book of Tiki*, 40.

31  Ibid., 39.

32  Ibid., 92.

33  H.v.d. Kraam, letter to Thor Heyerdahl, 27 Jan. 1955, KTA Oslo. And Thor Heyerdahl, letter to H.v.d. Kraam, 2 Feb. 1955, KTA Oslo.

34  Staszak, 'Primitivism and the other', 356–7. Ellen Furlough, 'Une leçon des choses: Tourism, Empire, and the Nation in Interwar France', *French Historical Studies*, 25/3 (2002), 441–8.

35  Richard Ruland, 'Melville and the Fortunate Fall: Typee as Eden', *Nineteenth-Century Fiction*, 23/3 (1968), 321.

36  Grimble, *A Pattern of Islands*, 222.

37  Ibid., 140.

38  Malcolm MacDonald, *Borneo People* (London: Jonathan Cape, 1956), 155.

39  Ibid., 65.

40  Eric Lundqvist, *Djungeltagen* (Stockholm: Bonniers, 1949), 18.

41  Ibid., 40–1.

42  Ibid., 157.

43  Ibid.

44  Wilfred Thesiger, *Arabian Sands* (1959; London: Penguin, 1991), 82.

45  Ibid.

46  Alain Gerbault, *Un paradis se meurt* (Paris: Éditions Self, 1949), 107, 264. The book has not been translated into English, so the translation of the title used here is my own.

47  Bronisław Malinowski, *Argonauts of the Western Pacific: An Account of Native Enterprise and Adventure in the Archipelagos of Melanesian New Guinea* (1922; reprint, London: Routledge, 1999), 518, cited in Jan Borm, 'In-Betweeners? –On the Travel Book And Ethnographies', *Studies in Travel Writing*, 4 (2000), 83.

48  George E. Marcus, 'Contemporary Problems of Ethnography in the Modern World System', in James Clifford and George E. Marcus, *Writing Culture: The Poetics and Politics of Ethnography* (Berkeley: University of California Press, 1986), 165 footnote.

49    Victor Segalen, *Essai sur l'exotisme: une esthétique du divers et Textes sur Gauguin et l'Océanie* (1978; Paris: Librairie Générale Français, 1986), 38.

50    Ibid., 76.

51    Lévi-Strauss, *Tristes tropiques*, 397.

52    Gavin Maxwell, *A Reed Shaken By the Wind* (London and New York: Longmans, Green and Co., 1957), 2–3.

53    Bengt Danielsson, *Den lyckliga ön* (1951; Stockholm: Albert Bonniers Folkbibliotek, 1953), 252.

54    Elspeth Huxley, *The Sorcerer's Apprentice: A Journey Through East Africa* (London: Chatto and Windus, 1948), xviii.

55    Ibid.

56    Christopher Isherwood, *The Condor and the Cow: A South American Travel Diary* (New York: Random House, 1948), 147.

57    Fussell, *The Norton Book of Travel*, 755–6.

58    Blanton, *Travel Writing*, 26.


## 9    The New Postwar Sea and the Pacific Frontier


1    Kroll, *America's Ocean Wilderness*, 96, 154–5.

2    In the Best Documentary category. Heyerdahl won in 1952, Carson in 1953, Cousteau in 1957.

3    Heyerdahl, *Kon-Tiki*, 97.

4    Ibid., 97, 123, 133.

5    Kroll, *America's Ocean Wilderness*, 5, 97. Kroll, 'Exploration in the Mare Incognita', 308.

6    Kroll, *America's Ocean* Wilderness, 155–6. Kroll, 'Exploration in the Mare Incognita', 30.

7    Herman Melville, *Mardi, and a Voyage Thither* (1850; Putney, VT: Hendricks House, 1990), 482.

8    Georges Carousso, '101 Days on a Raft: Kon-Tiki by Thor Heyerdahl', *Brooklyn Eagle Sun*, 19 Nov. 1950.

9    Friedman, *Creating an American Lake*, 147. Gibson, *Yankees in Paradise*, 343.

10    Graybar, 'The 1946 Atomic Bomb Tests', 890.

11  Steinberg, *The Social Construction of the Sea*, 138–50.

12  Elenor Lattimore, 'Pacific Ocean or American Lake?', *Far Eastern Survey*, 14/22 (1945), 314.

13  Jonathan Raban, *The Oxford Book of the Sea* (Oxford and New York: Oxford University Press, 1992), 30–1.

14  Nicholas Monsarrat, *The Cruel Sea* (London: Cassell & Company, 1951), 11.

15  Ibid., 392.

16  Kroll, *America's Ocean Wilderness*, 137.

17  Jacques-Yves Cousteau and Frédéric Dumas, *Le Monde du Silence* (Paris : Éditions de Paris, 1953), 236.

18  Cited in Raban, *The Oxford Book of the Sea*, 8–9.

19  Ibid.

20  Ibid., 14. Steinberg, *The Social Construction of the Sea*, 118–20.

21  Heyerdahl, *Kon-Tiki*, 101.

22  Ibid., 106–8. Kroll, *America's Ocean Wilderness*, 120.

23  Heyerdahl, *Kon-Tiki*, 101–2.

24  Jules Verne, *Vingt mille lieues sous les mers* (1870; Paris: Michel de L'Ormeraie, 1975), 91 (part 1, ch. 10).

25  Ibid., 347 (part 2, ch. 8).

26  As Nemo tells Arronax: 'Là seulement est l'indépendance! Là je ne reconnais pas de maîtres! Là je suis libre!', ibid., 95 (part 1, ch. 10).

27  Ibid., 484 (part 2, ch. 19).

28  Joseph Conrad, *Youth: A Narrative and Two Other Stories* (1902; London: The Gresham Publishing Co., 1925), 42. Joseph Conrad, *The Mirror of the Sea: Memories & Impressions* (1906; London: The Gresham Publishing Co., 1925), 136.

29  Ernest Hemingway, *To Have and Have Not* (1937; London: Arrow Books, 2004), 80, 90.

30  Bert Bender, *Sea-Brothers: The Tradition of American Sea Fiction from Moby-Dick to the Present* (Philadelphia: University of Pennsylvania Press, 1988), 171–2. Henry David Thoreau, *Thoreau: Walden and Other Writing* (New York: Bantam Books, 1971), 173.

31  Said by Brigadier General Thomas Farrell, present at the Trinity test in New Mexico in July 1945; cited in Margot A. Henriksen, *Dr. Strangelove's America: Society and Culture in the Atomic Age* (Berkeley: University of California Press, 1997), xv.

32  Heyerdahl, *Kon-Tiki*, 91.

33 Ibid., 26.

34 Ibid.

35 Ibid., 68.

36 Ibid., 80–1.

37 Ibid., 84.

38 Report, 'Kon-Tiki Usage check MAY 1, 1947 to JUNE 7, 1947', 19 June 1947, KTA Oslo. Article put out for distribution on 30 May with the full title: 'Kon-Tiki Raft Center of Fishy Social Life Attracted by Seaweed'.

39 Heyerdahl, *Kon-Tiki*, 155–6.

40 Ibid., 122.

41 Ibid.

42 Ibid., 110, 121. The aquarium reference is in the book, whereas the raft as basement is something that is mentioned in the film alone.

43 Ibid., 116.

44 Ibid., 158.

45 de Roo, 'Six Specks', 1033.

46 Thor Heyerdahl, 'Six Men on a Raft: A Tale for Statesmen', *New York Times*, 12 Sept. 1947.

47 '4 Men and a Girl Brave Rhone On Raft of Table Tennis Balls', *New York Herald Tribune*, 12 Aug. 1952.

48 'France: The Ken-Tooki', *San Francisco Chronicle*, 7 Sept. 1952.

49 Loren McIntyre, 'Rafting Fever', *Americas*, 52/5 (2000), 38–47. See also P. J. Capelotti, *Sea Drift: Rafting Adventures in the Wake of the Kon-Tiki* (New Brunswick, NJ: Rutgers University Press, 2001). Bengt Danielsson, 'Kon-Tiki-Thor, söderhavsfolkens nya gud', in Jacoby, *Thor Heyerdahl*, 28.

50 Joseph Conrad, 'Preface to the Shorter Tales of Joseph Conrad', in Richard Curle (ed.) *Last Essays* (London & Toronto: J. M. Dent & Sons, 1926), 211–12.

51 Ibid.

52 Herman Melville, *Moby Dick* (1851; Oxford: Oxford University Press, 1988), 3 ('Loomings').

53 Kroll, 'Exploration in the Mare Incognita', 308. Kroll, *America's Ocean Wilderness*, 112–13.

54 Rachel L. Carson, *The Sea Around Us* (London; Staples Press, 1951), 98.

55 Ibid., 38.

56 Ibid., 3.

57  Ibid., 101.

58  Ibid., 15.

59  Ibid., 37.

60  Ibid., 38.

61  Vera L. Norwood, 'The Nature of Knowing: Rachel Carson and the American Environment', *Signs*, 12/4 (1987), 741–6.

62  Heyerdahl's text is in the form of a short letter in which he talks mostly of small flying squid, the gempylus he encountered and phosphorescent plankton; see Carson, *The Sea Around Us*, 17–18.

63  Ernest Hemingway, *The Old Man and the Sea* (1952; London: Arrow Books, 2004), 19–20.

64  Ibid., 48.

65  Ibid., 73.

66  David Castronovo, *Beyond the Grey Flannel Suit: Books from the 1950s that Made American Culture* (New York: Continuum, 2004), 25.

67  Carlos Baker, *Hemingway: The Writer as Artist* (Princeton, NJ: Princeton University Press, 1952), 289 note 1.

68  Alain Bombard, *Naufragé volontaire* (Paris: Éditions de Paris, 1953), 67.

69  Ibid., 221.

70  Ibid., 310.

71  Cousteau, *Le Monde du Silence*, 11–12.

72  Ibid., 14–17.

73  Ibid., 8.

74  Ibid., 188.

75  Ibid., 211–14.

76  Verne, *Vingt mille lieues*, 122 (part 1, ch. 13), 94–5 (part 1, ch. 10).

77  Cousteau, *Le Monde du Silence*, 149. This incident is also left out of the film.

78  Ibid., 236.

79  As also argued by Kroll, 'Concluding Remarks and Speculations on a Theory of Frontier Replacement', in Kroll, 'Exploration in Mare Incognita', 397–409.

80  This was not solely an effect of the standing of the postwar sea, but also conceptual baggage that was applied to space exploration from the aviation 'frontier' of the early twentieth century; see David T. Courtwright, *Sky as Frontier: Adventure, Aviation, and Empire* (College Station: Texas A&M University Press, 2005), 133.

81  Ibid., 172.

82　It can be argued that Carson had moved somewhat away from the ocean (or returned to shore) and the 'ocean consciousness' of the postwar sea with the third book in her sea trilogy, *The Edge of the Sea* (1955).

83　John Gillis, *Islands of the Mind: How the Human Imagination Created the Atlantic World* (New York and Houndmills: Palgrave Macmillan, 2004), 109.

# Select Bibliography

Alleyne, Mark D. *Global Lies? Propaganda, the UN and World Order* (Houndmills: Palgrave, 2003).

Anderson, J. R. L. *The Ulysses Factor: The Exploring Instinct in Man* (London: Hodder & Stoughton, 1970).

Andersson, Axel. '*Kon-Tiki* and the Postwar Journey of Discovery', PhD thesis, European University Institute, Florence, 2007.

Andersson, Gunder. 'Unik boksamling tillgänglig', *Kulturrådet*, 6 (1995), 16–21.

Auerbach, Erich. *Mimesis: The Representation of Reality in Western Literature* (1946; Princeton, NJ: Princeton University Press, 2003).

Baker, Carlos. *Hemingway: The Writer as Artist* (Princeton, NJ: Princeton University Press, 1952).

Bandelier, Adolph F. 'Traditions of Precolumbian Landings on the Western Coast of South America', *American Anthropologist*, 7/2 (1905), 250–70.

Barsam, Richard M. *Nonfictional Film: A Critical History* (1973; Bloomington and Indianapolis: Indiana University Press, 1992).

Bascom, William. 'The Forms of Folklore: Prose Narratives', *Journal of American Folklore*, 78/307 (1965), 3–20.

Bazin, André. *Qu'est-ce que le cinéma?* (1958; Paris; Les Éditions du Cerf, 1994).

Bender, Bert. *Sea-Brothers: The Tradition of American Sea Fiction from Moby-Dick to the Present* (Philadelphia: University of Pennsylvania Press, 1988).

Benét, Stephen Vincent. *America* (New York: Overseas Editions, 1944).

Bennett, Wendell Clark. 'Excavations at Tiahuanaco', *Anthropological Papers of the American Museum of Natural History*, 34 (1934).

de Bisschop, Eric. *Cap a l'est: première expédition du Tahiti-Nui: Tahiti–Santiago du Chili* (Paris: Plon, 1958).

Blanton, Casey. *Travel Writing: The Self and the World* (New York: Routledge, 2002).

Blassingame, Wyatt. *Thor Heyerdahl: Viking Scientist* (New York: Elsevier/ Nelson Books, 1979).

Blaut, J. M. *The Colonizer's Model of the World: Geographical Diffusionism and Eurocentric History* (New York: The Guilford Press, 1993).

Blomberg, Rolf. *Vildar: En berättelse om aucaindiarnerna i Ecuador* (1949; Stockholm: Tiden, 1954).

Bomann-Larsen, Tor. *Roald Amundsen: En Biografi* (Oslo: J. W. Cappellens Forlag, 1995).

Bombard, Alain. *Naufragé volontaire* (Paris: Éditions de Paris, 1953).

Bordwell, David et al. (eds). *The Classical Hollywood Cinema: Film Style & Mode of Production to 1960* (1985; London: Routledge, 1988).

Borm, Jan. 'In-Betweeners? – On the Travel Book And Ethnographies', *Studies in Travel Writing*, 4 (2000), 78–105.

Brée, Germaine. 'The Ambiguous Voyage: Mode or Genre', *Genre*, 1 (1968), 87–96.

Burke, Edmund. *A Philosophical Enquiry into the Origin of Our Ideas of the Sublime and Beautiful* (1757; Oxford: Oxford University Press, 1998).

Burnett, Whit (ed.). *The Spirit of Adventure* (New York: Henry Holt & Company, 1955).

Bush Jones, John. *Our Musicals, Ourselves: A Social History of the American Musical Theatre* (Lebanon, NH: Brandeis University Press, 2003).

Campbell, Mary B. *The Witness and the Other World: Exotic European Travel Writing, 400–1600* (Ithaca, NY: Cornell University Press, 1998).

Capelotti, P. J. *Sea Drift: Rafting Adventures in the Wake of the Kon-Tiki* (New Brunswick, NJ: Rutgers University Press, 2001).

Capra, Frank. *The Name Above the Title: An Autobiography* (1971; New York: Vintage, 1985).

Cardinal, Roger. 'Primitivism', in Jane Turner (ed.) *The Dictionary of Art, xxxv: Pittoni to Raphael* (London & New York: Grove, 1996), 582–5.

Carlsen, G. Robert. 'To Sail Beyond the Sunset', *The English Journal*, 42/6 (1953), 300.

Carroll, Michael. 'Of Atlantis and Ancient Astronauts: A Structural Study of Two Modern Myths', *Journal of Popular Culture*, 11/3 (1977), 541–50.

Carson, Rachel. *The Sea Around Us* (London; Staples Press, 1951).

——*The Edge of the Sea* (Boston: Houghton Mifflin, 1955).

——*Silent Spring* (Boston: Houghton Mifflin, 1962).

Castronovo, David. *Beyond the Grey Flannel Suit: Books From the 1950s that Made American Culture* (New York and London: Continuum, 2004).

Charney, Davida. 'Lone Geniuses In Popular Science: The Devaluation of Scientific Consensus', *Written Communications*, 20/3 (2003), 215–41.

Chegaray, Jacques. *Mon tour du monde en bateau stop* (Paris: Amiot-Dumont, 1950).

—— *L'Afrique noir en auto-stop* (Paris: Amiot-Dumont, 1951).

Cherry-Garrard, Apsley. *The Worst Journey in the World: Antarctic 1910–1913* (London: Constable and Company, 1922).

Clifford, James and George E. Marcus. *Writing Culture: The Poetics and Politics of Ethnography* (Berkeley: University of California Press, 1986).

Coles, John. *Experimental Archaeology* (London: Academic Press, 1974).

Conrad, Joseph. *Youth: A Narrative and Two Other Stories* (1902; London: The Gresham Publishing Co., 1925).

—— *The Mirror of the Sea: Memories & Impressions* (1906; London: The Gresham Publishing Co., 1925).

—— *Last Essays*, ed. Richard Curle (London & Toronto: J. M. Dent & Sons, 1926).

Courtwright, David T. *Sky as Frontier: Adventure, Aviation, and Empire* (College Station: Texas A&M University Press, 2005).

Cousteau, Jacques-Yves and Frédéric Dumas, *Le Monde du Silence* (Paris: Éditions de Paris, 1953).

Crane, Stephen. *The Open Boat* (1898; London: Travelman, 1998).

Danielsson, Bengt. *Den lyckliga ön* (1951; Stockholm: Bonniers, 1953).

Dening, Greg. *Beach Crossings: Voyaging Across Times, Cultures and Self* (Philadelphia: University of Pennsylvania Press, 2004).

Derrida, Jacques. *Of Grammatology*, tr. Gayatri Chakravorty Spivak (Baltimore: Johns Hopkins University Press, 1974).

Derry, T. K. *A History of Modern Norway 1814–1972* (Oxford: Clarendon Press, 1973).

Douglas, Susan J. *Listening In: Radio and the American Imagination, from Amos 'n' Andy and Edward R. Murrow to Wolfman Jack and Howard Stern* (New York: Random House, 1999).

Dundes, Alan. 'Binary Opposition in Myth: The Propp/Lévi-Strauss Debate in Retrospect', *Western Folklore*, 56/1 (1997), 39–50.

Escobar, Arturo. *Encountering Development. The Making and Unmaking of the Third World* (Princeton, NJ: Princeton University Press, 1995).

Evensberget, Snorre. *Thor Heyerdahl: Oppdagaren* (Oslo: J. M. Stenersens Forlag, 1994).

Fawcett, P. H. *Exploration Fawcett: Arranged from his manuscripts, letters, log-book, and records by Brian Fawcett* (London: Hutchinson, 1953).

Finney, Ben. *Voyage of Rediscoveries* (Berkeley: University of California Press, 1994).

Friedman, Hal M. *Creating an American Lake: United States Imperialism and Strategic Security in the Pacific Basin, 1945–1947* (Westport, CT: Greenwood Press, 2001).

Furlough, Ellen. 'Une leçon des choses: Tourism, Empire, and the Nation in Interwar France', *French Historical Studies*, 25/3 (2002), 441–73.

Fussell, Paul (ed). *The Norton Book of Travel* (New York: Norton, 1985).

—— *Wartime: Understanding and Behavior in the Second World War* (New York and Oxford: Oxford University Press, 1989).

Gedin, Per I. 'Adam Helms – ett liv för boken', in Märta Bergstrand et al. (eds), *Stockholms universitetsbibliotek 25 år* (Stockholm: Universitetsbiblioteket, 2002), 53–7.

Gerbault, Alain. *Un paradis se meurt* (Paris: Éditions Self, 1949).

Gheerbrant, Alain. *L'Expédition Orénoque Amazone 1948–1950* (Paris: Gallimard, 1952).

Gibson, Arrell Morgan. *Yankees in Paradise: the Pacific Basin Frontier* (Albuquerque: University of New Mexico Press, 1993).

Gillis, John. *Islands of the Mind: How the Human Imagination Created the Atlantic World* (New York and Houndmills: Palgrave Macmillan, 2004).

de Gobineau, Arthur. *Essai sur l'inégalité des races humaines*, iv (Paris: Firmin Didiot, 1855).

—— *The Moral and Intellectual Diversity of Races*, tr. H. Hotz (Philadelphia: J. B. Lippincott & Co, 1856).

Golding, William. *Pincher Martin* (London: Faber, 1956).

Graybar, Lloyd J. 'Bikini Revisited', *Military Affairs*, 44/3 (1980), 118–23.

—— 'The 1946 Atomic Bomb Tests: Atomic Diplomacy or Bureaucratic Infighting?', *Journal of American History*, 72/4 (1986), 888–907.

——and Ruth Flint Graybar, 'America Faces the Atomic Age: 1946', *Air University Review*, 2 (Jan.–Feb. 1984), 68–77.

Green, Dudley. *Mallory of Everest* (Burnley: Faust, 1991).

Grieg, Harald. *En forleggers erindringer* (1958; Oslo: Gyldendal, 1971).

Grimble, Arthur. *A Pattern of Islands* (1952; London: John Murray, 1953).

—— *Return to the Islands* (London: John Murray, 1957).

Günther, Hans. *Rassenkunde Europas* (Munich: J. S. Lehmans Verlag, 1929).

—— *Mon témoignage sur Adolf Hitler* (Puiseaux: Pardès, 1990).

Hackett, Alice Payne. *80 Years of Best Sellers: 1895–1975* (New York and London: R. R. Bowker Company, 1976).

Hale, Christopher. *Himmler's Crusade* (London: Bantam, 2003).

Harbsmeier, Michael. 'Spontaneous Ethnographies: Towards A Social History of Traveller's Tales', *Studies in Travel Writing*, 1 (1997), 216–38.

Haugland, Knut and Svein Sæter. *Operatøren* (Oslo: Cappelen, 2008).

Haynes, Roslynn D. *From Faust to Strangelove: Representations of the Scientist in Western Literature* (Baltimore and London: Johns Hopkins University Press, 1994).

Heffer, Jean. *Les États-Unis et le Pacifique; Histoire d'une frontière* (Paris: Albin Michel, 1995).

Helms, Adam. *Kollektiv reklam: föredrag vid 'Vadstenamötet' Svenska Bokhandlar-föreningens studiedagar den 22–25 maj 1952* (Stockholm: Forum, 1952).

—— *En förläggare fattar pennan* (Stockholm: Forum, 1969).

Hemingway, Ernest. *To Have and Have Not* (1937; London: Arrow Books, 2004).

—— *The Old Man and the Sea* (1952; London: Arrow Books, 2004).

Henriksen, Margot A. *Dr. Strangelove's America: Society and Culture in the Atomic Age* (Berkeley: University of California Press, 1997).

Herzog, Maurice. *Annapurna premier 8.000* (Paris: Arthaud, 1951).

Heyerdahl, Thor. *På jakt efter paradiset: et år på en sydhavsø* (Oslo: Gyldendal, 1938).

—— 'Turning Back Time in the South Seas', *National Geographic Magazine*, Jan. (1941), 109–36.

—— *The Kon-Tiki Expedition* (1950; London: Flamingo, 1996).

—— *The Kon-Tiki Expedition: By Raft Across the South Seas*, tr. F. H. Lyon (London: George Allen & Unwin, 1950).

—— *American Indians in the Pacific: The Theory Behind the Kon-Tiki Expedition* (Stockholm: Forum, 1952).

—— *The Ra Expeditions* (London: Allen & Unwin, 1971).

—— *Fatu-Hiva: Back to Nature* (London: Allen & Unwin, 1974).

—— *Tigris. På lettning etter begynnelsen* (Oslo: Gyldendal, 1979).

—— *Påskeøya. En gåte blir løst* (Oslo: Gyldendal, 1989).

—— *Grønn var jorden på den syvende dag* (Oslo: Gyldendal, 1991).

—— *I Adams fotspor, en erindringsreise* (Oslo: J. M. Stenersens Førlag AS, 1998).

—— and Lilleström, Per. *Inga grenser* (Oslo: J. M. Stenersens Förlag, 2000).

—— *Jakten på Odin* (Oslo: J. M. Stenersens Förlag, 2000).

Hirdman, Arne. *Med äventyret i ryggsäcken* (Stockholm: Folket i Bilds Förlag, 1954).

Holton, Graham E. L. 'Heyerdahl's Kon-Tiki Theory and the Denial of the Indigenous Past', *Anthropological Forum*, 14/2 (2004), 163–81.

Howe, K. R. 'Maori/Polynesian Origins and the "New Learning"', *Journal of Polynesian Society* 108/3 (1999), 305–25.

Hunt, John. *The Ascent of Everest* (London: Hodder & Stoughton, 1953).

Huxley, Elspeth. *The Sorcerer's Apprentice: A Journey Through East Africa* (London: Chatto and Windus, 1948).

Isherwood, Christopher. *The Condor and the Cow: A South American Travel Diary* (New York: Random House, 1948).

Iversen, Gunnar, Tytti Soila and Astrid Söderbergh Widding (eds), *Nordic National Cinemas* (London: Routledge, 1998).

Jacob, Lewis. 'World War II and the American Film', *Cinema Journal, 7* (1967–8), 1–18.

Jacobsen, Nils Kare (ed.). *Erindringer om en forlegger: forfattere om Harald Grieg* (Oslo: Gyldendal Norsk Forlag, 1994).

Jacoby, Arnold. *Señor Kon-Tiki: boken om Thor Heyerdahl* (Oslo: J. W. Cappelen, 1965).

—— *Señor Kon-Tiki* (London: George Allen & Unwin, 1968).

—— (ed.) *Thor Heyerdahl: festskrift til 75-årsdagen* (Larvik: Sjøfartsmuseum, 1989).

Johansson, Anders. *Den glömda armén. Norge–Sverige 1939–1945* (Rimbo: Fischer & Co., 2005).

Judt, Tony. *Postwar: A History of Europe Since 1945* (London: William Heinemann, 2005).

Jünger, Ernst. 'On Danger', in Jay Kaes and Edward Dimensberg (eds), *The Weimar Sourcebook* (Berkeley: University of California Press, 1994).

Kant, Immanuel. *Observations on the Feeling of the Beautiful and Sublime* (1799; Berkeley: University of California Press, 1960).

Kasson, John F. *Houdini, Tarzan, and the Perfect Man: The White Body and the Challenge of Modernity in America* (New York: Hill and Wang, 2001).

Kater, Michael H. *Das 'Ahnenerbe' der SS 1935–1945* (Stuttgart: Deutsche Verlags-Anstalt, 1974).

Katz, Nancy and Robert Katz. 'Documentary in Transition, Part I: The United States', *Hollywood Quarterly,* 3/4 (1948), 425–33.

—— 'Documentary in Transition, Part II: The International Scene and the American Documentary', *Hollywood Quarterly,* 4/1 (1949), 51–64.

Kirsten, Sven A. *The Book of Tiki* (Cologne: Taschen, 2000).

Kock Johansen, Øysten. *Thor Heyerdahl: vitenskapsmannen, eventyreren og mennesket* (Oslo: Cappelen, 2003).

Korda, Michael. *Making the List: A Cultural History of the American Bestseller 1900–1999* (New York: Barnes & Noble Books, 2001).

Kowalewski, Michael (ed.). *Temperamental Journeys: Essays on the Modern Literature of Travel* (Athens: University of Georgia Press, 1992).

Kroes, Rob. *If You've Seen One, You've Seen the Mall: Europeans and American Mass Culture* (Urbana and Chicago: University of Illinois Press, 1996).

Kroll, Gary. 'Exploration in the Mare Incognita: Natural History and Conservation in Early-Twentieth Century America', PhD dissertation, University of Oklahoma, 2000.

—— 'The Pacific Science Board in Micronesia: Science, Government, and Conservation of the Postwar Pacific Frontier', *Minerva*, 41 (2003), 25–46.

—— *America's Ocean Wilderness* (Lawrence: Kansas University Press, 2008).

Kvam, Ragnar, Jr. *Thor Heyerdahl: Mannen og havet* (Oslo: Gyldendal, 2005).

—— *Thor Heyerdahl: Mannen og verden* (Oslo: Glydendal, 2008).

Lane Keller, Kevin. 'Branding and Brand Equity', in Barton Weitz and Robin Wensley (eds), *Handbook of Marketing* (London: Sage, 2002), 151–78.

Lattimore, Elenor. 'Pacific Ocean or American Lake?', *Far Eastern Survey*, 14/22 (1945), 313–16.

Leed, Eric. *The Mind of the Traveler: From Gilgamesh to Global Tourism* (New York: Basic Books, 1991).

—— *Shores of Discovery* (New York: Basic Books, 1995).

Lev, Peter (ed.). *History of the American Cinema*, vii: *Transforming the Screen 1950–1959* (New York: Charles Scribner & Sons, 2003).

Leverenz, David. 'The Last Real Men in America: From Natty Bumppo to Batman', in Peter F. Murphy (ed.), *Fictions of Masculinity: Crossing Cultures, Crossing Sexualities* (New York and London: University of New York Press, 1994), 21–57.

Lévi-Strauss, Claude. 'The Structural Study of Myth', *Journal of American Folklore,* 68/270 (1955), 428–44.

—— *Tristes tropiques* (1955; Paris: Plon, 1984).

—— *The Naked Man: Introduction to a Science of Mythology IV* (1971; London: Jonathan Cape, 1981).

Loe, Erlend. *L* (Oslo: Cappelen, 2000).

London, Jack. *The Call of the Wild, White Fang, and Other Stories* (New York and London: Penguin Books, 1981).

—— *The Sea Wolf* (1904; Oxford: Oxford University Press, 1992).

Lundqvist, Eric. *Djungeltagen* (Stockholm: Bonniers, 1949).

Lynton, Norbert. *The Story of Modern Art* (1980; London: Phaidon, 1999).

MacDonald, Malcolm. *Borneo People* (London: Jonathan Cape, 1956).

McIntyre, Loren. 'Rafting Fever', *Americas* 52/5 (2000), 38–47.

Malinowski, Bronisław. *Argonauts of the Western Pacific: An Account of Native Enterprise and Adventure in the Archipelagos of Melanesian New Guinea* (1922; London: Routledge, 1999).

Maufrais, Raymond. *Aventures au Matto Grosso* (Paris: René Julliard, 1951).

—— *Aventures en Guyana: Carnets* (Paris: Julliard, 1952).

Maxwell, Gavin. *A Reed Shaken By the Wind* (London and New York: Longmans, Green and Co., 1957).

Melville, Herman. *Mardi, and a Voyage Thither* (1850; Putney, VT: Henricks House, 1990).

—— *Moby-Dick* (1851; Oxford: Oxford University Press, 1988).

Mjøen, Jon Alfred. 'Der Mensch des Nordens', in *Nordland Fibel. Gerausgegeben von der Nordischen Gesellschaft* (Berlin: Wilhelm Limpert Verlag, 1938), 21–34.

Moitessier, Bernard. *Un vagabond des mers du sud* (Paris: Flammarion Éditeur, 1960).

Monsarrat, Nicholas. *The Cruel Sea* (London: Cassell & Company, 1951).

Montagu, M. F. Ashley. *Man's Most Dangerous Myth: The Fallacy of Race* (New York: Columbia University Press, 1942).

Munson, Gorham. 'Adventure Writing in Our Time', *College English,* 16/3 (1954), 153–9.

Murphy, John M. (ed.). *Branding: A Key Marketing Tool* (1987; Houndmills: Macmillan, 1992).

Newby, Eric. *A Short Walk in the Hindu Kush* (London: Secker & Warburg, 1958).

Norbeck, Edward. 'Book Review: American Indians in the Pacific: The Theory Behind the Kon-Tiki Expedition', *American Antiquity*, 19/1 (1953), 92–4.

Nordhoff, Charles and James Norman Hall. *The Bounty Trilogy: Comprising the Three Volumes, Mutiny on the Bounty, Men Against the Sea & Pitcairn's Island* (London: Corgi, 1983).

Norwood, Vera L. 'The Nature of Knowing: Rachel Carson and the American Environment', *Signs*, 12/4 (1987), 740–60.

Olson, Charles. *Call Me Ishmael* (New York: Reynal & Hitchcock, 1947).

Pagden, Anthony. *European Encounters with the New World: From Renaissance to Romanticism* (New Haven, CT: Yale University Press, 1993).

Parry-Giles, Shawn J. *The Rhetorical Presidency, Propaganda, and the Cold War, 1945–1955* (Westport and London: Praeger, 2002).

Perrin, Michel. *La tragédie du Haut-Amazone* (Paris: Éditions Denoël, 1954).

Perry, W. J. *The Children of the Sun: A Study in the Early History of Civilization* (London: Methuen & Co., 1923).

Porter, Dennis. *Haunted Journeys: Desire and Transgression in European Travel Writing* (Princeton, NJ: Princeton University Press).

Pratt, Mary Louise. *Imperial Eyes: Travel Writing and Transculturation* (London: Routledge, 1992).

Pringle, Heather. *The Master Plan – Himmler's Scholars and the Holocaust* (New York: Hyperion, 2006).

Propp, Vladimir. *Morphology of the Folk Tale* (1928; Austin: University of Texas Press, 1968).

Raban, Jonathan. *The Oxford Book of the Sea* (Oxford and New York: Oxford University Press, 1992).

Ralling, Christopher. *The Kon-Tiki Man: An Illustrated Biography of Thor Heyerdahl* (London: BBC Books, 1990).

Raspail, Jean. *Le Camp des saints* (Paris: R. Laffront, 1972).

—— and Andrieu Phillip. *Terrre de Feu – Alaska: L'éxpedition automobile de l'equipe Marquette* (Paris: Julliard, 1952).

Ridon, Jean-Xavier. *Le voyage en son miroir: essai sur quelques tentatives de réinvention du voyage au 20e siècle* (Paris: Éditions Kimé, 2002).

Ries, Al and Laura Ries. *The 22 Immutable Laws of Branding* (1998; London: HarperCollins, 2000).

Riesman, David. *The Lonely Crowd: A Study of the Changing American Character* (New Haven, CT: Yale University Press, 1950).

Robertson, David. *George Mallory* (1969; London: Faber & Faber, 1999).

Robertson, John Oliver. *American Myth, American Reality* (New York: Hill and Wang, 1980).

Room, Adrian. *Dictionary of Trade Name Origins* (London: Routledge, 1984).

Roosevelt, Theodore. *An Autobiography* (1913; New York: Charles Scribner's Sons, 1946).

Rørholt, Bjørn and Bjarne W. Thorsen. *Usynlige soldater: Nordmenn i Secret Service foreteller* (Oslo: Aschehoug, 1990).

Rosaldo, Renato. 'Imperial Nostalgia', *Representations*, 26 (1989), 107–22.

Rosenberg, David Alan. 'American Atomic Strategy and the Hydrogen Bomb Decision', *Journal of American History*, 66/1 (1979), 62–87.

Ruland, Richard. 'Melville and the Fortunate Fall: Typee as Eden', *Nineteenth-Century Fiction*, 23/3 (1968), 312–23.

Rutgers, David F. *Creating the Secret State: The Origin of the Central Intelligence Agency, 1943–1947* (Lawrence: University of Kansas Press, 2000).

Said, Edward W. *Orientalism: Western Conceptions of the Orient* (1978; London: Penguin, 1994).

——*Culture and Imperialism* (1993; London: Vintage, 1994).

Sandvik, Harald. *Frigjøringen av Finnmark 1944–1945* (Oslo: Gyldendal, 1975).

Sassoon, Donald. *The Culture of the Europeans: From 1800 to the Present* (London: HarperCollins, 2006).

Schaltz, Thomas (ed.). *History of the American Cinema*, vi: *Boom and Bust: American cinema in the 1940s* (1997; Berkeley: University of California Press, 1999).

Segalen, Victor. *Essai sur l'exotisme: une esthétique du divers et Textes sur Gaugain et l'Océanie* (1978; Paris: Librairie Générale Français, 1986).

Sklar, Robert. *Movie-Made America: A Cultural History of American Movies* (1975; New York: Vintage, 1994).

Skolmen, Roar. *I skyggen av Kon-Tiki* (Gjøvik: N. W. Damm & Søn, 2000).

Skorgen, Torgeir. *Rasenes oppfinnelse: Rasetenkningens historie* (Oslo: Spartacus, 2002).

Smith, G. Elliot. *In The Beginning: The Origin of Civilization* (1932; London, Watts & Co., 1937).

——*The Diffusion of Culture* (London: Watts & Co., 1933).

Smith, Marian W. 'Book Review: Aku-Aku: The Secret of the Easter Island', *Geographical Journal*, 124/3 (1958), 384–6.

Sontag, Susan. *Against Interpretation* (1966; London: André Deutsch, 1987).

Staszak, Jean-François. 'Primitivism and the other: History of art and cultural geography', *GeoJournal*, 60/4 (2004), 353–64.

Steinberg, Philip E. *The Social Construction of the Sea* (Cambridge: Cambridge University Press, 2001).

Tambs, Erling. *The Cruise of the Teddy* (London: Cape, 1933).

Théodore-Aubanel, Eduoard. *Comment on lance un nouveau Livre* (Paris: L'Intercontinentale d'édition, 1937).

Thesiger, Wilfred. *Arabian Sands* (1959; London: Penguin, 1991).

Thomas, Nicholas. *Marquesan Society: Inequality and Political Transformation in Eastern Polynesia* (Oxford: Clarendon Press, 1990).

Thoreau, Henry David. *Thoreau: Walden and Other Writing* (New York: Bantam Books, 1971).

Tiika, Ensio. *Raft of Despair* (London: Hutchinson, 1954).

Todorov, Tzvetan. 'Structural Analysis of Narrative', *Novel*, 3/1 (1969), 70–6.

—— *Genres in Discourse* (Cambridge: Cambridge University Press, 1990).

—— *The Morals of History* (Paris: Grasset et Fasquelle, 1991).

Torgovnick, Marianna. *Gone Primitive: Savage Intellects, Modern Lives* (Chicago and London: University of Chicago Press, 1990).

Trumbull, Robert. *The Raft* (New York: Henry Holt & Co., 1942).

Twain, Mark. *The Innocents Abroad* (1869; New York and Oxford: Oxford University Press, 1996).

Ustvedt, Yngvar. *Det skjedde i Norge, i: 1945–52: Den varme freden, den kalde krigen* (1978; Oslo: Gyldendal, 1981).

Vanderbilt, Arthur T., II. *The Making of a Bestseller: From Author to Reader* (Jefferson, NC: McFarland, 1999).

Verne, Jules. *Vingt mille lieues sous les mers* (1870; Paris: Michel de L'Ormeraie, 1975).

Vogt, Evon Z. 'Anthropology in the Public Consciousness', in *Yearbook of Anthropology* (Chicago: University of Chicago Press, 1955), 357–74.

Vold Hurum, Gerd. *En kvinne ved navn 'Truls': Fra motstandskamp til Kon-Tiki*, ed. Cato Guhnfeldt (Oslo: Wings, 2006).

Wagnleitner, Reinhold. *Coca-Colonization and the Cold War: the Cultural Mission of the United States in Austria after the Second World War* (Chapel Hill: University of North Carolina Press, 1994).

Wauchope, Robert. *Lost Tribes & Sunken Continents: Myth and Method in the Study of American Indians* (Chicago and London: University of Chicago Press, 1962).

Waugh, Evelyn. *When the Going was Good* (London: Duckworth, 1946).

Wheeler, John N. *I've Got News for You* (New York: E. P. Dutton, 1961).

Whyte, William H., Jr. *The Organization Man* (1956; London: Jonathan Cape, 1957).

Wilson, Sloan. *The Man in the Gray Flannel Suit* (New York: Simon and Schuster, 1955).

Wouk, Herman. *The Caine Mutiny, a Novel of World War II* (Garden City, NY: Doubleday, 1951).

Zizek, Slavoj. *Jacques Lacan in Hollywood and Out: Enjoy Your Symptom!* (1992; London: Routledge, 2001).

# Index